DAILY LIFE IN WARTIME JAPAN, 1940–1945

Modern War Studies

Theodore A. Wilson
General Editor

Raymond Callahan
Jacob W. Kipp
Allan R. Millett
Carol Reardon
Dennis Showalter
David R. Stone
James H. Willbanks
Series Editors

Daily Life in Wartime Japan, 1940–1945

SAMUEL HIDEO YAMASHITA

University Press of Kansas

Chapter 5 reprinted by permission of the publishers from "The 'Food Problem' of Evacuated Children in Wartime Japan, 1944–1945," in *Food and War in Mid-Twentieth-Century East Asia*, edited by Katarzyna J. Cwiertka (Farnham: Ashgate, 2013), pp. 131–148. Copyright © 2013.

Published by the University Press of Kansas (Lawrence, Kansas 66045), which was organized by the Kansas Board of Regents and is operated and funded by Emporia State University, Fort Hays State University, Kansas State University, Pittsburg State University, the University of Kansas, and Wichita State University

Library of Congress Cataloging-in-Publication Data
Yamashita, Samuel Hideo, 1946– author.
Daily life in wartime Japan, 1940–1945 / Samuel Hideo Yamashita.
  pages cm. — (Modern war studies)
Includes bibliographical references and index.
ISBN 978-0-7006-2190-3 (cloth : alk. paper) — ISBN 978-0-7006-2195-8 (ebook)
1. World War, 1939–1945—Social aspects—Japan. 2. Japan—Social life and customs—1912–1945. 3. World War, 1939–1945—Japan. I. Title.
D744.7.J3Y36 2015
940.53'52—dc23

                                        2015032192

British Library Cataloguing-in-Publication Data is available.

Printed in the United States of America
10 9 8 7 6 5 4 3 2 1

The paper used in this publication is recycled and contains 30 percent postconsumer waste. It is acid free and meets the minimum requirements of the American National Standard for Permanence of Paper for Printed Library Materials Z39.48-1992.

To my teachers
Whose example inspired me to become a teacher

CONTENTS

ACKNOWLEDGMENTS

This book never would have found its way into print without the help of many others. I owe a huge intellectual debt to my friend Stefan Tanaka. Some years ago, he introduced me to *Alltagsgeschichte* (history of everyday life), an approach developed to explore the contributions of ordinary Germans to the Nazi regime that proved useful when I began to read and analyze wartime Japanese diaries, letters, and memoirs. I am deeply indebted as well to Michael Briggs, editor in chief at the University Press of Kansas, whose unwavering interest in this project gently spurred me on to finish this manuscript.

I would like to thank the many librarians who helped me as I gathered material for this book. At the International House of Japan in Tokyo, Izumi Koide helped me find wartime diaries written by women; Keiko Higuchi gave me advice on copyright issues; and Rie Hayashi and her staff were indispensable when I was searching for photographs for this book. Kenji Niki, curator of the Japanese collection at the University of Michigan, allowed me to copy a part of a rare 1946 edition of *Kuni no ayumi* (The country's progress). Isamu Miura, curator of the Asian studies collection at Honnold/Mudd Library at the Claremont Colleges, gathered biographical information about several of my diarists and identified obscure places and items mentioned in the diaries. In addition, the staff at the interlibrary loan service at Honnold/Mudd Library arranged for me to use scholarly articles and books not available locally.

I presented parts of this book at the University of California, Los Angeles; the University of Iowa; the University of Southern California; the University of Hawai'i at Manoa; the University of North Carolina at Chapel Hill; and the University of California, Santa Barbara, and benefited from the questions, criticisms, and comments of faculty and students at these institutions. I would like to thank Fred Notelhelfer, Stephen Vlastos, Joan Piggot, Miles Fletcher, Lonny Carlile, Christine Yano, and Luke Roberts for making these visits possible. I delivered what became the introduction of this book as the keynote address at a "Symposium on Asia and the Liberal Arts," held at the University of Puget Sound in April 2009 and am grateful to Suzanne Barnett, whose invitation to speak at the symposium prompted me to reflect on the significance and limitations of my research. I presented parts of my book as the Grant Goodman Distinguished Lecture in Japanese

Studies at the University of Kansas in April 2009 and would like to thank Grant Goodman, Bill Tsutsui, and Eric Rath for this special honor and for their hospitality during my visit to Lawrence. Adam Rosenkranz invited me to present my findings on coercion, compliance, and resistance in wartime Japan as a Claremont Discourse Lecture in October 2009. And I had the pleasure of presenting a preliminary version of chapter 7 as the Steine Jonasson Lecture at Linfield College in April 2012 and thank Peter Buckingham, John Sagers, Lissa Wadewitz, and their colleagues for the invitation to speak in McMinnville.

In addition, several chapters of this book were greatly improved after I presented them at conferences in the United States and abroad: chapter 5 at a symposium, "Food in Zones of Conflict," organized by Katarzyna Cwiertka and held at Leiden University in August 2011; chapter 7 at a conference, "Japan's World War II in Asia: Seventy Years On," organized by Richard Smethurst and held at the University of Pittsburgh in September 2011; and early versions of chapter 4, first at a conference, "World War II: How It Transformed America, the Pacific and Asia," organized by Paul Heintz and Frank Middleton and held in Honolulu, and then at a conference, "Children, Education and Youth in Imperial Japan, 1925–1945," organized by Peter Cave and Kyoko Itagaki and held at Kyoto University in January 2014.

Many others offered advice and comments about the contents of this book. I would like to thank Peter Cave, Angelina Chin, Katarzyna Cwiertka, Liza Dalby, Ayako Ebara, Miles Fletcher, Elaine Gerbert, William Hauser, Robert Hellyer, James Huffman, Shoko Imai, Masako Koike, Yoshiaki Koike, Lynne Miyake, Eriko Miyazawa, Aaron Moore, C. T. Nishimoto, Michiko Kodama Nishimoto, Warren Nishimoto, Albert Park, Luke Roberts, Richard Smethurst, Osamu Tagaya, Hisashi Takahashi, Kazumi Takahashi, Stefan Tanaka, Yuma Totani, Lisa Tran, and Stephen Vlastos; and the late Mark Peattie and George M. Wilson. Food historian Ayako Ebara shared hard-to-find information about the number of evacuated children who perished during the war. I am grateful as well to Theodore Cook, Edward Drea, Akira Iriye, and Louise Young for their thoughtful and encouraging comments on the proposal for this book.

My student Yuki Numata spent a month confirming the wartime locations of every individual cited in my book and produced preliminary drafts of the maps that cartographer Bill Nelson made for each chapter, a task that proved far more difficult than any of us imagined it would be.

When I was deciding how to render in English the names of Japanese fish, plants, vegetables, foods, and so forth, I relied heavily on Richard Hosking's

A Dictionary of Japanese Food: Ingredients and Culture and consulted Shizuo Tsuji's *Japanese Cooking: A Simple Art.*

Also indispensable to the completion of this book were the timely grant I received from the Northeast Asia Council of the Association for Asian Studies and a steady stream of grants from Pomona College, including three Fred Sontag Research Fellowships that funded many trips to Japan and paid for the photographs and maps in this book. I would like to thank Gary Kates, former dean of the college, and former associate deans of the college Cynthia Selaissie, Jonathan Wright, and Elizabeth Crighton as well as the Research Committee at Pomona.

In addition, I would like to express my thanks to the *Mainichi* and *Yomiuri* newspapers and the National Shōwa Memorial Museum (Shōwakan) in Tokyo for allowing me to use their photographs in my book.

Finally, I owe more than it is possible to say to my wife, Margaret Barrows Yamashita, whose high standards have always prompted me to do my best work and whose sharp professional editor's eye greatly improved this book.

DAILY LIFE IN WARTIME JAPAN, 1940–1945

Introduction

On July 4, 1992, I started reading the "last letters" of special attack pilots—known outside Japan as *kamikaze*—that I had been collecting for several years. I remember the date because it seemed ironic that I was reading these letters on that most patriotic American holiday. Over the next two years I read and translated about 130 of these letters. But my close reading of these last letters revealed that they were not truly private documents, so I began searching for wartime diaries, first servicemen's diaries and then those of the home-front population.

During the next two decades, I found about 160 published diaries. Some were complete and others were fragments, but all were interesting and revealing. When the managing editor at the University of Hawai'i Press, Pat Crosby, expressed an interest in publishing my translations of these diaries, I chose eight and composed them as a book.[1]

As I prepared the diaries for publication, I wondered whether I could use them to write what German historians call an *Alltagsgeschichte*, a "history of everyday life." *Alltagsgeschichte* emerged in the mid-1970s as a critique of the studies of the Nazi phenomenon that looked only at the larger social and economic "structures, processes, and patterns" that were thought to have created it and the leadership that directed it. These studies left out the *kleine Leute*, literally, "little Germans," which I would translate as "ordinary Germans." In response, the practitioners of *Alltagsgeschichte* called for an examination of ordinary Germans and the part they played during the war.[2]

The Japanese diaries that I had read seemed to provide enough material for a history of everyday life in wartime Japan. They offered what one historian labeled the "inner perspective" on the war, revealing exactly how the wartime government, from 1937 onward, mobilized the populations of Japan's home islands and its colonies (Taiwan and Korea) to fight, against first the Chinese and then the United States and its allies. In addition, the diaries tell us how ordinary Japanese responded to mobilization; the outbreak of war; Japan's early victories; the demands of the neighborhood associations and community councils for obedience, compliance, and sacrifice; the horrifying impact of the Allied bombing of Japanese cities and towns; and, finally, the prospect and reality of defeat.

The diaries also show that the impact of the war on ordinary Japanese varied. For example, those living in the big cities—Tokyo, Yokohama, Osaka, Nagoya, and Kobe—were the first to feel the effects of the war, and those living in the countryside never experienced the physical destruction and hardships that the urban population did. Class is another dimension of the war that emerges clearly in the diaries: high-ranking officials, military men, and the rich were better off than most of their fellow Japanese, and they also had enough to eat. Finally, the diaries reveal the desperate conditions on the home front in the last months of the war.

Why has it taken so long for these wartime Japanese diaries to be translated, given that they contain so much information about the war? And why have historians in the English-speaking world been so slow to use them to write a history of everyday life in wartime Japan? First, the diaries came to light only slowly. The Allied forces occupied Japan for nearly seven years, from August 1945 through April 1952, and those Japanese who kept diaries during the war undoubtedly were reluctant to come forward and publish them, as they might incriminate the diarist and his or her family. Moreover, the diaries had to clear the Allied censors before they could be published, and this was not an insignificant barrier. For example, I found a young woman's diary that had been published during the Occupation but that showed unmistakable signs of having been worked over by Allied censors. It thus had been reduced to virtually nothing more than her impressions of the weather, blossoming flowers, and so forth.[3] I wondered what objectionable things the original had said. Another diary that I translated and published in *Leaves from an Autumn of Emergencies* was written by Yoshizawa Hisako, a single working woman from Tokyo who first released her diary under her husband's name.[4] Was this because he was a writer and had the requisite credentials? Or were there other reasons?

A remarkable collection of letters and diaries published during the Occupation, entitled *Kike wadatsumi no koe*, consists of letters and diaries written by university students who had died in the war. After many years it finally was translated, first into French. Then in 2000 Midori Yamanouchi, a professor of Japanese at the University of Scranton, and Joseph Quinn translated the collection into English, published as *Listen to the Voices from the Sea*.[5]

Would American, Australian, Canadian, or British readers have read these diaries if they had been available in English translation after the war? Maybe not. After all, the Japanese enemy was so hated and caricatured that it might have been impossible for, say, an American to be interested in the personal diary of a Japanese. Moreover, the Japanese had been characterized as primitive, infantile, pagan, insane, subhuman, and nonhuman, and described as apes, dogs, bees, sheep, and vermin.[6] Indeed, American readers might have asked: Do fanatics keep personal journals? Do monkeys keep diaries? Do vermin write? Besides, we Americans had John Hersey, Frank Gibney, and Richard Tregaskis.[7] Why would we need anything else?

Another problem was that the official Allied interpretation of what happened in Japan in the 1930s and during the war was that Japan's "military leaders suppressed the people, launched a stupid war, and caused this disaster!"[8] This judgment was first articulated in 1946 and later affirmed by the International Military Tribunal for the Far East in its indictment of Japanese class A war criminals. This view—that Japan's wartime leaders were solely responsible for the war and that ordinary Japanese were innocent—became an orthodoxy. Why, then, would anyone need to read the wartime diaries of ordinary Japanese?

Moreover, the prevailing American view of "Japan" and "the Japanese" in the 1950s and 1960s was that they were an inferior and backward people whose women were loose and easy and whose factories made cheap, shoddy goods that broke easily. The best thing that could be said about the Japanese was that they were little people who made little things, such as transistor radios, miniature cameras, and, later, small cars.

Another explanation for the slowness with which wartime Japanese diaries were translated and read is patriotism, which made it hard for Americans to see the Japanese as they saw themselves. This was revealed at a display at the Smithsonian Institution commemorating the dropping of the atomic bombs on Hiroshima and Nagasaki. The exhibition of a section of the *Enola Gay*, the B-29 that dropped the atomic bomb on Hiroshima on August 6, 1945, prompted a fierce debate between those who wanted to celebrate the atomic annihilation of Hiroshima and Nagasaki and those who felt it should be condemned. As Susan Sontag wrote about the perspective of the former group: "A museum devoted to the history of America's wars . . . that fairly represented the arguments for and against using the atomic bomb in 1945 on the Japanese cities, with photographic evidence that showed what these weapons did would be recognized, now more than ever, as a most unpatriotic endeavor."[9] According to this thinking, translating and publishing wartime Japanese diaries would have been unpatriotic as well.

Another reason why the diaries were slow to be translated was that they would have been subversive in the eyes of many. Indeed, the wartime diaries challenge many of the prevailing myths about the Japanese: that they were an innocent people misled by their "military leaders" (International Military Tribunal for the Far East narrative), that they were a backward and inferior people who pulled themselves up and out of the ashes of the wartime rubble to become an economic superpower (Cold War narrative), that Japan was a feudal kingdom that succeeded in modernizing itself beginning in the mid-1660s (modernization narrative) and even outperformed the United States in the 1970s and 1980s.[10] The wartime diaries challenge these myths by revealing what one scholar called the "doubleness of knowledge": the diaries reveal that postwar narratives of "Japan" were fabricated to serve American geopolitical interests in the Cold War.[11] This analysis also made me wonder whether the *absence* of a narrative of everyday life in wartime Japan was itself a narrative of the war in which "everyday life" was absent, a narrative in which ordinary Japanese do not appear. Like the images of Nagasaki and Hiroshima after they were destroyed, this would be an account in which no humans appear.

Fortunately, wartime Japanese diaries have begun to be translated into English. We now have a translation of the diary of a Japanese army officer on Iwo Jima, Lieutenant Sugihara Kinryū, thanks to the editors of the *Journal of Military History*, who published it in 1995.[12] Eugene Soviak and Tamie Kamiyama translated the wartime diary of a leading Japanese journalist, Kiyosawa Kiyoshi, which Princeton University Press published as *A Diary of Darkness: The Wartime Diary of Kiyosawa Kiyoshi* in 1999.[13] But diaries like these raise difficult questions: How are we to read them? Which should we avoid?

At first, we might think that these diaries give historians exactly what they need. A diary like the one kept by Yoshizawa Hisako tells us how an ordinary Japanese woman felt about the war, her government, her military, and the enemy. Isn't this what historians want and need? Diaries like

Yoshizawa's give us an abundance of what philosopher Arthur Danto calls "true descriptions of the world."[14] A "true description" is a statement like the following from Yoshizawa's diary: "Just before two o'clock, an air-raid warning sounded, and a bombing raid followed."[15] Danto points out that historians *always* configure "true descriptions" and that their configurations are *their* representations of the facts contained in each "true description." So Danto might say of those of us who use wartime Japanese diaries in our research that we necessarily configure the true descriptions contained in these diaries, that this is how we make sense of what we read and what "gives us access" to the wartime Japanese. Frank Ankersmit, one of Danto's contemporary interpreters, reminds us that when we configure the true descriptions found in wartime diaries and generate a representation of life on the Japanese home front during the war, we do something that the writers of the diaries could never "do themselves," because these diarists were not aware of "their own representations of the world."[16] Moreover, when we "enclose" wartime Japanese in our representations, to use Ankersmit's terms, we also distance them, because our "representations have no counterpart in how they experience[d] their lives and the world."[17] To say that "*our* representations have no counterpart in how [wartime Japanese] . . . experience[d] their lives and the world" seems strangely paradoxical and demands explanation.

What Danto and Ankersmit are saying is that no matter how hard we historians try to recover the wartime experiences of ordinary Japanese, we are destined to fail. That is, our "history of everyday life in wartime Japan" is necessarily *our* version of the history of everyday life in wartime Japan, a voiceover that drowns out the voices of ordinary Japanese. Perhaps we historians should assume that the wartime diaries do not give us "true descriptions" but, rather, "experiences," the raw, unmediated experiences of the war.

Here historian Joan Scott offers us some guidance. In a brilliant essay entitled "The Evidence of Experience," she disagrees with the historians who, as she puts it, "have argued that an unproblematized 'experience' is the foundation of their practice."[18] "Experience," she contends, is of questionable value because it is not simply what an individual undergoes at a particular moment in time. Nor is it the product of an immaculate intellectual conception: pure, unsullied, and simply as it is. Instead, experience is more complex than that. "It is not individuals who have experience," she explains, "but subjects who are constituted through experience. Experience in this definition then becomes not the origin of our explanation . . . but rather that which we seek to explain, that about which knowledge is produced."[19]

This is her response to historians who regard "experience" as unproblematic. Thus, even experience is a construction and first must be understood on its own terms, analyzed, and explained before historians can use it.

I would argue that in order for wartime Japanese diaries to be useful, they first must be understood as the work of wartime Japanese subjects whose very existence was carefully shaped by their government through their community councils and neighborhood associations, through hundreds of wartime propaganda broadcasts, through the many hours of air-raid drills, and, in the case of children, through classroom and out-of-class instruction. Accordingly, even the diarists' language was in some sense learned and neither natural nor spontaneous. Therefore, when historians read wartime Japanese diaries, they also must locate them in a specific time and place and understand them as a product of that time and place, heeding Scott's cautionary advice about "experience."

Sontag's book *Regarding the Pain of Others* offers a third perspective on reading wartime Japanese diaries. Her fascinating discussion of war photography poses another set of questions about wartime Japanese diaries. What is distinctive about a war diary? What do such diaries include and exclude? Are they literalist? Sontag reminds us that the great war photographers always composed their shots very carefully. The great Civil War photographer Alexander Gardner, for example, moved the body of a Confederate soldier to compose the photograph that became known as the "Home of a Confederate Sharpshooter." He, and also Mathew Brady, did this to capture what they regarded as the horror of that war.[20] Were wartime Japanese diaries "staged" as well? Where was artifice introduced, and how did it shape diary entries and even whole diaries?

Following Sontag's suggestions, we also might ask, What do wartime Japanese diaries include and exclude? Do they really give us a close-up of the war? How did what diarists wrote about in their journals shape their experience? For example, Sontag observes that the "enemy" who appears in war photographs always has the same quality: anonymity. When we can recognize the enemy, she writes, we are shocked because they look a lot like us.[21] Maybe this is why the enemies in *our* photographs of the Pacific War are barely recognizable as human beings and why, for so long, we were never shown their faces. The Japanese were represented as human beings like us only when they surrendered and accepted our superiority. But a recently published album of photographs taken during the battle for Iwo Jima suggests that this has changed, for it gives us "full-frontal views" of both Japanese and American dead.[22] Was this possible because the passage of time has dissolved some of our feelings about our former enemy? Is it because there now are fewer Americans who lived through and remember the war? Or because we Americans now have new enemies who are caricatured and dehumanized in the same way the Japanese once were and thus have displaced them?

Borrowing from Sontag, I would suggest that the Japanese enemy was long "regarded only as someone to be seen, not someone (like us) who also sees"—and, I would add, who keeps diaries.[23] This may be another reason why it took so long for Japanese wartime diaries to be translated into English. In the same way that the enemy does not see, he or she does not keep diaries. Thus reading the wartime Japanese diaries requires that we recognize our former enemies as fellow human beings, with families, passions, preferences, and even a sense of humor. It means recognizing that the enemy is like us and that, in a sense, we are the enemy.

Those of us who write the history of everyday life in wartime Japan face a challenge. We have to search for diaries that represent the entire spectrum of Japanese and their range of wartime experiences; we need to look for diaries written by both servicemen and civilians, city folk and country folk, women and children as well as men, ordinary people as well as the powerful and rich, and ethnic Chinese, Koreans, Taiwanese, and Pacific Islanders as well as Japanese. We have to understand the complicated network of military and home-front organizations that enveloped these diarists as they wrote, as well as the endless ways in which ordinary Japanese were encouraged to comply with their government's policies and to support the war effort. We also must remember how special and privileged our position is as those who "see," and we must recognize that it is we who will configure the material from the diaries and we who will represent the Japanese, not in *their* voices, but in *ours*. Our history of everyday life in wartime Japan will be just that: *our* history of everyday life in wartime Japan.

PART I

The Home Front

I

We Are All Home-Front Soldiers Now

Japan had done much to prepare its people for war. By December 7, 1941, the country had been at war for almost three and a half years already. This began in July 1937 when men from a Japanese army unit stationed outside Beijing provoked a firefight with Nationalist Chinese troops, and the Japanese government used the incident as a pretext for invading China. Japanese forces then streamed into north China from Korea, a Japanese colony, taking both Beijing and Tianjin by the end of the month. In November the Japanese opened a second front in Shanghai and took that city and then Nanjing, committing horrible atrocities in the process. A year later, Japanese forces had taken Guandong and Wuhan, and by December 1938 they controlled all of the Chinese littoral, and Chiang Kai-shek had moved the Nationalist government to Chongqing in southwestern China. During the first three years of the war, the Japanese military drafted nine hundred thousand men, and more than a million Japanese servicemen were stationed overseas at the time of the Pearl Harbor attack in December 1941.

Popular support for war existed well before July 1937. The Japanese takeover of Manchuria (1931–1932) generated what historian Louise Young terms "war fever" and "imperial jingoism," which, she points out, was the work of the commercial media, particularly the newspapers and radio.[1] Indeed, the government seemed to have learned something from them, and perhaps even from the Nazi regime in Germany, because beginning in January 1938, ten minutes of war news was broadcast every night at 7:30 P.M.[2]

Even before the outbreak of war in China, the government had taken steps to control the media, by reducing the number of

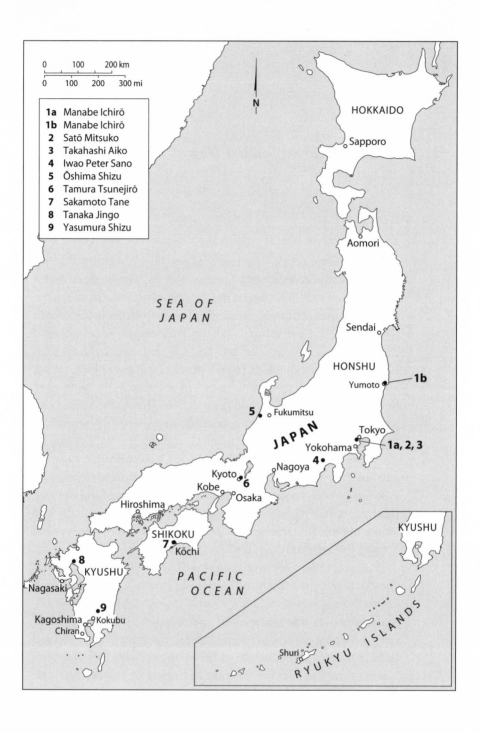

0 100 200 km
0 100 200 300 mi

1a Manabe Ichirō
1b Manabe Ichirō
2 Satō Mitsuko
3 Takahashi Aiko
4 Iwao Peter Sano
5 Ōshima Shizu
6 Tamura Tsunejirō
7 Sakamoto Tane
8 Tanaka Jingo
9 Yasumura Shizu

N

HOKKAIDO

Sapporo

Aomori

SEA OF JAPAN

Sendai

HONSHU

Yumoto — 1b

5 Fukumitsu

JAPAN

Tokyo
Yokohama — 1a, 2, 3
Nagoya 4

Kyoto 6
Kobe
Osaka

Hiroshima

KYUSHU

SHIKOKU
7 Kōchi

8 KYUSHU
Nagasaki

PACIFIC OCEAN

9
Kagoshima Kokubu
Chiran

Shuri

RYUKYU ISLANDS

newspapers and magazines, creating new government agencies to oversee the press and manage news reporting, and issuing new guidelines for reporters.[3] Then the day after the Pearl Harbor attack, journalists were urged to write articles about Japan's military superiority, its enmity for the United States and Britain, and the prospects for a long war.[4]

With the outbreak of war, the Home Ministry initiated a series of spiritual mobilization campaigns designed to generate popular support for the war. These assumed many forms: citizens were encouraged to avoid extravagance and to save for themselves and the state; women from the National Defense Women's Association sent off recruits, made talismanic thousand-stitch belts for them to wear in battle, and enlisted schoolgirls to write letters to servicemen serving overseas; and streetcars paused in front of the imperial palace so that passengers could bow to the emperor. On the first anniversary of the Marco Polo Bridge Incident that opened the Sino-Japanese War, the *Asahi* newspaper sponsored a parade of ten thousand patriotic citizens that went from Yasukuni Shrine to the imperial palace.[5]

The Ministry of Education also created what might be called an "official ideology." Taking the lead, it published in the mid-1930s a fourth edition of ethics textbooks that was decidedly more nationalistic and militaristic.[6] This edition was guided by a new pedagogical strategy: the children were now "to be affected on an emotional level," as education ministry policymakers put it. A fifth edition, published during the war, simply intensified the changes initiated in the fourth edition.[7] Even more telling were the government agencies' statements of the official ideology for popular consumption. In 1937 the education ministry published *Kokutai no hongi* (*The Principles of Our National Polity*), intended for teachers, and *Shinmin no michi* (*The Way of the Subjects*), disseminated among the general population. In 1941 the war ministry issued the *Senjinkun* (*Field Service Code*), which laid out the ideal values and behaviors of servicemen, including the no-surrender clause that would lead many thousands of Japanese servicemen to commit suicide rather than surrender. Every serviceman was expected to memorize the *Senjinkun* and follow its precepts.

In 1940 the Home Ministry began mobilizing the entire home-front population, as well as Japan's colonial subjects, for the war. It created new organizations called "community councils" (*chōnaikai*). In the cities each council consisted of a few hundred households, and in the countryside they consisted of whole villages. By the end of the year, more than 180,000 of these bodies had been formed.[8] In addition, the Home Ministry created neighborhood associations (*tonarigumi*), subordinate to the community councils. Because this was a much larger task, it took longer to implement, but by July 1942 there were more than a million neighborhood associations in Japan, Taiwan, and Korea, each consisting of eight or nine households.[9] By design, the functions of the two organizations overlapped slightly: the community councils relayed government policy to neighborhoods and discussed the topics to be addressed by neighborhood associations, which included air defense, savings bonds, metal collection drives, comfort kits for servicemen, and commemorative rituals and events.[10] The neighborhood associations met several times a month to discuss issues that the home ministry relayed to them through the community councils—issues such as food rationing, the distribution of commodities, the collection of materials for the war effort, savings-bond campaigns, air defense, and labor service. Typically, each family sent a representative, usually the mother of the household, to these meetings, which started after dinner and often lasted until just before midnight.

The government's first step in transforming the domestic economy into a war economy was to create a "new economic order," which included control over the import and export of crucial raw materials. In 1938 the government pushed the National General Mobilization Law through the Diet, which empowered the Ministry of Commerce to create in each industry "control associations" that allocated raw material and capital, set prices, and determined output and market share. The government also created a "new labor order" in order to bring the labor unions under its control.[11]

In addition, rationing was extended to scarce commodities and food. Rationing had been a fixture of life in Japan since 1938, when the government launched two types of austerity campaigns. "Imposed" austerity referred to the controlled availability of gasoline, coal, telephones, and leather goods. "Voluntary" austerity was purely hortatory. In 1939, for example, showy, flashy fashion styles were condemned; men were urged to wear the national civilian uniform; and women were encouraged to wear *monpe*, the baggy pants worn by farm women. Cosmetics were banned, and women's permanents were limited to three curls per customer.

In 1940 the government began to control food distribution, which immediately affected people in the big cities. The first foods to be rationed were sugar, milk, and rice, and, starting in 1941, cooking oil, meat, and fish as well.[12] An adult living in Tokyo or one of the other big cities (Yokohama, Nagoya, Kyoto, Osaka, Kobe) was entitled to the following daily allotments: 11 ounces of hulled rice, 1.8 ounces of fish, and between 1.3 and 1.8 ounces of meat, plus 3.2 ounces of cooking oil per month.[13]

Finally, in October 1940, the government created a mass party to usher in what Prime Minister Konoe Fumimaro called the "new political order." But the new party, the Imperial Rule Assistance Association, never became anything like the mass-totalitarian Nazi Party in Germany, because there were too many would-be policymakers in Japan and too many disparate voices. In any case, by this time Japan was being governed by conservatives, mainly the army and its supporters in the bureaucracy and the Diet. Nonetheless, elections were still held, and members of political parties—chiefly the Seiyūkai and Minseitō—continued to challenge or question government policies and even military decisions, and cabinets were still formed and dissolved.

After the Pearl Harbor Attack

After the attack on Pearl Harbor and the outbreak of war with the Allies, the Japanese government further intensified everything it had done up to that point. It issued orders and regulations that affected all Japanese in some way, shaping their actions and influencing their views of the war. The government launched metal drives that collected teapots, hibachi, and even religious objects, ostensibly for the war effort.[14] Sunflower seeds were distributed so that their flowers could be pressed for oil, and pine roots were dug up, because "two hundred pine roots [could] keep a plane in the air for an hour."[15] The government also tightened its control of the news media, closing more newspapers and magazines.[16] Censorship was systematized so that the army and navy now vetted all articles on military affairs, and the foreign ministry and the Ministry of Greater East Asia controlled international news. Home Ministry censors monitored everything: books, newspapers, magazines, and films.[17] Even baseball terminology was changed, with *honkyū* (center ball) and *gaikyū* (outside ball) replacing *sutoraiki* and *bōru*, respectively. Music, too, was censored, and jazz was outlawed and consequently went underground.[18]

The home front felt these changes immediately. The monthly meetings of neighborhood associations were moved from the first of every month to the eighth, to commemorate the day the emperor announced the start of the war with the United States and its allies. The community councils and neighborhood associations met more often to discuss topics such as war bonds, contributions to the war effort, and air-defense training. Neighborhoods were subjected to more and more inspections, most having to do with air-defense preparations. In addition, each community and neighborhood was expected to see off local men who had been conscripted for military service, which in the cities meant that at least one person from each family had to show up for the send-offs.

Teenagers mobilized for war work, April 1944. Photo courtesy of the National
Shōwa Memorial Museum, Tokyo.

The greatest and most widespread change in the first two and a half
years of the Pacific War was the government's tightening control of food. In
January 1942 staples such as miso, salt, and soy sauce began to be rationed.
Each person's monthly ration of miso was 2.3 ounces; salt, 7 ounces; and
soy sauce, 1.5 pints.[19] In August 1942 the government added dried noodles
to the rice allocations, at a six-to-five ratio, and promoted the consumption
of brown rice (*genmai*), and in November 1942 the government limited the
consumption of vegetables.[20] Although these allotments applied to both
the urban and the rural populations, those in the cities obviously suffered
more than did those in the countryside.

The war affected the home-front population in another way. Late in 1941,
the government mobilized one million men and one million women between the ages of sixteen and twenty-five for war work. Then in September 1943 the government mobilized girls fourteen and older. By March 1944
nearly three million girls had been mobilized, and labor service for girls (in
the Girls' Volunteer Corps) was made compulsory.[21]

On October 15, 1943, anticipating Allied attacks on the Japanese home islands, the government began evacuating people from the big cities. All "non-
essential" (the elderly, mothers, and children) urban dwellers were told to
leave the cities and to move in with their relatives in the countryside. Large

numbers of adults and three hundred thousand children left the big cities, and in 1944 another eight hundred thousand children were evacuated as well.

Popular Responses to the Wartime Regime and Its Policies

The wartime government assumed that all Japanese were loyal and patriotic citizens who would follow orders and obey regulations, make sacrifices for the war effort, and fight the nation's enemies, even to death. A careful reading of wartime diaries and letters reveals that this generally was true. What explains the loyalty, patriotism, obedience, and selflessness of ordinary Japanese? The first reason is obvious: Japan was at war. However, even though the patriotism of ordinary Japanese would be expected in a time of war, it still was impressive. The string of Japanese military victories in Southeast Asia and the Pacific inspired powerful patriotic feelings. Indeed, every night Sakamoto Tane, a housewife in Kōchi on the island of Shikoku, and her husband, a local judge, huddled in front of their radio to hear the latest reports on the fighting. On December 25, 1941, Sakamoto joined others in her community to celebrate the success of the Japanese military. "The town was full of waves of rising sun flags," she wrote in her diary, "and we [celebrated] together the string of imperial army victories. Today at 7:30 Hong Kong finally fell." On January 3, she reported that Japanese forces took Manila.[22]

These military successes made many Japanese want to contribute, in their own small ways, to the war effort. Sakamoto was typical. Writing on December 31, 1941, as she prepared food for the New Year celebration, she wrote: "For fish, the community council gave us a distribution of only shrimp and swordfish; we can't get either pork or beef. I have the feeling that little by little there will be shortages but that in war, we must aim for frugality even in small ways and we must be careful about waste—for the sake of the country."[23]

She also noted, with some pride, that this year's New Year celebration was simpler than in the past: "The ceremonies that take place in ordinary years have become even simpler, and it appears that there are none of the usual New Year's preparations. At 6:30 P.M., after we finished dinner, we went into the bath and then spent the evening working on the household account and [my] diary." As proof of this, she wrote that she received only three New Year cards and observed that "the government's call for the stopping of empty ritual has been carried out for the first time." A week later, she offered further confirmation when she described her family's *zōni* (rice cake soup), a traditional New Year's dish: "The seven-herb *ozōni* today was porridge without rice cakes, and although it feels as though something is missing, the radio broadcasts the imperial army's splendid military achievements, and with the firm resolve of the imperial country's subjects, we must look forward to the end of this war and persevere."[24]

Sakamoto and her husband spent the next day, January 8, listening to a reading of the Imperial Declaration of War and a broadcast from the Yoyogi parade grounds in Tokyo, where the emperor reviewed the troops. She wrote, "The town was filled with rising-sun flags, and the sky was clear. . . . We passed a day of deep gratitude."[25]

Not everyone, though, was so happy about the victories. Ōshima Shizu, a housewife in the city of Kanazawa, was less enthusiastic, perhaps because she had a son approaching draft age. She simply listed the things her family did on January 8, 1942: "Today is the first remembrance day. It is the day we revere the Imperial Declaration of War. We listened to a broadcast of a parade on the radio. The children had an opening ceremony at school."[26] Missing from Ōshima's diary entry is the ardent patriotism expressed by Sakamoto Tane.

On February 13, 1942, Japanese troops attacked Singapore, and a day later Sakamoto heard that the British were retreating. When Singapore fell, a day after that, she wrote in her diary: "At 7:50 P.M. Singapore fell, and at 10 P.M. hostilities ceased. Banzai!" On February 20 there were reports that Japanese forces had bombed Australia and occupied the city of Darwin. About a week later, Sakamoto heard that Japanese naval forces racked up more victories, prompting her to write in her diary: "Today a special news report at four o'clock [said that] our navy, once again, had produced great military results. It referred to the sea battles around Java, Surabaya, and Batavia. Truly we can only be grateful for, and excited by, our imperial forces' magnificent power." The report stated that twenty-three enemy vessels had been sunk in the Java Sea. Six days later, Sakamoto wrote that 93,500 Dutch and Indian troops and 5,000 British and Americans had surrendered. At this time, because the news was so good, Japan's radio audience reached its highest point during the war, with an estimated 7.34 million following these victories on their radios.[27]

All the while, communities happily sent off more and more men and boys to war. After all, Japan was still winning. On January 8, 1942, Ōshima Shizu joined others to see off conscripts,[28] and on February 1, the Ōshimas saw off the Ōgaki family's third son.[29] The Sakamotos, too, regularly saw off conscripts.[30] No one looked forward to these send-offs more than the schoolboys who were too young to be drafted. They not only joined the processions; they stayed with the recruits and their families all the way to the train station. Manabe Ichirō, a ten-year-old Tokyo schoolboy, wrote in his diary about a neighbor's send-off: "Afternoon—there was a going-off-to-war farewell party for Nakamichi at 7:30 P.M. It was pitch black and a little gloomy. Nakamichi said, 'I will fight with enthusiasm!' and eighteen people went with him as a group as far as Kōenji Station."[31] Manabe's was a typical schoolboy response.

This ritual of seeing off the troops was the same throughout the country—in big cities, towns, and country villages. *Nisei* Peter Sano, who was conscripted in 1944, described his send-off from the rural village where he was living:

> The house was crowded that evening with guests who gathered for the farewell party. This party was much like the others, with animated conversation and bursts of laughter. It was surprising that everyone had more than enough to eat and drink; the food shortage had become severe even in this farming community. The kinds of food suitable to serve at parties had long been unavailable, I thought.
>
> Early the next morning, I was ready to leave for Tokyo to report for duty but felt somewhat restless. Soon people would arrive to say their goodbyes, deliver their good wishes and words of encouragement. Two women came to the door in the uniform of the National Defense Women's Association. . . . The relatives who had attended the party arrived. "Iwao, stay well. We know you'll be a strong and brave soldier," said an aunt. More neighbors and schoolchildren joined us and were served a cup of saké or tea with which to drink a farewell toast to me.
>
> Three men from the Veterans Association arrived in their khaki uniforms. This signified that it was time for everyone to line up behind them for a procession to the neighborhood shrine. The village people had gone through the ritual repeatedly in recent months and were accustomed to the practice.[32]

Sano joined the infamous Kwantung Army and was sent to Manchuria, but the war ended before he saw any action and even before he had a chance to fire his weapon. He was captured by Soviet troops and spent nearly three years in a work camp in Manchuria. Nonetheless, he was one of the lucky ones, as he survived the war and was repatriated.

In December 1944 Tokyo housewife Nakamura Chiyoe wrote to her son Shigetaka, who had been evacuated to a village in Okayama Prefecture:

At this end, there is one enlistment and send-off after another. At 7:30 P.M. yesterday, there was a farewell party for draftees. Mizuno Mitsuo, the physician, left for the front, and you know the café next to the bakery. The seventeen-year-old from there was conscripted for the Naval Preparatory Flight Training Program, and the day before yesterday, Harada-san was conscripted in Kure, and yesterday evening someone named Ashida Akira . . . was conscripted; [all] seemed to be energetic servicemen, and there was lots of crying. You probably know about Watanabe Shiro [who is reported to have died in battle]. An honor, isn't it?[33]

The enthusiastic send-offs continued into 1945. Even in June 1945 Satō Mitsuko, a Tokyo housewife, traveled some distance to say goodbye to a conscript and later wrote about her trip in a letter to her daughter:

Shizuko, on June 10 Katayanagi Hideo was mustered into the familiar Thirty-Sixth Division of the Eastern District Army. Because it is the infantry, your mother went, on the ninth, to Ibaraki on the train that left Ueno at 6:40 A.M. I thought they would be extremely busy and went to help. In the evening more than thirty people appeared, and it was a grand farewell party; the kitchen was so busy that my eyes were spinning. I returned home on the train that left Ibaraki at six in the evening.[34]

To send off young Katayanagi, Satō got up well before dawn and returned late that night.

Japanese also mourned those who died in battle, in elaborate national and local ceremonies in both the cities and the countryside. Sakamoto Tane described the service that took place in Kōchi on March 26, 1942, when "every household in the city flew a mourning flag to express its compassion [for the families who had lost loved ones]."[35] Ōshima Shizu mentioned another service that was held on April 25.[36] There was a report that even the emperor and empress prayed for the war dead at the Yasukuni Shrine in Tokyo on April 25.[37] The Ōshima family celebrated the emperor's birthday on April 29 by listening to a broadcast of his review of the troops. By this time, because the country had been at war since July 1937, the rituals of mourning were familiar to most Japanese. The same communities that saw off their young men and boys also met their remains—"heroic spirits"—when they were brought home. The Sakamotos, for example, met the returning "heroic spirits" on March 28 and October 8.[38]

The members of neighborhood associations often did several things on the same day, as on October 8, 1942, when Sakamoto Tane joined her local group to read the imperial rescript, send off conscripts, and receive the remains of the war dead.[39] Naturally, those who saw off conscripts also worried about them, and the news media kept them informed about the war. In contrast to the first year of the Pacific War, when all the news was good and the Japanese looked forward to the latest battle reports, 1943 brought disturbing news. On May 23, the nation was stunned by the news that Admiral Yamamoto Isoroku, commander-in-chief of the Combined Fleet, had been killed when his plane was shot down by American aircraft.[40] Five weeks later, the Japanese public was informed that the Imperial Japanese Army garrison on Attu Island in the Aleutian chain had been decimated.[41] Sakamoto copied the military's official announcement about Attu into her diary:

On the evening of May 29, the force defending Attu, under extremely difficult conditions from May 20 onward and while continuing a desperate battle against overwhelmingly superior forces, decided to strike a final decisive blow against the main force and to display the divine mettle of the Imperial Army and delivered a brilliant attack using all their forces, after which communications ceased. We recognize that all our forces "shattered the jewel." Recognizing that they would not be able to participate in the attack, all the wounded and sick decided to kill themselves; our garrison numbered well over 2,000 men, and was commanded by Yamazaki [Yasushiro]; the enemy consisted of 20,000 crack forces and, up through May 28, suffered 6,000 casualties. Second, "Kiska" was defended.[42]

The news said that the men on Attu died "honorable deaths," or in wartime parlance, they performed *gyokusai*, "shattered the jewel."[43]

Later that summer came the news that Italy had surrendered. Sakamoto wrote in her diary:

The government of our imperial country already expected this and took the appropriate steps, and something like this event will not influence the course of the war. The imperial country simply will firm up even more the belief in certain victory.

The imperial country will tighten even more the alliance and cooperation with Germany, the various Western countries in the alliance, and the various countries and peoples of Greater East Asia and will fight to the bitter end to annihilate our old enemies, America and England.

The 100 million of our citizens cannot but expect to elevate even higher the 3,000-year tradition of our fighting spirit and our iron will; to display, with the single heart of the "One Hundred Million," the greatest military power; and to put the Sage Mind at ease by achieving the goals of this sacred war.[44]

The surrender of Italy also prompted Tokyo housewife Takahashi Aiko to write:

Today in the afternoon, there was a radio broadcast that Italy had surrendered unconditionally. Some people blanched when they heard this report and were surprised, and yet when the Mussolini government was overthrown a month and a half earlier and the Badoglio government was established, the surrender was just a matter of time. Is there really any need to be surprised just because we hear that Italy has surrendered? Nonetheless, the newspapers report that although Italy has surrendered, Mussolini is holed up in the north and has proclaimed the establishment of "North Italy." Thus, nothing has changed in the secure three-country [Axis] alliance. Recently, all newspaper reports have been written in this style, so we have to use our intuition and much more when reading the papers. If we don't work at discovering the truth, we may see all this as incredible mistakes, but I feel that nothing is more dangerous than this.

Even so, though, the collapse of one of the countries in the three-country alliance of Japan, Germany, and Italy makes us feel more and more uneasy.[45]

As Takahashi notes in her long entry, the home-front population spent a lot of time reading between the lines of news reports. What encouraged this was the foreign ministry's not censoring its news releases quite as strictly as the war ministry did, or not waiting as long to report what had happened.

The Routinization of War

In the first three years of the Pacific War (1941–1944), even when Japan's military fortunes began to sag, the general population remained patriotic and supported the war effort. The nationwide system of collective responsibility represented by the neighborhood associations and community councils may help explain this, because these institutions not only subtly shaped the behavior of wartime Japanese but also served to keep them in line. In this way, these neighborhood groups also ensured, as German historian Peter Borscheid put it, that "everyday thinking and action became pragmatic" and "functioned to 'relieve' the individual of constant uncertainty or doubts."[46] Consider, for example, the cycle of daily, weekly, and monthly meetings, drills, and rituals that took place in each neighborhood. Every month began with War Remembrance Day on the eighth, when families turned on their radios to hear a broadcast of the imperial rescript that announced the start of the war. Often families in a neighborhood association gathered at the local shrine, where the rescript was read aloud and they prayed for their country's success in the war.[47] Schoolchildren were asked to stand at attention while the imperial rescript was read.

The diaries kept by home-front adults reveal precisely how the neighborhood associations insinuated themselves into their members' lives. Consider, for example, how the war affected Sakamoto Tane, the judge's wife in Kōchi:

9/1/1943: In the evening at 6:40 P.M. air-raid warning and alert [were] issued; with the blackout system we could not do a thing. . . . At 6:15 P.M., according to Imperial Headquarters, "Today before dawn many enemy aircraft attacked Minami-Tori Shima, and the enemy [warships] shelled the island."[48]

9/2/1943: The air-raid alert has not been lifted, and the neighborhood association meeting [was] held at the Uehara residence.

9/3/1943: Mrs. Uehara came to our house to discuss the national savings-bond campaign. Mrs. Shimamura and Mrs. Tokuhiro also came and responded to various points. The burden for the neighborhood association is the large amount of ¥271, and naturally we will have to buy lots more than expected.

9/8/1943: At 4:00 A.M. an air-raid warning and alert [were] issued; I changed immediately into my monpe and had the relief team prepare to assemble. From 5:30 A.M. there was a one-hour drill. At 11:00 A.M. the second drill [was held]. From 6:30 P.M. [the community council met] for an hour. Seventy-four attended, and because everyone was enthusiastic, the community council head seemed extremely pleased. Everyone pledged to make every effort to respond well when we have a real attack. Today there was a distribution of fish for the first time in a while.

9/9/1943: Because tomorrow is a holiday I went to buy directly from farmers but did not find anything special; just vegetables, as usual. Twenty yen is the allotment per neighborhood association, so each family will have to give ¥2.

9/10/1943: Today was really hot and muggy, and it was unbearable. Unexpectedly, the consumers' union came to take orders, and I ordered soy sauce, *sōsu* [Worcestershire sauce], and *mizuame* [a kind of candy] and returned home.

9/12/1943: This morning I finally wrote to the older Kodera sister. I have worried every day about her illness, but overwhelmed by everything I have had to do each day, my letter of condolence will be late, and I am really sorry about this.

9/13/1943: Because a surprise air-defense drill will take place at some point soon, I will have to prepare.

9/15/1943: The last few days have been the dog days of summer, and the heat has been killing. Late morning I went in the direction of Fifth Avenue, but there was just eggplant and ginger. I had the feeling that the lines of buyers were longer after the co-ops appeared in each ward. From 7:30 P.M. I hosted a meeting of officials at our house. We discussed Council Head Yamamoto's requisition order and the problem of succession after the survey is completed and the requisition is decided on. We decided on cooperating after everything is decided. The meeting broke up just before 10 P.M. Attending were eleven people, beginning with Councillor Uehara.[49]

The entries for May 1944 in the diary of Ōshima Shizu, the housewife and mother from Kanazawa, reveal a similar pattern but also differ slightly because Ōshima, unlike Sakamoto, who had no children, was caring for three children as well as a husband:

5/1/1944: Father went off on business and returned late in the evening. I calculated our neighborhood association's national savings and savings bonds.

5/4/1944: Asano-san and Matsuda-san visited . . . to talk about [my] becoming head of the neighborhood association's housewives association. I had no choice but to accept the position.

5/5/1944: In the evening there was the usual meeting of officials of the housewives association [and discussions of] housewives' labor, comfort [packages], etc. The Ōshima house passed the Great Cleanup Inspection.

5/7/1944: From 10 A.M., I attended a parents association meeting, had a school meal for lunch, visited a class in the morning, had chats in the afternoon, and then a general meeting. There was a discussion of the mobilization of the third-year students for a work brigade. Papa finished the air-raid shelter in the garden.

5/15/1944: I was busy making the rucksack. I am doing it with the [sewing machine], but the foot pedal is not in good shape. I ground up sardines, sesame, nori, kombu, etc., to make *furikake* [topping for rice]. I will make sushi for Masa's farewell party.

5/17/1944: Masatada left in the morning with more than forty pounds of stuff crammed into his rucksack. He left at seven. In the evening, dinner was somehow lonely.

5/20/1944: We celebrated Papa's birthday with red-bean rice. . . . [Received] the first letter from Masa at his mobilization site [Tsubata in Ishikawa Prefecture]. He reported that their work started without incident. Sixty of them live in a thirty-eight-*tatami* [mat] room. He also reported that he couldn't sleep the first night. In the evening an air-raid warning was issued. He reported that enemy aircraft came to Minami-Tori Shima.

5/22/1944: I dried boiled bamboo shoots, short-neck clams, Japanese asparagus, bracken, etc., for preservation. That evening I made *mame-iri* [roasted beans] and dried sardines, made small packages for mobilized Kō and Masa, and it took until midnight. . . . I also got pumpkin squash seedlings from the Tarōdas.

5/25/1944: My leg, with yesterday's strain, was not in good shape. I will try to get cotton fabric and a chemise at the cooperative. . . . Takako cried a lot and I didn't know what to do. An evacuee, Sakashita-san, came to the house across the street.

5/28/1944: Work for the Housewives Labor and National Service Brigade. I went in the afternoon to work at the Hirano Manufacturing Company. I went with the two children, and Taeko helped a lot. It was easy work, cutting small, delicate things with scissors. In the evening the squad had its regular meeting. Work and the distribution of needles—three per person.

5/29/1944: I washed the winter clothes. Leaves came out on both the pumpkin squash and castor bean plants. In the evening I made the ingredients for *furikake*, salting and drying the gizzard shad.

5/30/1944: In the afternoon I went out to do Serving the Country Brigade work. . . . In the evening I roasted beans with soybean flour and received the tofu distribution, the first in a month.

5/31/1944: Kō returned home: he was well, completely black, and had finished a month's worth of work. We celebrated his homecoming with Imperial Japanese Navy Commemoration rice cakes, the *okara* [bean curd lees] he brought as a homecoming present, yellowtail from the distribution, and bamboo shoots. It felt like early summer.[50]

The diaries of housewives with children suggest how busy they were during the war and explain why many were often on the verge of collapse. Satō Mitsuko reported in September 1944 that she and other members of the housewives association were told they now must do the "work of soldiers," and she soon found that she was so busy that she had trouble finding the time to write to her evacuated daughter or to send packages to her. "Mother recently has been really busy with housewives association work," she wrote to her daughter Shizuko, "and each of us is doing ninety [things], and I'm doing everything I possibly can because it's for the soldiers."[51]

The community councils and neighborhood associations also had a gender dimension. Most of the community council leaders were male, between the ages of forty and sixty, and small-businessmen in the community, and they usually had no more than a middle-school education. Each neighborhood association head was a husband and/or father of one of its member families, and every month one of the families assumed responsibility for whatever had to be done in the neighborhood. Since the husbands usually worked and were gone during the day or were at war, the burden of managing the neighborhood association's affairs usually was left to the wife in the family on duty for the month. She would be responsible for distributing food and commodities, collecting contributions to campaigns, or informing everyone of an upcoming visit or inspection by community council officials. Since the women who had families also had to worry about securing enough food for meals for them, the burden of neighborhood association duties was truly onerous and unwanted. In her September 2, 1943, entry, Takahashi Aiko, the wife of a Tokyo doctor, expressed her feelings about being on neighborhood association duty:

Our household is on neighborhood duty for the month, and this is causing us a lot of anxiety. The reports that enemy planes will be coming increase daily, and if this should happen, we would have full responsibility for the neighborhood association. For those who are not very good at leading people, the thought of having to do this is depressing. Although it must seem quite irresponsible to have these thoughts, we are terrified and pray that nothing will happen during our month of duty. When a commodity has to be distributed, the person on duty, representing the neighborhood, picks it up and divides it up among the various households based on the number of people in each family. Is there a circular to be sent around? Do we have to have someone run around the neighborhood? I have everyone come to get the various commodities but am at a complete loss as to [what to do about] the vegetables distributed by the greengrocer. When dividing things up based on the number of people in a household, I find that if I don't include the bundled straw sheaths and the completely yellowed leaves, the distributions don't work out by weight. But if I do include the straw and the dried leaves, I have the feeling I'll hear the criticism "she's probably taking the good ones for herself." This is irritating to everyone, and it's really unbearable and difficult for us. When you're on monthly duty, you can do what everyone else has done, but you can't do anything about people who think about things only from the perspective of the present. You can't become a god who thinks of everything, nor can you do something for the sad people and show compassion. In distributing things in this way, you waste a lot of time and have hurt feelings, and you go to pick up things at the distribution center and have to work hard.[52]

Takahashi's anxiety is understandable and also not unusual.

In the cities, the community councils and neighborhood associations had an important class dimension as well. The fact that the men who headed the community councils were not well educated made a huge difference to the better-educated and richer families of more elite status. Takahashi Aiko, the doctor's wife, repeatedly expressed her contempt for the leaders of her community council. At the end of June 1942, her neighborhood had an air-defense equipment inspection for which each house was asked to make a list of what they had in the way of hoses, steel helmets, fire dampers, ladders, sand, buckets, and shovels and to post the list on the door of their residence. "In the afternoon," Takahashi wrote in her diary, "two officials with stern faces conducted the inspection. I really don't like the attitude of these sorts of people and their way of speaking." Nine months later, Takahashi's neighborhood had another air-defense inspection, which she described in this way: "Today we had an air-defense drill again. The community council's big shots put on their pompous clothes and their pompous faces and strutted about with a pompous number of people." Her feelings about the leaders of her community council are clear.[53]

In the rural communities, the gender and class dimensions of the community councils and neighborhood associations differed from those in the cities. Here community council leaders were men from families that had served as village headmen for decades, even centuries, with the result that everyone in those villages knew his or her place, and the interactions between the distinguished and the ordinary did not cause the kind of resentment that Takahashi expressed. In fact, village headmen and their cronies really formed a single unit vis-à-vis the wartime state. Tanaka Jingo, a farmer in Kyushu, gathered with other men from his village once a month to eat and drink, and since seafood and saké always were available, they ate and drank well despite the wartime rationing. These gatherings took place even as Tanaka complained repeatedly in his diary about the government's demands for more and more of what he produced and the growing shortages of labor and fertilizer.[54]

Rural communities displayed much more cooperation between the well-to-do farmers and those less well off. An example is Yasumura Shizu, a young mother in Okinawa. Yasumura's father had served in the military, and he was sure that Okinawa would soon be attacked and warned, "It'll be terrible."[55] For this reason, in 1944 he urged his daughter to move with her two children from Okinawa to Takaharu, her husband's home village in western Kyushu. She did move and kept a diary the whole time she was there, recording the generosity of the well-to-do families in that village. During her first week in Takaharu, Yasumura and her two children received food from the neighborhood association there, which she paid for by working for designated families. Once her debt was repaid, she continued to work for these families but now was compensated.[56] Because she was there with two children, it would have been difficult for her to survive without the side work and food these families offered.

The neighborhood associations allowed local officials to monitor their support for the war. Whether families participated fully or not at all was noted, as was their representative's punctuality at meetings. Takahashi wrote in her diary on March 27, 1943: "Each time there is an air-defense drill, we are made to line up in single file, call out our names, and roll is taken, with lots of muttering about which houses are not represented, who was late, and which wife sent her maid in her place."[57]

Whether families showed up to see off local men and boys conscripted for military service also was noticed. Tamura Tsunejirō, a seventy-five-year-old man from Kyoto, was visited by a community council representative, who urged him to come to his grandson's send-off. He related in his diary what happened:

On the morning of the scheduled visit to Imamiya Shrine, Community Council Captain Kataoka came to urge us to participate. We had a responsibility to do this. We had to pray for the success of [our grandson] Inao, who had enlisted and was being sent to the front. We couldn't say we can't go because it's raining . . . and luckily we got Toshie [Tamura's granddaughter] to go at 7:30 A.M. and stand in for us and march to the Imamiya Shrine with the people from the community council.[58]

Tamura's grandson was sent to New Guinea, where he was killed in action in December 1944.

The government also demanded the labor of its citizens. Sakamoto Tane's diary is full of references to labor service and whether she and other members of her neighborhood association contributed as much as they were expected to. When and whether they offered their labor for the war effort clearly was being recorded by their community council. Ōshima wrote that this was the case in Kanazawa too, writing on November 21, 1943: "Today we assumed that we had to turn out for labor service, according to the community council, but my husband was busy . . . and could not go. Not a single person showed up from the number one neighborhood association [Sakamoto's neighborhood association], so it was decided that tomorrow the wives will go out."[59]

The next day she and fellow members of her neighborhood association tried to make amends:

I woke up at five o'clock in the morning, prepared a *bentō* lunch, and reported for labor service together with these three—Uehara, Tokuhiro, and Tamura—to the Shimeda Improvement Construction in Shionoe. From our community council, approximately thirteen turned out—one male and twelve women. Our task was to dig a culvert in the middle of a rice paddy, and we put a bamboo pipe approximately one meter down to drain water. Today we were able to dig four feeder lines, and we had more than enough female labor; we all were very tired, but we fulfilled our responsibility; there was no greater happiness. After finishing dinner, I went right to bed and rested my tired body.[60]

Then two weeks later, Sakamoto stood in for her husband:

It was little different from the last place, and it involved digging a culvert at the foot of Mount Takami. From the number one neighborhood association, five of us participated—Uehara (maid), Shimamura, Tamura, and Abe. All together, there were fifteen of us, six males and nine females. The soil was softer than the other day, and because of this and the fact that it was Sunday, students were mobilized as well, and the part of the culvert we had to dig was small, so as a result we finished extremely early and left at about 1:30. Walked home with the Nagano wife from the number five neighborhood association.[61]

Labor service was another way that the wartime state controlled and monitored the lives of its citizens.

Whether citizens contributed materially to the war effort was noted as well. As the leader of her neighborhood association, Sakamoto Tane knew exactly how much each family contributed over the course of the war. In her diary entry for December 23, 1942, for example, she reported that she deposited ¥238 at the post office for the savings-bond campaign and dropped off ¥30 at the community council, adding that the Uehara and Miyamoto families gave ¥10 each and the Hatakeyama and Sakamoto families gave ¥5 each.[62]

Similarly, Sakamoto recorded exactly how much in savings bonds each family bought: "For the number one neighborhood association, the designated amount was ¥320, and the Ueharas bought ¥100 worth; the Tokuhiros, Shimamuras, and Sakamotos each bought ¥50 worth; and the others bought ¥70 worth; and it looks as though we will be able to handle this."[63]

She added, when the April savings bonds went on sale in the form of ¥50 certificates, "I had no choice but to decide to buy one."[64] In her September 3, 1943, diary entry, she again wrote what each of the ten families in her neighborhood association contributed to the current savings-bond campaign:

Mrs. Uehara came to see me about the national savings-bond allotments. Mrs. Shimamura and Mrs. Tokuhiro also will participate and were responsive to various deliberations. The current amount for the number one neighborhood association is the large amount of ¥271. Naturally, we must buy more than is specified.

Generally, the contributions were as follows:

Uehara: ¥98
Sakamoto: ¥35
Tokuhiro: ¥30
Shimamura: ¥24

Maeda: ¥20
Tamura: ¥20
Abe: ¥14
Horiuchi: ¥10
Yanagigawa: ¥10
Matsumura: ¥10[65]

Sakamoto continued to work for some time, writing in her December 11, 1943, entry: "For our meeting about the community council's savings-bond allotment, I polled each house in the neighborhood association about the amounts they hoped to contribute and reported to Uehara what I learned. This month we have to reach a goal of ¥600 million in savings, so we applied to purchase ¥50."[66] The careful recording of how much each neighborhood association member contributed shows how closely the authorities tracked the wartime behavior of ordinary people.

Individuals who did not do what they were supposed to were punished in some way. For example, their wartime powers enabled local officials to embarrass and humiliate those who did not toe the line. Tamura Tsunejirō, the elderly man from Kyoto, never forgot being humiliated by community council officials during a blackout in January 1945:

A neighborhood association meeting to discuss savings bonds, December 1942. Photo courtesy of the *Mainichi shinbun*.

It was an unusually cold night, and I turned on the light in the hall so I could see my feet during a fire prevention drill. Unfortunately, unbeknown to me, the Karaku civilian air-raid warden was making his rounds. It was dark and I was grubby, but I thought he was a customer. "Please come in," I said, which was the wrong thing to say. At that instant I felt sharp pains in my chest, and before too long someone shouted, "Hey! Who's in charge? Don't you know about the Civilian Air-Raid Patrol? What's this fire? This is not allowed today! Come to the station! Now!"

> "I'm sorry. Now if you let me, I'll put out that light right away!"
> "No! That's not permitted. Come to the station!"
> "Don't you think the Matsubara bomb damage was a terrible shame?"
> "You idiot! Don't you know it's because of one house that many are inconvenienced?"

An overbearing guy with a drooping moustache came in from the street and shouted.

> "This old guy is still not the age when he'd be senile. Isn't there a young person here?"

Were these the words of a fellow human being? Because I recognized that I was in the wrong, I fell to my knees and lowered my head, but he insisted, "This old guy's not senile." . . . In my seventy-five years, I've never been called a "senile old guy" or humiliated to this extent.[67]

No doubt the fear of being humiliated or embarrassed encouraged ordinary Japanese to police themselves and to monitor their behavior so that everything they did conformed to government guidelines.

Compliance of the Home Front

The many wartime institutions that the government created to mobilize the home-front population were effective because they were interlocking, by design; that is, they were what one government document described as "an essential part of the controlled economy."[68] Thus neighborhood associations were intended to monitor morale and war support, to implement government directives, to distribute rationed foods and commodities, and to be the first line of defense against espionage and enemy attacks.

The system worked too well. Already by August 1941, some community council leaders in Tokyo had punished people who became angry during air-raid drills by taking their names off the community council rolls, which meant, of course, that they could not receive any rationed foods or commodities. To resolve this situation—the poor relations between community councils and their members—the government continued to issue the usual warnings to community council leaders, and it also made shopkeepers post the following sign:

OUR SHOP'S PLEDGE

We are home-front soldiers.
The sellers and buyers are war buddies.
Let's cooperate with smiling faces.
All Japanese are now home-front soldiers.[69]

This system of interlocking institutions encouraged ordinary Japanese to internalize the values and behaviors that the wartime government promoted in the print and broadcast media. They were encouraged to become good Japanese subjects who were completely willing to do whatever was asked of them, to do everything they could to support the war, to send off their husbands and sons to fight in the war, and even to give their own lives. The government's efforts paid off. On January 22, 1942, for example, Sakamoto Tane reported that a new system for rationing clothes was to go into effect on February 1, and she added, "I resolved to make an effort to live without waste."[70]

This self-policing intensified as the war continued. On December 8, 1943, the second anniversary of the start of the Pacific War, Sakamoto and her husband commemorated the event with what she called "dawn mobilization":

Got up at four in the morning. Finished breakfast and went with my husband at 6:00 A.M. to Kainan Middle School, where each house sent at least one person, and we assembled, in other words, in dawn mobilization. To commemorate the second anniversary of the start of the war, we performed the ritual reading of the emperor's declaration of war rescript. Beginning with the head of the community council and including adviser Uehara; my husband, who was the deputy head;

Nakakado, the head of the savings section; and Miyamoto, the head of the housewives' section—everyone offered their opinions about the decision for war, and at the end, we shouted 'banzai' three times, and the meeting broke up at 7:30 A.M.[71]

Even after a year, the Sakamoto family's support for the war was undiminished. Indeed, in their wartime correspondence with one another, entire families affirmed and encouraged the same values and behaviors and even rehearsed the official ideology. Knowing that teachers, friends, and relatives were fighting somewhere for the country had a huge effect on the home-front population. By this time, they had internalized the militarization of daily life, so gathering to commemorate the start of the war was not simply a "meeting"; it was "mobilization." All Japanese were now home-front soldiers.

2

"No Luxuries until the War Is Won"

The horrors of World War II are well known: historian John Dower tells us that nearly fifty-five million people died in that conflict and estimates that "several million to fifteen million" died in Asia alone.[1] But the huge losses suffered by the Japanese and Japanese colonial subjects during the war are not so well known. Dower estimates that 3 percent of the Japanese population—2.1 million people—perished. Of the approximately two million Japanese who served in the armed services, 1,740,955 were killed, many hundreds of thousands were wounded, and many of those repatriated to Japan needed medical attention; and the firebombing of Japanese cities and towns and the atomic bombing of Hiroshima and Nagasaki killed almost four hundred thousand.[2]

Japanese and Japanese colonial subjects suffered in another way as well. It is well known that many did not have enough to eat, especially in the last year of the war, but what the English-language scholarship on the war does not cover in much detail is the impact and extent of the food shortages.[3] To remedy this, I examine next the impact of the wartime food shortages on the urban and rural populations in the Japanese home islands during the last three years of the war. I will attempt to answer three questions: First, how did the food shortages affect the home-front population? Second, how did the food situations in the cities and the countryside differ? And third, why did the food situations in the cities and countryside differ as they did?

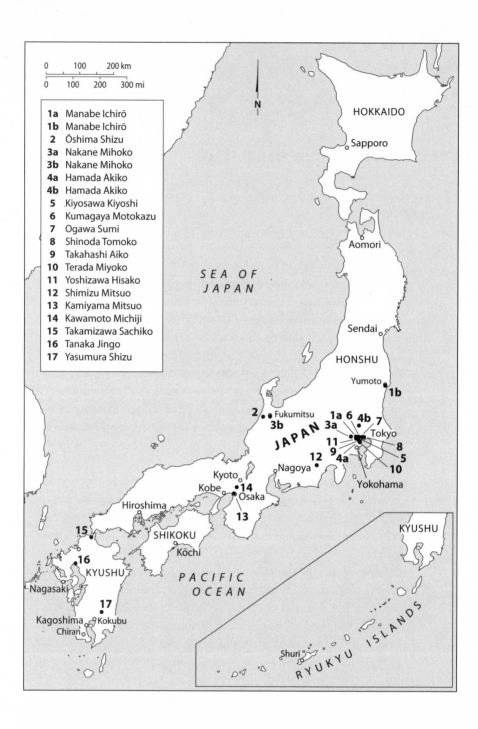

0 100 200 km
0 100 200 300 mi

N

1a Manabe Ichirō
1b Manabe Ichirō
2 Ōshima Shizu
3a Nakane Mihoko
3b Nakane Mihoko
4a Hamada Akiko
4b Hamada Akiko
5 Kiyosawa Kiyoshi
6 Kumagaya Motokazu
7 Ogawa Sumi
8 Shinoda Tomoko
9 Takahashi Aiko
10 Terada Miyoko
11 Yoshizawa Hisako
12 Shimizu Mitsuo
13 Kamiyama Mitsuo
14 Kawamoto Michiji
15 Takamizawa Sachiko
16 Tanaka Jingo
17 Yasumura Shizu

HOKKAIDO

Sapporo

Aomori

SEA OF
JAPAN

Sendai

HONSHU

Yumoto **1b**

2 Fukumitsu

3b   **1a 6**   **4b 7**
       3a   Tokyo
       11   **8**
      9   **5**
   12   **4a**   **10**
Nagoya

Kyoto
Kobe **14**
Osaka

Yokohama

Hiroshima

13

15   SHIKOKU

Kōchi

KYUSHU

16
KYUSHU

PACIFIC
OCEAN

Nagasaki

17

Kagoshima Kokubu
Chiran

Shuri

RYUKYU ISLANDS

JAPAN

Government Food Controls

Any discussion of the wartime food situation in the Japanese home islands has to begin in 1940, the year the government began to control food distribution. In June it created a rationing system for sugar and milk products in Yokohama, Nagoya, Kyoto, and Kobe, although participation was still voluntary.[4] In August the government fixed the prices of forty vegetables and fruits in an effort to stop their dramatic rise—they had risen 400 percent the previous year—and in September the government imposed a limit on seafood prices.[5]

In October 1940 the government assumed control of rice distribution after a drop in production that summer and fall resulted in shortages.[6] At first the government responded to the shortages by mixing foreign rice with domestic rice, but this was not sufficient; so in January 1941 it prohibited the buying and selling of rice altogether.[7] A month later it set up a rationing system that based rice allotments on age, occupation, and gender.[8] Then in April 1941 the government initiated a food distribution system in the six biggest cities that gave citizens coupons entitling them to buy fixed amounts of what were termed "daily necessities." Each adult was allotted just over eleven ounces of hulled rice a day, a system that was later introduced to other cities as well.[9] Despite these measures, the rice shortages persisted through the spring of 1942, prompting the government to take other steps: in August dried noodles were added to rice allotments at a six-to-five ratio, and in November the government began to promote the consumption of brown rice (*genmai*). Rice production rose by 2 percent in 1942 and then fell by 6 percent in 1943, 7 percent in 1944, and then by a huge 33 percent in 1945.[10] As this happened, Allied surface ships and submarines made matters worse by interdicting the flow of rice, first from southeast Asia and then from Manchuria.[11]

Annual Rice Production

1939	10,345,000 tons
1940	9,131,000
1941	8,263,000
1942	10,016,000
1943	9,433,000
1944	8,874,000
1945	5,872,000

Distributing the vegetable ration, Osaka, July 1944. Photo courtesy of the *Mainichi shinbun.*

The government imposed similar controls on other staples. Beginning in September 1941 it fixed meat and fish allotments, with the daily allotment of meat set at 1.3 to 1.8 ounces per person (1.8 ounces per person in a two-person family, and 1.3 ounces in a five-person family) and fish at 1.8 ounces per person. The government did the same with miso, salt, and soy sauce, fixing the monthly per-person allotment at 2.3 ounces of miso, 7 ounces of salt, 3.2 ounces of cooking oil, and 11 ounces of soy sauce.[12] These were not generous allotments, and they would shrink over the next four years.

In the eighteen months from January 1943 through the early summer of 1944, the government reduced daily food allotments even further. In 1943 the daily fish allotment was reduced to less than an ounce per person;[13] and in 1944 the daily vegetable ration fell to 2.5 ounces per person and the monthly oil allotment was reduced to just over one ounce per person.[14] In addition, the authorities routinely added soybeans to the rice ration and promoted rice substitutes such as soybeans, sweet potatoes, barley, and wheat flour.

The last year of the war brought even more dramatic changes. In the fall of 1944 the government replaced fresh fish with dried anchovies (*niboshi*) and fish preserves (*tsukudani*), delivered once every four days.[15] Usually dried anchovies were used to make stock and preserves were eaten as a condiment, most often with hot cooked rice, but now they were a main source of protein. In January 1945 the authorities cut the rice ration again, even as the actual amount of rice in the allotment dropped from 87 percent in May to 51 percent in June and to 41 percent in July.

The government reduced the quantities of other foodstuffs as well. In January 1945 it cut fish allotments to one ounce per person every six days and, in March, to half an ounce per person. The daily vegetable allotment dropped to less than one ounce per person in February and March, and in May the monthly cooking oil ration shrank to less than one ounce per person. Then in July 1945, the government reduced even these meager allotments by 10 percent.[16] Not surprisingly, the average daily caloric intake fell to just below 1,900 calories and was as low as 1,677 calories in Kyoto.[17]

Impact of the Food Controls on the Urban Population

How did the government's food controls affect ordinary Japanese? The urban populations felt their impact almost immediately. They found that there was simply less food available and that they now had to shop more aggressively. For example, in February 1942 Takahashi Aiko was elated when she found tempura being made at a department store while shopping in Tokyo. Recognizing that it had been some time since her family had had tempura, she bought some and brought it home. When she got home, she made a distressing discovery: "When I tried a piece, whew! It had the horrible smell of something that had begun to go bad. . . . I was surprised that they were selling something bad!"[18] Urban families also found that they had to spend more time shopping—a second effect of the new food controls. A

A rice gruel cafeteria, May 1944. Photo courtesy of the *Mainichi shinbun*.

survey conducted in 1942 revealed that a family of five spent an average of four and a half hours a day standing in line for food.[19] This was true in provincial cities as well. In Kanazawa, Ōshima Taeko stood in line for cutlass fish on August 4; two days later she queued for beef; and eight days after that she "stood in line at the fishmonger's, but no fish were delivered, and no one received anything."[20] By 1944 Tokyo had "lines of about a hundred people" in front of food shops and even lines at the rice gruel restaurants.[21]

After the reduction in food allotments in 1943, those living in the big cities began to not have enough to eat. That year, rice production fell by 6 percent—from 10,016,000 to 9,433,000 tons—and not only was rice adulterated with dried noodles and, later, soybean bran and soybeans, it also was very hard to get. Tokyo journalist Kiyosawa Kiyoshi observed, "Everywhere there is a shortage of rice," and a month and a half later he noted that "there is only rice for two meals a day, and a third meal is unthinkable."[22] Kiyosawa's comment is telling because he was well off and could afford to buy rice. Indeed, it was necessity that forced many urban Japanese to do as the government recommended: to consume greater quantities of rice substitutes like soybeans, sweet potatoes, barley, and bread. The result was a dramatic shift from what one scholar called a "granular diet" to a "powder diet."[23]

As meat and fish disappeared from their diets, urban families substituted vegetables. In 1944 a family of five in Kyoto was expected, we are told, to split "one Kamo eggplant and one Japanese radish" for dinner, and eight months later the same family stretched half a radish over two days.[24] A Tokyo family of four had half a radish for two days' worth of meals, and the daily allotments for a family of six were "a handful of bean sprouts" on one occasion and a "handful of greens" on another. Some even "boiled chrysanthemum leaves" for two days' worth of meals.[25] When the government cut the vegetable ration further, it compensated by distributing dried radish (kiriboshi daikon), bean sprouts, and konnyaku and encouraging people to eat more pumpkin squash and to cultivate home gardens. Pumpkin squash was one of two vegetables whose production rose during the war; the other was sweet potatoes.[26] Despite these countermeasures, vegetable consumption continued to fall, and by the summer of 1945 it was less than 60 percent of what it had been in 1937.[27]

Most city folk simply learned to make do with less. They continued to buy what their neighborhood associations offered them, even though what they paid for these distributed foodstuffs could be, at the same time, both reasonable and absurd. In July 1944, for example, Kyoto resident Tamura Tsunejirō paid only eighty-five sen for just over eight pounds of potatoes, and three months later he paid ¥30 for just over eight pounds of sugar.[28]

Many urban families were driven to shop on the black market, but they quickly discovered that increased demand had driven up black market prices. In desperation, many families began going to the countryside to buy directly from farmers, which the government did not encourage, but they found that the farmers were asking even more than the official prices offered by their neighborhood associations and those in the black market.[29] Nonetheless, the shopping trips to the countryside continued because most city dwellers had no other choice. On September 12, 1943, a Sunday, an estimated sixteen thousand Tokyoites took trains to Funabashi and Matsudo, on the eastern edge of the city, to buy from farmers.[30] Later that same month, Kanazawa housewife Ōshima Shizu spent five hours in transit to get more than sixteen pounds of potatoes.[31] In December 1944 Tamura Otsuru journeyed from Kyoto to Tokyo and back to buy sweet potatoes for her family.[32] And on any given day in 1944—whether a weekday or a weekend—an estimated eight thousand to twenty thousand Tokyoites went to nearby Chiba or Saitama to buy directly from farmers. About 40 percent of these shoppers were women, and the other 60 percent were children. Families sent their children because the authorities were said to be more lenient with children, and children were better at eliciting sympathy from callous or stingy farmers.[33] Because the wartime inflation made farmers less inclined to accept money, shoppers also had to take things to barter, such as kimono, "Western clothes," and household goods.[34]

Yet some Tokyoites continued to eat well. Through the spring of 1944, many still frequented favorite restaurants, but in time they discovered that cooked rice was no longer served at these eateries either. By summer, therefore, many had to join the many thousands who stood in line for rice gruel, and by the early fall of that year, many restaurants simply closed. In September Kiyosawa Kiyoshi tried to take a friend to a favorite Chinese restaurant only to discover that it had closed.[35]

Good food was still available in the big cities, but it was served in the homes of families with the means to pay the high prices asked for fowl, fish, and vegetables. In May 1944, for example, Kiyosawa and his wife had Rōyama Masamichi and his wife for dinner and served chicken sukiyaki.[36] Hamada Akiko, a young teacher evacuated with her students from Tokyo to a village in Saitama Prefecture, had surprisingly good meals on trips back to Tokyo throughout the fall and early winter of 1944: on October 19 she had a sumptuous dinner of "sashimi, a fried dish, and a simmered flounder dish," and in late November she visited relatives in Ōmori and "was treated to a fine meal." Hamada even had a restaurant meal in December, which she described as her "first served meal in a long time" and reported that "it was wonderful."[37] That same month, in Osaka, Kamiyama Mitsuo was invited to a friend's home to have chicken sukiyaki, and went even though he had a cold.[38]

In January 1945 some urban families even managed to have the usual New Year's food. Terada Miyoko, a Japan Women's University student mobilized for war work, reported that her family had zōni (rice cake soup) with fish, black beans, herring roe, shrimp, kinton (a sweet), tangerines, kelp rolls, nishime (a simmered dish), and carrots, plus Japanese radish namasu (a vinegared dish).[39] Satō Mitsuko and her family had rice cakes, tatsukuri (sardines fried in soy sauce), and herring roe, which she described in a letter to her evacuated daughter as "a wasted repast in this time of decisive war."[40] Kawamoto Michiji, who lived on the outskirts of Osaka, could hear his neighbors pounding glutinous rice to make rice cakes.[41] To have such a sumptuous New Year's meal in the midst of the worsening food situation was not typical, however.

The New Year's meals in the provinces were even more sumptuous. Sakamoto Tane described the rice cake soup she served her husband at New Year's in January 1942: "The seven-herb rice cake soup today was gruel without rice cakes, and although it feels like something is missing, the radio

Making rice cakes in Tokyo, January 9, 1945. Photo courtesy of the National
Shōwa Memorial Museum, Tokyo.

broadcasts the imperial army's splendid military achievements, and with the firm resolve of the imperial country's subjects, we must look forward to the completion of this war and persevere."[42]

In Kanazawa in January 1944 Ōshima Shizu served rice cakes and yellow-tail to her family, and the following year she served rice cakes and herring roe.[43]

As a result of these food shortages, most of the urban population began to have serious health problems, with weight loss the most common and conspicuous. In Tokyo in late June 1944 Kiyosawa Kiyoshi commented that "of late, everybody is extremely emaciated. When I encountered Ohata of the foreign ministry after an absence of one month, he was completely emaciated. When I met my neighbor Koike on the street, he was so thin I didn't recognize him. It seems that everybody is like this. The reason is the inadequacy of nutrition."[44] A week later, he wrote, "For the first time since he was born, Professor Kuwaki is emaciated. This is also true of Professor Makino. Everybody is talking about becoming emaciated. It is clear that it is a matter of inadequate nutrition."[45] In Kyoto in October 1944 Tamura Tsunejirō's barber insisted, "You've changed; you've lost weight," and finally in late January 1945 Tamura came to the same conclusion.[46]

Fatigue and illness were other effects of the food shortages. The elderly Tamura noticed that he tired easily,[47] but it was even worse for those who had physically demanding jobs. Takamizawa Sachiko, who had been mobilized for war work in a factory making balloons, remembered:

We worked on these [balloons] through the frigid winter, and the food was very poor. We worked two twelve-hour shifts, standing the entire time. Those on the night shift were forced to take two stimulant pills to stay awake. It was a constant struggle against drowsiness. Our dormitory, which slept twelve to a ten-tatami-mat room, was a place where we went only to flop down to sleep.

In these vile conditions almost everyone got athlete's foot and frostbite. Nearly one-tenth of our number died soon after graduation. Many suffered from tuberculosis, neuralgia, rickets, and overexhaustion.[48]

In July 1945 a man from Kyushu who had been assigned to move a shipment of rice from Karatsu Harbor to nearby warehouses put it even more bluntly. "Although there is all this rice," he observed, "we're starving to death and our stomachs get emptier and emptier. We lack energy, and [some rice] would give us the energy to help."[49] That same month, Shimizu

Mitsuo, an eighteen-year-old substitute teacher, wrote in his diary that he felt "dizzy from hunger while teaching class," and on August 4 Yoshizawa Hisako, a single working woman in Tokyo, wrote in her diary: "Recently we've been working hard, eating little, and not getting enough sleep, and it's really beginning to be a source of concern."[50]

With food in such short supply, many urban Japanese were desperate. In January 1945 Yoshizawa admitted that with all the reductions in food allotments, very little was available, and she wondered, "What are we to do?" A week earlier, she had watched her neighbor go off to stand in line for scraps of *udon* (noodles). Because this neighbor had a ten-person household to feed, she had no other choice but to stand "in line to buy *udon* scraps to supplement their rations."[51]

In the big cities that had been bombed repeatedly—Tokyo, Osaka, Yokohama, Nagoya, and Kobe—the situation was even worse, and the residents were even more desperate. On the morning of March 10, 1945, after 279 B-29s had firebombed central Tokyo, Shinoda Tomoko and her family returned to find that their house had burned down, but they also found the rice that they had washed and had left to soak before the attack. "It was now charred," she remembered, "but we ate it."[52] Kumagaya Motokazu described his life in Tokyo after the May 24, 1945, firebombing raid:

I was staying at a friend's house a bit beyond Rikkyō University. This house was burned completely in an air raid on the night of May 24, and I lost everything. With no other place to go, I stayed with a colleague who lived alone nearby. Food rationing was so strict then that we had no salt or soy sauce, and only a thumbnail-size dollop of miso paste per person each day. For vegetables we were lucky to be able to eat the leaves grown in a vacant lot.

These were my materials to cook with—since I was the hanger-on. I soon used up the small amount of firewood that we had. After trying to think of a good alternative, we decided to tear and use the old magazines stored in the house. Ripping out twenty pages or so and burning them made the flame rise up too quickly. So we had to watch the fire constantly. Twisting the pages together made it last a little longer. With a three-hundred-page magazine I could cook a cup and a half of rice. But it took one and a half magazines to cook miso soup.

This amount of rice and miso was what the two of us ate for our three meals. For lunch we took a small sushi-size ball of rice and a bit of miso wrapped in paper. I was so hungry that it was a chore to climb the stairs. At night we stuck it out by eating cold leftovers.[53]

Later Kumagaya reported that one day their small cache of rice and miso was stolen. "We looked dumbfounded at each other," he wrote, "amazed that someone was worse off than we [were]." Like Kumagaya and his friend, other people, too, foraged, picking greens in cemeteries and vacant lots.[54]

Impact of the Food Controls on the Populations of Provincial Cities and Towns

Outside the big cities, the food situation was quite different. In provincial cities and towns food was plentiful through the fall of 1944. Kiyosawa Kiyoshi traveled often to these provincial cities and towns, and his diary confirms the availability of food. For instance, in January 1944 on a trip to Atami, a resort town sixty miles southwest of Tokyo, he reported that "at noon there was a meal at the hotel. They put out an extraordinary spread." A month later he visited Hakone and stayed at the Fujiya Hotel, where "the food was good, but the quantity was small." At the end of May, Kiyosawa went south to Kyushu, where he visited Shimonoseki and reported that "food supplies are still more abundant here than in Tokyo." He also found "a place that serves its customers sweet *mitsumame* [a dish made with sweet beans, fruit, and jellied agar-agar]," but he also mentioned that "a sea urchin shop and close to half of the others were shuttered." On the same trip Kiyosawa also visited Hakata, where he had wonderful meals: "I lunched at the Hakata Hotel," he writes. "I ate things that could not be found in Tokyo." But he did recognize that what made possible these "extraordinary feasts" in Hakata was the fact that the restaurant had become a "munitions factory club." That fall Kiyosawa visited the Matsumoto-Toyoshina area in central Japan and wrote that "we have been treated to dishes that are rare nowadays. Indeed, the countryside is well provided for."[55]

Once the Allied bombing of the home islands began in earnest in late November 1944, however, the populations of the provincial cities that were bombed also faced severe shortages. The bombing destroyed the facilities that produced and distributed foodstuffs in these cities, and Allied warships and submarines stopped the flow of rice from abroad. In fact, because they were smaller cities, the bombing did proportionately more damage. Nearly all of Toyama City, 90 percent of Aomori, 86 percent of Fukui, 85 percent of Tokushima, 78 percent of Kōfu, and 72 percent of Hitachi had been reduced to "burned out fields."[56] So when Kiyosawa visited provincial cities in March 1945, he now had to bring his own rice to the inns where he stayed, and he complained that after accepting a pint of rice, one such inn in Asama served him only two *onigiri* (rice balls).[57] Ogawa Sumi, who left Tokyo after the devastating March 10, 1945, firebombing for Atami, on the east coast of Japan, found "food shortages worse than we'd known in Tokyo."[58]

In contrast, the populations of provincial cities and towns that were not bombed fared much better. The diary of Ōshima Shizu in Kanazawa reveals just how much better. Like families in the big cities, the Ōshimas received rationed food allotments from time to time, which they paid for. The following is a list of some of what the family received through their neighborhood association:

Date	Item	Quantity
12/31/1941	kelp	NA
	fishcake (*hanpen*)	half piece
4/23/1942	saké	6.4 ounces
	glutinous rice	2 quarts
4/30/1943	freshwater eel	2
8/6/1943	*sōmen* noodles	NA
	crackers	NA
9/11/1943	*niboshi*	NA
10/18/1943	sweet potatoes	83 pounds
11/26/1943	Japanese radish	4.1 pounds per person
12/5/1943	preserves (*tsukudani*)	NA
	saké lees (*kasuzuke*)	NA
3/6/1944	chub mackerel (*saba*)	1.5 fish
4/11/1944	dried cuttlefish	NA
4/26/1944	sauce squares	NA
	seaweed topping (*furikake nori*)	NA
5/17/1944	rice mixed with soybeans	11 pounds (4 days)
5/30/1944	tofu	NA
5/1944	yellowtail	NA
	bamboo shoots	NA
7/9/1944	beans and other vegetables	NA
7/11/1944	potatoes	NA
10/6/1944	sweet potatoes	96 pounds (6 days)
10/7/1944	potato substitute	NA
10/10/1944	soybean lees (*okara*)	NA
11/1/1944	*kuzu* potatoes	NA
2/3/1945	rice	NA

2/20/1945	Japanese radish	half
	tangerines	16
3/10/1945	frozen apples	1 per person
4/27/1945	ground sardine dumplings	NA
5/25/1945	sardines	2 per person per day
7/8/1945	rice	2.5 quarts
	preserves	NA

The Ōshimas supplemented these allotments with aggressive shopping. When they heard that this or that food was available, Ōshima Shizu or her daughters immediately set out to buy some for the family. Most of the time they were successful: in June 1943 Ōshima waited in line for two hours for fish and got one mackerel, in August her daughter lined up for fish, and in 1944 her patience was rewarded when she managed to get some soy sauce and vinegar. Early in 1945 she was able to find, outside their town, soybean flour, millet, and *chirashi sushi*. Sometimes, though, she or her daughter waited in line for hours only to come home empty-handed. This happened on February 4, 1943, when she went out to buy sugar but found that it had been sold out by the time she got there. A month later the same thing happened with sweet potatoes. "We heard they were selling sweet potatoes and we lined up from early in the morning," she wrote, "but in the end couldn't get any." Her daughter lined up at a fish shop in mid-August, but "nothing was delivered and no one received anything."[59] Nonetheless, the Ōshimas managed reasonably well, and certainly better than families in the cities that had been bombed. Like others living away from the big cities, they bought more of the vegetables, fish, and meat that they consumed on the black market than was the case in Tokyo.[60]

When adding the items the Ōshimas managed to buy or exchange to what they received through their neighborhood association, the following is what they had (the purchased items are in italics):

Date	Item	Quantity
12/31/1941	kelp	NA
	fishcake (*hanpen*)	half piece
2/26/1942	oysters	NA
4/23/1942	saké	6.4 ounces
	glutinous rice	2 quarts
4/30/1943	freshwater eel	2
6/8/1943	*mackerel*	*half a tail*

8/4/1943	*fish*	NA
8/6/1943	*sōmen* noodles	NA
	crackers	NA
9/11/1943	*niboshi*	NA
10/18/1943	sweet potatoes	83 pounds
11/26/1943	Japanese radish	4.1 pound per person
12/5/1943	preserves (*tsukudani*)	NA
	saké lees (*kasuzuke*)	NA
12/23/1943	whitebait	NA
3/6/1944	chub mackerel (*saba*)	1.5 fish
4/11/1944	dried cuttlefish	NA
4/26/1944	sauce squares	NA
	seaweed topping (*furikake nori*)	NA
5/17/1944	rice mixed with soybeans	11 pounds (4 days)
5/30/1944	tofu	NA
5/1944	yellowtail	NA
	bamboo shoots	NA
6/8/1944	*soy sauce*	NA
	vinegar	NA
7/4/1944	*ham*	NA
7/9/1944	beans and other vegetables	NA
7/11/1944	potatoes	NA
10/6/1944	sweet potatoes	96 pounds (6 days)
10/7/1944	potato substitute	NA
10/10/1944	soybean lees (*okara*)	NA
11/1/1944	*kuzu* potatoes	NA
1/21/1945	*mushrooms (kinoko)*	NA
	millet	NA
	chirashi sushi	NA
2/3/1945	rice	NA
2/20/1945	Japanese radish	half
	tangerines	16
3/10/1945	frozen apples	1 per person
3/25/1945	*turnips*	NA
	green onions	NA
4/27/1945	ground sardine dumplings	NA
5/25/1945	sardines	2 per person per day
7/8/1945	rice	2.5 quarts
	preserves	NA

Also greatly supplementing the Ōshimas' diet were the foods that friends and relatives gave them from time to time (these gifts are in boldface):

Date	Item	Quantity
12/31/1941	kelp	NA
	fishcake (*hanpen*)	half piece
2/26/1942	oysters	NA
4/23/1942	saké	6.4 ounces
	glutinous rice	2.5 quarts
4/30/1943	freshwater eel	2
5/30/1943	**preserves**	**NA**
6/8/1943	*mackerel*	*half a tail*
8/4/1943	*fish*	*NA*
8/6/1943	*sōmen* noodles	NA
	crackers	NA
9/11/1943	*niboshi*	NA
10/18/1943	sweet potatoes	83 pounds
11/26/1943	Japanese radish	4.1 pounds per person
12/5/1943	preserves (*tsukudani*)	NA
	saké lees (*kasuzuke*)	NA
12/17/1943	**sweets**	**NA**
2/6/1944	**rice crackers**	**NA**
3/6/1944	chub mackerel (saba)	1.5 fish
4/3/1944	*sweets*	*NA*
4/11/1944	dried cuttlefish	NA
4/26/1944	sauce squares	NA
	seaweed topping (*furikake nori*)	NA
5/17/1944	rice mixed with soybeans	11 pounds (4 days)
5/30/1944	tofu	NA
5/1944	yellowtail	NA
	bamboo shoots	NA
6/8/1944	*soy sauce*	*NA*
	vinegar	*NA*
7/4/1944	*ham*	*NA*
7/9/1944	beans and other vegetables	NA
7/11/1944	potatoes	NA
8/14/1944	**tomatoes**	**NA**
	eggplant	**NA**
	roasted barley flour	**NA**

10/6/1944	sweet potatoes	96 pounds (6 days)
10/7/1944	potato substitute	NA
10/10/1944	soybean lees (*okara*)	NA
10/16/1944	**mushrooms (*kinoko*)**	**NA**
	chestnuts	**NA**
10/22/1944	**apples**	**NA**
	preserves	**NA**
11/1/1944	*kuzu* potatoes	NA
12/29–30/1944	**rice cakes**	**NA**
1/21/1945	*mushrooms (kinoko)*	*NA*
	millet	*NA*
	chirashi sushi	*NA*
2/3/1945	rice	NA
2/20/1945	Japanese radish	half
	tangerines	16
3/10/1945	frozen apples	1 per person
3/25/1945	*turnips*	*NA*
	green onions	*NA*
4/27/1945	ground sardine dumplings	NA
5/25/1945	sardines	2 per person per day
7/8/1945	rice	2.5 quarts
	preserves	NA
8/15/1945	pumpkin squash	half

Their most generous benefactors were their neighbors, the Tarōdas, who routinely gave them something every three or four months, such as kelp and *tsukudani*, rice crackers, pumpkin squash seeds, tomatoes, eggplant and fried barley flour, and rice cakes.[61] The eldest Ōshima daughter, Takako, who worked in Tokyo, sent sweets from time to time, and on one occasion in the spring of 1944, the family even used some of these sweets in place of the sugar they had run out of. Still other neighbors or friends gave them rice cakes, preserves, apples, and pumpkin squash, or sold them things they could not get.[62]

Yet even the Ōshimas had some bad stretches. Already in April 1943, they had trouble getting meat, fish, and vegetables, and Ōshima Shizu admitted that she was "at her wit's end." But the spring and summer of 1945 were absolutely the worst time for the family. "We're short on vegetables and really in a tight spot," she wrote on March 25, 1945. Two months later she wrote, "Rice is scarce, as are beans, and we can't even manage to get *okara* or other substitute foods." At one point in early June 1945 they did not even have enough firewood to cook dinner: "We are helpless without any firewood," Ōshima lamented in her diary. "Recently everybody in the family has been dog tired, and after dinner we all feel faint. The reality is we don't have enough food."[63]

All things considered, however, the Ōshimas fared much better than most urban dwellers, especially those living in cities that had been bombed repeatedly. Three things suggest this. First, Ōshima Shizu still managed to make special occasion meals from time to time. For the 1943 winter solstice, for instance, she made red-bean rice and a pumpkin squash dish, and for New Year's in 1944 she made a simmered dish, probably *nishime*. In April she made red-bean rice to celebrate her children's matriculation ceremonies, and a month later, she made red-bean rice for her husband's birthday. What is even more remarkable is that she continued to make these special occasion dishes in the last year of the war. At New Year's 1945, she served rice cakes, soybean flour, Japanese radish, carrots, and burdock root, and for the Doll's Festival in March she made red-bean porridge. To celebrate her daughter Taeko's admission to middle school, she added red beans to *udon* and served this with tangerines and bread. And for the emperor's birthday, she combined rice and quail eggs to make a mixed rice dish. She was still making special occasion food as late as the summer of 1945, when she made potato rice cakes (*ohagi*) in mid-July.[64]

The second thing that reveals how well the family was faring is what Ōshima Shizu prepared for her teenaged sons when they were mobilized for war work. In late May 1944 she made small packages of roasted soybeans and *niboshi*. A week later she salted and dried some fish and then chopped up the ingredients for a seaweed topping (*furikake nori*); and the next day she roasted soybeans and dried clams, Japanese asparagus (*udo*), and bracken. Finally, the Ōshimas occasionally sent food to others or gave it as gifts. For example, when her daughter gained admission to middle school, the family prepared a gift of red beans, dried *udon*, tangerines, and small loaves of bread for a certain teacher.[65]

Nonetheless, Ōshima did have to improvise in 1944. She added curry powder to the vegetable porridge she made with boiled greens and rice. As noted earlier, she made her own *furikake nori* by chopping up dried anchovies, seaweed, and kelp and adding sesame seeds. She even made her own preserves, boiling and preserving bamboo shoots, dried clams, Japanese asparagus, and bracken for future meals. In March 1945 she added what the government called "perseverance flour" to rice, which could not have been very appetizing.[66]

Impact of the Food Controls on the Rural Population

What about the rural population? Not surprisingly, they had more food than did families like the Ōshimas and much more than those in the cities that had been bombed repeatedly. An example is Yasumura Shizu, who left Okinawa with her two children in the fall of 1944 to live with her husband's family in Takaharu, a village in eastern Kyushu. As an outsider, Yasumura was completely dependent on the kindness of her in-laws and fellow villagers. Arrangements were made for her to do odd jobs for local families, such as gathering mulberry leaves for the silkworms, spreading manure, threshing grain and rice, and harvesting potatoes. Not only was she paid for this work, she also was usually given fresh produce. Yasumura kept a careful record of what she was given, no doubt so she could reciprocate in the future, and her diary describes precisely what foods were available in one rural community in Kyushu in the fall of 1944. For example, the following is what she received from September 12 to October 9, 1944:

Date	Item	Quantity
September 12	vegetables	NA
September 14	persimmons	NA
September 16	taro (*satoimo*)	NA
	eggplant	NA
	tofu	NA
September 19	pumpkin squash	NA
September 20	potatoes	NA
	red beans	half gallon
September 21	persimmons	NA
	rice	1.5 gallons
September 24	vegetables	NA
September 27	potatoes	NA
	Chinese chives	NA
October 7	potatoes	NA
	barley	NA
	tofu	NA
October 9	tea	NA

In addition, Yasumura also bought rationed rice, fish, *udon*, soy sauce, and wheat through the village's neighborhood association. Her September rice allotment—four and a half gallons for a ten-day period—was far more than

Yasumura and her children needed and shows the abundance of food in this community.[67]

What rural communities served at New Year's is telling. In Saitama, Tokyo teacher Hamada Akiko enjoyed a New Year's repast that included *nishime* and rice cakes that were whiter than any rice cakes she had had in Tokyo.[68] Yamanaka Ryōtarō, a teacher who accompanied students from an Osaka school to Tsuda-machi, northeast of Osaka, had "a veritable mountain of wonderful food" at the Shōnenji Temple—chicken, sushi, *nishime*, slices of yellowtail, canned goods, and tangerines—and remembers being "embarrassed."[69] Kyushu farmer Tanaka Jingo noted that the official ration for New Year's consisted of two pints of saké, herring roe, fifty dried persimmons, twenty tangerines, two pieces of salted trout, and 450 grams of sugar. He also served a sea bream and a sea cucumber.[70]

What was served on other special occasions also is revealing. In April 1945, when Tanaka's daughter entered primary school, a special meal was prepared that included chicken.[71] At the end of that month, the village of Fukumitsu in Toyama Prefecture celebrated the emperor's birthday with a special lunch of beans, lotus root, bog rhubarb, sweet potato stems, cold tofu, and red-bean rice.[72] On July 15, 1945, for the Sōbyōsai Festival, Tanaka's family served rice cakes, *udon*, tofu, and a fava bean jam spread made with honey. Tanaka reported that the last dish was the most popular: "Everyone was pleased, and they muttered, 'This is so sweet!' and the children were very happy."[73] On August 7, the Fukumitsu school authorities served their students a special Seventh Night Festival lunch of eggplant fried with miso, mashed cucumber, miso soup with eggplant, and sweet potato rice.[74] At the time of the Harvest Festival, on November 23, Yasumura Shizu made 150 rice cakes, which she shared with others, and received "lots of good food" in return.[75] In the countryside, the departure of local men for military service also called for red-bean rice, a traditional festive dish, and visitors always became an occasion for *gochisō*, or "delicious food," usually fish or chicken.[76]

The reasons that the rural population had more food is obvious: most farm families still were largely self-sufficient, growing or producing nearly everything they ate. They grew their own rice, wheat, and an assortment of vegetables, including cucumbers, pumpkin squash, soybeans, taro, and Irish potatoes.[77] They also made their own miso, soy sauce, tofu, *udon*, fermented soybeans (*natto*), and pickles, and brewed their own saké.[78] Because many farmers raised chickens, they had a steady supply of eggs and, occasionally, fowl, and they also fished for carp, trout, or sweetfish. Another, less obvious, reason for the abundance of food in the countryside was the unintended effect of the government's food-rationing program: it brought rice to villages where it could not be grown and where residents had traditionally eaten millet.[79]

Since most modern farm families typically bought their sugar, salt, cooking oil, and seafood, wartime rationing made these items harder to get. In the last year of the war, for example, sugar was not available, and meat was a rare item. Accordingly, the unexpected distribution of meat to Tanaka Jingo's family on July 3, 1945, was a special treat. "For that night's meal we had a meat dish, which we had not had for some time," Tanaka wrote. "Shōgo [his son] exclaimed 'Hoorah! A beef dish!' Everyone was pleased with the long-awaited feast." Seafood and saké were another matter. People living near the coast still served seafood on special occasions or gave it as a gift, and home-brewed saké always was available for village festivals and meetings.[80]

Japanese farmers also responded ingeniously to the food shortages. They increased their production by cultivating land that had not been used before, such as school yards, alleys, the areas along railway lines, and unclaimed land. They also made some extra money by selling their produce. For instance, Tanaka Jingo's wife and daughter grew fava beans, and when word spread that they were selling them, "every day many people came to buy them." Farmers also had no trouble finding substitutes for scarce commodities; for example, honey was gathered and used in place of sugar. When the supply of fish ran out, Tanaka simply made a net and went fishing for freshwater eel.[81] And they also did as they always had done when times were hard: they foraged for wild vegetables, grasshoppers, and frogs.

Nonetheless, Japanese farmers had their share of problems during the war. Conscription was especially hard on their communities, and many fathers, brothers, and sons were drafted and never returned. In fact, the war so depleted the rural workforce that the authorities sent evacuated children, mobilized teenagers, Korean day laborers, or locally based servicemen to help the farmers plant and harvest their crops. In early July 1945, when Tanaka fed one group of mobilized students who had helped his family plant their crops, one of them exclaimed, "Mr. Farmer's rice is delicious!"[82]

As the war progressed, the government also requisitioned more and more of what farmers produced, especially rice, barley, and wheat, and the farmers began to wonder whether they would have enough for themselves. In addition, the authorities took their livestock, and fertilizer was in short supply, which reduced productivity.[83] As one farmer observed, "There is no fertilizer, no resources, and no harvesting of rice, and the government is a stickler about deliveries." Work clothes, work socks (*chikatabi*), buckets, bridles, and so forth were hard to get as well. Finally, the farmers had the added problem of "relatives [from the cities] that they had never heard of visiting to talk about rice."[84]

The Effect of the Wartime Food Controls

Clearly, the government's food controls and the resulting shortages greatly affected the wartime population, but their impact varied by social class, location, gender, and age. The rich, powerful, and well connected in the major cities had enough to eat through the end of the war, as their wealth and power allowed them to buy what they needed, to acquire scarce commodities, and to frequent the few inns and restaurants that offered fine dining opportunities. Many, like Kiyosawa Kiyoshi, also had villas or farms in the countryside where they could grow their own food. Hardest hit were the urban middle and lower classes in the biggest cities, who faced shortages from the moment that controls were imposed on food distribution and who began to experience real deprivation once the Allied bombing of Japanese cities began in late November 1944. In fact, the situation was so bad in the big cities that were bombed that by the last several months of the war many were on the verge of starvation.

The provincial cities and towns had more food until the early winter of 1945, when those that were bombed began to experience food shortages comparable to those in the big cities. However, the situation in provincial cities and towns that were not bombed could not have been more different: the residents there had sufficient food resources, although it was hardly life as usual, as the experience of the Ōshima family in Kanazawa reveals so clearly.

Women in the cities and towns, as their diaries show, bore the heaviest burdens on the home front: they not only provided and cooked for their families; they also did double duty as members of their neighborhood associations and often were assigned the onerous but important task of overseeing food and commodity distributions. In addition, they journeyed to the countryside with goods to barter for food, and with the wartime call-up of men and the mobilization of teenagers, they became the sole providers for their families.

In contrast, the rural areas had plenty of food, largely because farmers were able to grow or produce what they needed. But as the diary of Tanaka Jingo reveals, this required a heroic effort, as they did this without adequate labor, fertilizer, tools, and beasts of burden. Furthermore, like Tanaka, many farmers resented, and resisted, the government's production quotas, which struck them as unreasonable.

PART 2

The Evacuated Children

3

Making "Splendid Little Citizens"

In December 1943 the Japanese Ministry of Education encouraged those living in metropolitan areas to send their primary school–aged children to live with relatives in the countryside. Accordingly, four months later, in April 1944, when Tokyo officials made the same recommendation, 64,659 students were sent to live with relatives. Osaka officials made similar recommendations early that summer. Then on June 30 the cabinet issued a plan for evacuating third- through sixth-grade students from thirteen cities, using Tokyo's plan as a model.[1] By the end of the war, 1,303,200 children had been evacuated: 857,000 moved in with relatives, and 446,200 were housed in inns or Buddhist temples or, often, with local families.[2] Those who did not evacuate to relatives' homes were accompanied by a number of administrators and teachers, and local men and women were hired as teachers and "dorm mothers" (*ryōbo*).[3]

The evacuation of Japanese children in wartime Japan has not received much treatment in the English-language scholarship on the Asia-Pacific War.[4] This lacuna is surprising because many of those who were evacuated have written memoirs about their experiences and because thousands of the diaries that the children were asked to keep during their time in the countryside have survived, as have the diaries of many of the administrators and teachers involved in their evacuation.

This chapter is an attempt to begin to fill this lacuna. I have used the textbooks, letters, diaries, and memoirs of the evacuated children and teachers to analyze a specific dimension of their evacuation: their transformation into what the wartime authorities called "splendid little citizens" (*rippana shōkokumin*). I believe that the

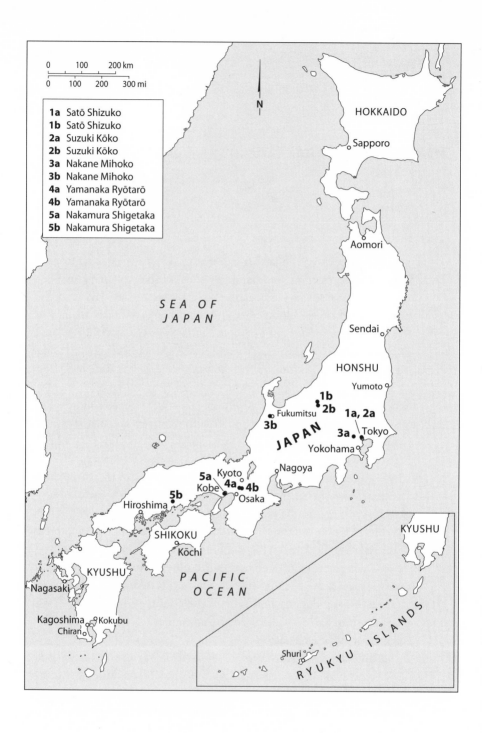

0   100   200 km

0   100   200   300 mi

1a   Satō Shizuko
1b   Satō Shizuko
2a   Suzuki Kōko
2b   Suzuki Kōko
3a   Nakane Mihoko
3b   Nakane Mihoko
4a   Yamanaka Ryōtarō
4b   Yamanaka Ryōtarō
5a   Nakamura Shigetaka
5b   Nakamura Shigetaka

N

HOKKAIDO

Sapporo

Aomori

SEA OF
JAPAN

Sendai

HONSHU

Yumoto

1b
Fukumitsu **2b**   **1a, 2a**
3b   **3a**   Tokyo
JAPAN   Yokohama

Nagoya

5a   Kyoto
Kobe **4a** **4b**
5b   Osaka
Hiroshima

SHIKOKU

Kōchi

KYUSHU

KYUSHU

PACIFIC
OCEAN

Nagasaki

Kagoshima   Kokubu
Chiran

Shuri

R Y U K Y U   I S L A N D S

making of "splendid little citizens" was the result of the following: (1) the carefully designed textbooks that communicated the official wartime discourse promoted by the Ministry of Education during the war, especially the fourth and fifth editions of national ethics textbooks, which appeared between 1934 and 1945; (2) the instructional and out-of-class programs at the evacuation sites that prepared the children for the expected "decisive battle"; (3) the close monitoring of the children's behavior, morale, and health by their teachers; and (4) the purposeful and continual exhortations of the evacuees' families as well as their teachers and representatives of national organizations, members of the imperial family, and veterans. In this chapter I examine the content of the government-issued textbooks, the instructional and out-of-class programs at the evacuation sites, and the children's responses to their new lives in the countryside.

Teaching the Children through Their Textbooks

A careful analysis of the transformation of the evacuated children must begin with the history of children's education in modern Japan, because what was done with the evacuated children during the war was partly the result of developments that began in the late nineteenth century. Shortly after the Meiji Restoration in 1868, the new government recognized the importance of children's education for a modern, Westernizing Japan. The Ministry of Education was created in 1871, and the next year a national education system was established, based on the American model of primary, middle, and high schools, as well as universities. In the 1880s the Ministry of Education, under Mori Arinori (1847–1889), turned to Prussian models, and Mori's successor, Inoue Kowashi (1843–1895), added vocational schools and girls' schools. By 1898 all children were required to attend elementary school, and attendance reached 69 percent. Then in 1907, compulsory education was increased to six years, and by 1919 attendance was 99 percent.

The moral education of school-aged children was a continuing concern for Ministry of Education officials. The problem was that the ethics textbooks being used in schools were written by private individuals and published by commercial houses, so they were not regulated in any way. What brought this problem to the attention of government officials and educators was the divergence of many of these textbooks from the Imperial Rescript on Education, the government's attempt in 1890 at articulating a national ideology.[5] After a vigorous debate in the Diet (the newly established national assembly), the Ministry of Education took steps to solve this problem. It formed a textbook compilation committee in 1902 and wrote the first national ethics textbooks in 1903 using British and American textbooks as models.[6] The "Principles of Compilation" that accompanied the new textbooks clarified their purpose:

> These texts were compiled to serve as a textbook for the primary school ethics course. They were based on the principles in the Imperial Rescript issued on the thirteenth day of the tenth month of Meiji [1890]; they nourish the moral character of the youngsters and direct their practice of morality; and they have as their goal the teaching of the essentials of the morality necessary for a sound Japanese citizenry.[7]

In April 1904 the new ethics textbooks began to be used in schools across the country.[8]

The first ethics textbooks concentrated on personal hygiene and physical fitness: youngsters were told to watch what they ate, to stay fit, and to exercise.[9] Diligence and industriousness were the next most frequently mentioned topics, followed by "independence and initiative."[10] After the sections on "enterprise" and "starting industries" were added, this complex of work-related values was the most frequently mentioned of the modern secular topics.[11] Other topics were "honesty," "obeying rules," "not falling prey to superstition," "universal love," "keeping promises," "not inconveniencing others," and "being orderly."[12]

The new ethics textbooks made ample use of history. Roughly two-thirds of the material features historical figures from nearly all periods of Japanese history, with those from the Tokugawa period (1603–1867) being the most numerous. Interestingly, the historical figure most often cited is Uesugi Yōzan (1757–1822), the reformist lord of Yonezawa Domain, who is described as the aggressive initiator of new local industries such as horse breeding, sericulture, and weaving.[13] The selfless fourteenth-century warrior Kusunoki Masashige (1294–1336), famous for his loyalty to the emperor, is the second most frequently mentioned historical figure.[14] The warrior Katō Kiyomasa (1562–1611); the Confucian scholars Nakae Tōju (1608–1648), Kaibara Ekken (1630–1714), Arai Hakuseki (1657–1725), and Ogyū Sorai (1666–1728); the popular eighteenth-century educator Ninomiya Sontoku (1781–1856); and the political activist Yoshida Shōin (1830–1859) each appear three or four times.[15] Even Americans and Europeans are presented as exemplars: Florence Nightingale is remembered for her "compassion," "kindness," and "universal love"; Abraham Lincoln for his "studiousness," "honesty," and "sympathy"; and Benjamin Franklin for his "independence and initiative," "public-spiritedness," "inventiveness," and "orderliness." Also mentioned are George Washington's "honesty," Christopher Columbus's "perseverance" and "confidence," William Jenner's "resolve," and Socrates's "respect for law."[16]

The ethics textbooks introduced what historian Carol Gluck has called the new "civic morality."[17] Created by the leaders of the Meiji state, this new morality was designed to instill in the general population "a sense of the nation and a civic ethos."[18] Reflecting this, the textbooks refer frequently to members of the imperial family, both past and present; to "Japan," "our country," "Greater Japan," and "Greater Imperial Japan"; to the "public good"; the "duties of citizens"; the major Shintō shrines; and the national flag. Next to the imperial house, "patriotism" is the most frequently mentioned theme of the new national morality. It is almost never presented abstractly but is represented by selfless patriots, chiefly modern military men.[19] The favorite is a certain "Comrade Kiguchi," who, as "he approached the enemy did not flinch one bit and blew his bugle three times," enabling Japanese troops "to advance and wipe out the enemy"; he "was hit by a bullet, dying with his bugle pressed to his lips."[20] Kiguchi is representative of a platoon of selfless individuals praised in the texts for, in some cases, giving their lives for their monarch and country.

Confucian virtues are prominent in the new ethics textbooks as well. "Learning" and "study" are the most frequently mentioned Confucian topics, and were valuable not only in themselves but also to the nation. "In order for our country to prosper," says the first edition, "each and every citizen must become a good person. What is important here is that everyone receive an education, cultivate his virtue, and polish his knowledge."[21] "Filial piety" is the second most common Confucian topic, followed by "loyalty" and "courage." The importance of courage is not surprising, given Japan's long history of warrior rule and the value of warrior precepts to the state. The famous historical figures named include Kusunoki Masashige, whose name was nearly synonymous with these qualities.[22] Even emperors and courtiers were pressed into service.[23] But the favored subjects of this genre were, like Comrade Kiguchi, the heroes of Japan's last two wars: the Sino-Japanese War (1894–1895) and the Russo-Japanese War (1904–1905).[24]

In addition, the textbooks introduced the five cardinal Confucian social relationships, with, not surprisingly, that between parents and children receiving the most attention. This theme is treated explicitly in descriptions of filial piety, and the family is implicit in much else covered in the texts. Also predictable is the attention given to the relationship between rulers and subjects, which appears in discussions of loyalty, patriotism, and courage. The relationship between siblings, especially between older and younger brothers and sisters, is emphasized as well. Friendship, too, was encouraged, and readers were urged to help their friends whenever possible. The last of the five relationships, that between husband and wife, is not given as much space as the other four relationships, although it is implicit in much else that is discussed.[25]

The ethics textbooks changed over the life of the series (1903–1944) in both obvious and subtle ways. Chapter titles were continually revised, illustrations were redrawn, emphases were altered, and sections were moved around, with both additions and deletions. Even the style of the texts changed, gradually at first and then dramatically in the 1940s. The first revisions appeared in the second and third editions, published between 1910 and 1918 and between 1919 and 1933, respectively. The entries in these editions are fuller or more focused than those in the first edition. Consider this excerpt from the section entitled "Learning" in the 1903/1904 edition: "When he lived in his uncle's house, [Ninomiya] Kinjirō gathered rapeseed and exchanged it for rapeseed oil, and he studied every night. When his uncle said, 'Instead of studying, how about doing your chores?' Kinjirō thereupon studied after he finished the things he was ordered to do."[26] The version in the second edition reads: "[Ninomiya Kinjirō's] uncle said, 'It would be better for you to do your chores instead of reading.' Accordingly, Kinjirō worked well into the evening and then studied."[27] The third edition then substitutes two young and obviously modern men for Ninomiya Kinjirō: "Here are two people. Both were once in the same school. One never heeded his teachers' admonitions and instead loafed and, as a result, became a pathetic person. The other listened to his teachers' instructions and studied, and he became a fine person."[28] The appended comment reads: "Seeds that are not sown do not sprout." The contrast represented in the text and the accompanying illustration leaves little doubt about the course that readers were to follow and what would happen if they did not.

The entries in the second and third editions also are more realistic: characters are more lifelike and "rounder," as the novelist E. M. Forster once put it, with personal histories and even personalities.[29] This is true even of august personages. For example, the empress is barely a presence in this entry from the second edition: "The empress went to a hospital to visit wounded and sick soldiers. Every single person there shed tears and felt the deepest gratitude."[30] But in the third edition, we even get a glimpse of her personality: "From her childhood onward, the empress was modest and felt compassion for lesser beings. When she became crown princess, she attended the openings of schools and, in wartime, made bandages and offered them to the soldiers. After she became empress, she turned her attention to education and industry and showed compassion for the poor. Many are the things for which one should be grateful."[31]

Direct discourse, too, is used more often in the second and third editions than in the first, perhaps because characters who speak directly seem more credible. Compare the lesson "Not Inconveniencing Others." The first edition reads "This child's father has spotted her throwing some trash away at the side of the road and stops her, saying, 'If you throw trash out there, you'll inconvenience people.'"[32] In the third edition, the same passage reads: "Ochiyo was about to throw out some trash at the side of the road. Her father stops her, saying 'If you throw trash out there, you'll inconvenience others.'"[33] These changes in the second and third editions—fuller biographical narratives, greater realism, more extensive use of direct discourse—made the exemplars and behaviors presented in these texts more believable and thus more persuasive. They were meant to encourage the children to adopt the norms presented in the texts and to work at becoming "good Japanese." The second and subsequent editions also include at the end of each chapter a composite picture of a "good Japanese" (yoi nihonjin). The expectation was that the children who read these lessons would transform themselves into approximations of the ideal, becoming "good Japanese" and seeing themselves and others in these terms. Michel Foucault calls this process of self-transformation "subjectification" and describes it as "the way a human being turns him- or herself into a subject."[34]

The most dramatic revisions appear in the fourth and fifth editions, which were published from 1934 to 1939 and from 1941 to 1945. The first major change was that direct discourse was used even more extensively than in earlier editions, and exemplars made longer and longer statements. Hortatory in nature, these lessons were obviously written to be recited, remembered, and mimicked. In the fourth edition, for example, when the warrior Kusunoki Masashige is commanded by Emperor Go Daigo "to attack [Hōjō] Takatoki and bring peace to the realm," he responds: "No matter how strong the rebel army is, I believe that by using clever strategies when attacking it, victory is certain. When our forces engage each other, even though there is one in ten thousand chances that we will be defeated, if you hear that Masashige alone has survived, you may be assured that the way will be opened for [your] sacred forces."[35] Of course, the entry continues, Masashige's forces wiped out Takatoki's.

Second, beginning in the fourth edition, the exemplars' thoughts are cited, something missing in earlier editions. Readers are told, for instance, what two students, Tarō and Takeko, thought about a rousing speech given by the principal of their school: "After hearing the speech, Tarō and Takeko thought, 'We ourselves have become third-year students, and thus we should unite our hearts, obey our teachers' instructions, and try to make our school even better.'"[36] This innovation opened up another dimension of state-sponsored moral instruction. The late Maruyama Masao contended that an independent moral conscience was not legally protected in Japan before 1945, as it was in the West, and that consequently the Japanese state from the Meiji Restoration to the end of World War II intruded freely into the private, "interior, subjective sphere" of its citizens' lives.[37]

Third, models were more important in the fourth edition than they had been before. Paragons of particular virtues parade through the textbooks, and if their value as exemplars once was tacit, it now was explicit. The word "model" (*tehon*) appears for the first time, and readers are advised "to become models" for others.[38] The reader for second-year students, for example, features Tarō and Takeko:

When the whole class was assembled, Tarō and Takeko became second-year students. They are completely familiar with everything; school is like home. The cute first-year students have entered the school, and Tarō and Takeko, feeling like an older brother and sister, look after them. When they get to school in the morning, they call them over and play with them. The new second-year students, Tarō and Takeko, study well and play hard and have become even better children and believe that they will probably be models for the first-year students.[39]

The message is clear: one should not only imitate the behavior of the models but also be a model for others.

Finally, the Ministry of Education was now more concerned with the state than the individual. This was in keeping with the guidelines for revision issued by the Ministry of Education, which said that the new text was "to transmit the essentials of a morality appropriate to a loyal and good Japanese subject" and "to clarify further the concept of a national polity."[40] The state was now everything, and Tarō and Takeko counted for very little except as its subjects.

The most dramatic revisions came in the fifth edition of the textbooks, which started to appear in 1941. The content of this edition is highly nationalistic, which is hardly surprising, given that the Japanese had been at war in China since July 1937, were on the verge of war with the United States and its allies when the first volume was issued, and were fully at war with the Allied forces when the other volumes were published. There are repeated references to "Japan," "the country," and "our country."[41] Various representations of Japan appear often: the rising sun; the flag; the emperor, empress, imperial house, and divine ancestors; the national anthem; and the Ise, Izumo, and Yasukuni shrines.[42] The Japanese are described as the politest people in the world. Indeed, they are said to take such special care when they speak that they are able to express the deepest and most profound sentiments.[43] Even the change of seasons in Japan is described with such enthusiasm that naive readers might have believed that spring and fall in Japan were unlike these seasons anywhere else in the world. This passage from "The Country of Japan," a chapter in the second-year reader, is typical:

A bright and pleasant spring has arrived. Japan is a country with beautiful spring, summer, fall, and winter scenery. It is a country with beautiful mountains and rivers and seas. And it is in this fine country that we were born. Both Father and Mother were born in this country as well, and Uncle and Aunt were born here, too.

Japan is a fine country,
a pure country.
The only divine country
in the world.

Japan is a fine country,
a strong country.
A glittering and great
world country.[44]

As in this passage, Japan is frequently described in the fifth edition as superior to all other countries because it is divine.[45]

A second important change was the proliferation of references to war. The imagery, symbols, and language of war are introduced at regular intervals, as are the paraphernalia of war—helmets, canteens, fire drills, tanks, aircraft, and other items that suggest combat.[46] Servicemen often appear as conquerors and occupiers, as ordinary citizens fulfilling their national duty, and as selfless heroes willing to die for their monarch and country.[47] All these allusions and references to war form what Edward Said labeled "a structure of attitude and reference" within which the children reading the texts could locate themselves.[48]

The wartime edition of the ethics textbooks brought a third change with profound implications. The first-person pronouns "I" and "we" replaced named figures as the texts' main subjects, the only exceptions being historical figures, who could not be elided very easily with the reader. This change is especially conspicuous in the readers for first- and second-year students, in which "I" (*watakushi*) and "we" (*watakushitachi*) replace Tarō, Takeko, Masao, and others who had appeared in earlier editions. Here the "I" "does not make his or her parents worry"; "sweeps the garden"; takes care of the house while another runs an errand; "politely bows to a visiting aunt, helps her mother, and carries out the tea"; "gets her own schoolbag together"; "tries on a lord's helmet"; "goes fishing for minnows"; "plays hard"; brings water to the house; and writes a letter to a soldier.[49] The "we" of these texts is described as looking after younger students; "truly feeling gratitude" for the kindness of the emperor and empress; trudging to school in a blizzard; "joining together to collect all sorts of things to sell so planes and tanks can be made"; watching a portable shrine pass by; and going on a school excursion.[50] As these examples suggest, the children were now encouraged, even expected, to make the leap from self to family, then to school, and finally to the nation. The structure of this progression echoes the commentary in the teacher's manual accompanying the text: "The new national morality encompasses the so-called social morality and individual morality."[51] The use of first-person pronouns also means that the texts addressed their student readers directly and in effect instructed them to be like those described in these pages.[52]

Finally, the last editions of the ethics textbooks attempted to engage the children on an affective rather than a conceptual level by introducing highly poetic language designed to elicit emotional responses. Consider the opening section of the second-year text:

> The classrooms have changed.
> The desks have changed.
> How wonderful!

> The first-year students have started school.
> [We] have lots of younger brothers and sisters.
> How wonderful!

> The books are new.
> The notebooks are new.
> [We] have become second-year students and are happy![53]

This is a far cry from the descriptive narratives opening the chapters in earlier editions. "The Rising-Sun Flag," a chapter in the third-year text, is typical:

> A blue, clear sky.
> Flying just at the eaves,
> the rising-sun flag
> is truly dignified.
>
> Snowbound houses.
> Flying just at the eaves,
> the rising-sun flag
> somehow seems warm.[54]

Engaging students on an affective level was the stated aim of the compilers of the fourth edition, who wrote that "emphasis will be placed on developing the affective and volitional aspects of the youngsters' moral character . . . and special care will be taken to affect their feelings."[55] Their intention was fully realized in the fifth edition of the ethics textbooks, whose impact on Japanese children during World War II is revealed clearly in their correspondence and diaries.

Disciplining the Children: A Teacher's Perspective

When the nearly half-million Japanese children who were evacuated with their teachers arrived at their new homes in 1944, they found that they now were at school twenty-four hours a day. Almost all aspects of their lives as evacuated children (*sokaiji*) were designed to protect their health, to keep up their morale, to sustain their support for the war, and, above all, to transform them into "splendid little citizens." Moreover, each evacuation location was virtually an enclosed site, and they were not supposed to leave without official permission, though many did and most were apprehended and returned. A few children were allowed to return home because of illness or other reasons.

The novel living situation was new to the teachers as well. They now were with the children around the clock and could not leave them at the end of the day. Their responsibilities were greatly expanded, as they not only had to teach the children but also had to worry about their meals, morale, discipline, and, above all, their health. The teachers had become,

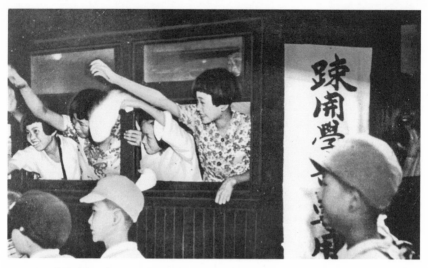

Evacuated children leaving Ueno Station in Tokyo, August 1944. Photo courtesy of the *Yomiuri shinbun*.

in effect, full-time agents of the Ministry of Education, and much, if not most, of what they did was done in accordance with official regulations or orders issued from Tokyo. Education ministry officials presented the evacuation as an opportunity to realize the "training of imperial citizens" (*kōkokumin no rensei*) ideology that had been bandied about in discussions of how best to protect Japanese children during air raids.[56]

Yamanaka Ryōtarō was one of these teachers. He taught at Ōmiya National Citizens School in Osaka and was one of several teachers who in September 1944 accompanied a group of 135 students from that school to a village in the Fujisaka area, in the northeastern corner of Osaka Prefecture. He dutifully performed this role until he received his draft notice in January 1945.[57] Yamanaka had been keeping a diary from 1937 and continued to do so during his time in the countryside. His diary is a record of his feelings about this experience, as well as a catalog of the many problems he and his fellow teachers encountered, their frustrations, and their episodes of poor health.

Yamanaka had been enthusiastic about the planning for the evacuation taking place in the summer of 1944, declaring that "as an educator in a country that is at war, I am ready to go off to the front." But once his departure date approached, he confessed that he "felt tense about the enormity of the responsibility" of caring for a large group of children. Nonetheless, he found comfort in thinking that he was simply doing what warriors had done in the past. "Although it was only a temporary parting," he wrote, "there was nothing happy about it, and I had the fondest thoughts. Together with thinking of this and that, it made me think of the feelings of brave warriors being called up and going off to war." This was Yamanaka's thinking from the moment he began to prepare for his group's evacuation.[58]

On September 16, the day of his departure from Osaka, his wife served him freshly made red-bean rice for breakfast, and then he put on his national citizen's uniform and service cap, wrapped puttees around his legs, and went off to school in his "'decisive victory' uniform." Even though the thirteen-mile journey to the evacuation site in Fujisaka was uneventful, Yamanaka described his departure and arrival in some detail in his diary. For example, he wrote that the evacuees' first dinner was "four pieces of bread." He also described how the day ended: "After making a round of the sleeping children, I readied my bed, sat on my futon, paid my respects to the palace, and expressed my pleasure at putting up with pain and pleasure together with His Majesty's children. I then faced my home and reported to my ancestors that I had not had any shameful thoughts." The next morning, Yamanaka and the children sat down to a hot breakfast that included homemade pickles (tsukemono) given to them by the local community council.[59]

What is important for our purposes is that Yamanaka dutifully recorded what he taught to his students, including the "national citizens' quotation of the day" and the topics he presented to the students, together with his own commentary and personal reflections. The "quotations of the day" were taken from a wide range of material and offer snippets of the official wartime discourse. On October 12, 1944, for instance, Yamanaka introduced the poet Matsuo Bashō's line "thinking of morning, thinking of evening" to his students and asked them to reflect on this line, adding his own personal commentary: "The strong American demons are attacking our southwestern islands. The divine country will not be destroyed. What will happen with the attacks of the foreign devils? We must harden our spirits and resolve to launch a great counterattack. I pledged this together with the children, and we will follow our ancestral country."[60]

On November 7, Yamanaka began his diary entry with a line from the Chinese Classic of Changes: "The movement of heaven is full of power, and the superior person makes himself strong and untiring."[61] He commented that "non-action is nature, and planning and working are a very good thing, but putting something into practice is difficult. No matter what humans do, selfish desire emerges. Everything is for the sake of the fighting country, and in order to win, I want to advance while experiencing pleasure and pain together with the children. They are separated from their parents, and cherishing them is my first task."[62] Although the selection of lines from Bashō and the *Classic of Changes* is unexpected, Yamanaka manages to relate these passages to the war and to affirm the need for perseverance, sacrifice, and pain.

Two weeks later the principal of Ōmiya National Citizens School visited the evacuees and gave a lecture on the Great Thanksgiving Festival (Daijō-sai). Yamanaka summarized the lecture's main points in his diary:

First, Great Thanksgiving Festival. Amaterasu Ōmikami and the emperor consumed the feast together. The emperor was able to become a god from the day of his ascension. Second, the citizens who are ruled by this god emperor also progress and approach the gods. The members of the divine wind unit of the Shikishima Special Attack Unit and the Banda Unit of the Tomigatake Special Attack Unit were youths and already have become divine spirits and reached the territory of understanding. Third, we hope to defend the divine country. We will pray that we will find pleasure in farming or in housework, volunteer, and go forward.[63]

Notice the reference to the special attacks (*tokubetsu kōgeki*) then taking place in the South Pacific and to the kinds of activities that made up the "training" program that Ministry of Education officials highlighted as one of the features of the evacuation.[64]

Early in 1945, the national citizens' quotation of the day was a line from "The Wall Writing" of sixteenth-century warrior lord Date Masamune (1567–1636): "Even if the morning and evening meals are poor, one should eat them and savor their flavor." Yamanaka added: "It would be hard to say that we have reached that point. It is a time of fighting . . . it is not the time to talk about what we're eating. Because we hear that at the front they are eating everything—the roots of grasses, thorns, snakes, etc. Even the aircraft we need for battle are not sufficient. No matter what we are eating, we should think it is the best."[65]

Also recorded in Yamanaka's diary are quotations of the day drawn from the writings of medieval and early modern historical figures: Zeami (1363–1443), Ikeda Mitsumasa (1609–1682), Yamaga Sokō (1622–1685), Kaibara Ekken (1630–1714), Dazai Shundai (1680–1747), and Maki Izumi (1813–1864), as well as the *Classic of History* and the *Laozi*, both ancient Chinese classics, and his thoughts on the special attack tactics that the Japanese military began to use in October 1944.[66] Yamanaka also had his students memorize poems from *Aikoku hyakunin isshu* (A patriot's one hundred poets, one hundred poems), a wartime version of the *Hyakunin isshu* (*One Hundred Poets, One Poem Each*), and awarded prizes to the students who made the best recitations.[67]

Yamanaka's enthusiastic support of the war did not wane over time. Typical are his thoughts on the first day of 1945: "As my words for the new year, I gave an admonitory lecture saying that we should rise up and greet the year of decisive battles and do what we do with the spirit of the divine wind special attack units."[68] His invocation of the sacrifices of the pilots who flew off on what were called "special attacks" is not at all surprising, as their willingness to die became a recurring trope in the official wartime discourse. These pilots were held up as models of complete loyalty to the emperor and total sacrifice for the country, and the accounts of their deaths in the wartime media were meant to elicit deep feelings of gratitude from the home-front population and even a willingness to make the same sacrifice. In fact, military men began to speak publicly about the "Suicide of the One Hundred Million," as Lieutenant General Nakai Ryōtarō did in a radio broadcast on January 1945.[69]

However, teachers like Yamanaka had the evacuated children do more than think about selections from the official wartime discourse. They had the children participate in various out-of-class activities, most tied to the war in some way. Arguably the most important for our purposes were what might be called official events, which included the reading of the imperial rescript that declared war on the Allies on the eighth day of every month. Often these ritual readings of the imperial rescript took place at local Shintō shrines, which the children visited regularly for war-related events or festivals. Other official events were sending off local conscripts, greeting what were termed the "spirits of the dead," and watching the flyovers of local men who buzzed their home villages on their way to the battle zones. The children also had many visitors—including members of the imperial family, veterans, and representatives of the local chapter of the Women's Patriotic Society—who encouraged them to support the war in every way possible and to become "splendid little citizens."

The children's days were also filled with a variety of physical activities that Ministry of Education officials saw as forms of "training." Their teachers had them take frequent conditioning hikes, forage for wild vegetables and grasshoppers, collect and move firewood, work in victory gardens, and pick up food distributions. They also militarized the children's lives: they had them perform war work, write "comfort letters" to servicemen, receive rudimentary military training, and periodically undergo spiritual training sessions. They even asked their charges to endure their homesickness, the indignities and unpleasantness of collective living, and the shrinking size of their meals "until the country prevailed" (*katsu made*). Unbeknownst to the children, their teachers also were preparing them for the "decisive battle" (*kessen*), expected when the Allies invaded the Japanese home islands in the fall of 1945.

Becoming "Splendid Little Citizens": Nakane Mihoko

The children evacuated to the countryside were required to keep diaries and to submit them to their teachers for diary checks (*nikki kensa*) every seven to ten days. These diaries offer full and detailed accounts of their lives as evacuated children. Typical is the diary of a nine-year-old school-girl named Nakane Mihoko (1935–), who was evacuated from Tokyo in the spring of 1944. Nakane, the daughter of a Tokyo civil servant, was a student at the primary school attached to Ochanomizu Women's University in central Tokyo. In accordance with government orders, her school moved third-, fourth-, fifth-, and sixth-graders to Kumekawa in the Kita-Tamagawa area south of Tokyo. Then, when Allied bombing raids intensified in the early months of 1945 and threatened the Tamagawa area, Nakane and her group were moved on April 10, 1945, to the town of Fukumitsu in Toyama Prefecture. Apparently Fukumitsu was chosen because a teacher at Nakane's school had ties with that community. Unlike most of the children evacuated from Japanese cities, who lived in temples and inns, Nakane's group lived with prominent local families—school principals, businessmen, and doctors—usually three or four to a family.

Nakane was a faithful diarist. She never missed a day and always recorded "her honest and true feelings."[70] Her diary reveals precisely how she was affected by the wartime evacuation, what she was taught and asked to do, and how she responded. In the days leading up to the evacuation, for instance, she could hardly contain her excitement. "Today, it was finally decided that we will go to Toyama Prefecture. I am so happy I can't bear it," she wrote in her diary. She continued:

In the evening I ate dinner and then packed. I probably won't be able to see my younger sisters and brothers. My kid brother said, "Hō-chan, come back quickly, OK?" I said, "I'm leaving. Good-bye. Take care of yourselves," and went with father, mother, and the baby to Ueno [Station]. A lot of people were already there. After some time we went into the station. I said, "Itte kimasu [I'm leaving and will return]." Father and Mother waved to me. The train came. We'll board this train. After some time it was 10:51 P.M. Then the train began to leave. With a clang, clang. The train sped along, Saitō-sensei said, "Good night."[71]

The next entry, dated April 10, finds Nakane waking up after her first night away from home:

I opened my eyes. It was light gray outside, and everyone was still asleep. After some time, Maeno, Tanaka, and Kobayashi woke up. They had told us, "No talking. If you don't go to sleep quickly, you'll be tired tomorrow!" So I fell asleep again. When I opened my eyes, it already had gotten light. Kobayashi was still asleep and snoring loudly. After some time she woke up. At that point the fifth- and sixth-grade boys said they were hungry, and Hori-sensei said, "Those who are so hungry they could die should eat!" After standing for a long time, he got down. Then we boarded the luggage train. It seemed as though we were going to be squashed. We got off the train. At that point, Iwamaru-sensei and the people from Fukumitsu National Citizens School greeted us and carried our luggage. Because my luggage didn't arrive, I stayed at the Setō house.[72]

Nakane described her first day at school in Fukumitsu:

April 11, 1945 (Wednesday) rain then cloudy
Today we washed our faces at the Setō house. Then we were fed. Together with delicious hot rice, we were given hot miso soup, pickles, and something else that had been boiled in grated radish. Then, with our eating utensils in hand, we went off to school. We had an admissions ceremony and afterward had lunch in the sewing room. After lunch, the second-, third-, and fourth-graders went off to see various things with Hori-sensei and others. The scenery was very nice. It looked like a picture. I thought how really nice the scenery was and how really happy I was to be in such a nice place.[73]

These diary entries show that her transition to her life as an evacuated child went smoothly.

Nakane had been keeping a diary since she was four and was a skilled diarist. Her diary entries are full and highly descriptive, offering an extremely valuable record of exactly what she and her classmates did (and were asked to do) from day to day. Prominent are the official events that occurred with some regularity. On April 29, for example, they celebrated the emperor's birthday:

> Today was the emperor's birthday, and it was a happy day! In the morning we put on our school uniforms. Beautiful rising-sun flags were flying at every house. They fluttered in the morning breeze and were beautiful. I thought I wanted to have a heart as beautiful as those beautiful flags. We arrived at school. From the back I could hear happy voices reciting the lines "The flowers bloom like a storm in Yoshino. If I am bórn a Yamato man . . ." The words seemed to sail on the wind. When I turned around, it was the third-section sixth-graders, who were all smiling more than usual. We entered one after another. The sewing room was brighter than usual. After some time passed, it was lunchtime. Lots of different delicious foods were served: beans, lotus root, bog rhubarb, sweet potato stems, cold tofu, and red rice. It was delicious. We played for a long time. Then we could hear the emperor's birthday song being sung solemnly, and we bowed our heads. After some time it ended, and we entered the lecture hall, which had been decorated beautifully. Then after some time we performed the emperor's birthday ceremony. It was a happy, happy emperor's birthday.[74]

The passage "Beautiful rising-sun flags were flying at every house. They fluttered in the morning breeze and were beautiful. I thought I want to have a heart as beautiful as those beautiful flags" echoes the passage in the third-year ethics textbook:

> A blue, clear sky.
> Flying just at the eaves,
> the rising-sun flag
> is truly dignified.
>
> Snowbound houses.
> Flying just at the eaves,
> the rising-sun flag
> somehow seems warm.[75]

The Ministry of Education's attempt to engage the children emotionally was working. A little more than a week later, on May 8, 1945, Nakane and her classmates celebrated Imperial Rescript Observance Day, the day of every month when Nakane and her classmates were asked to write letters to Japanese soldiers and sailors:

> Today was Imperial Rescript Observance Day. When I went to school in the morning, the beautiful rising-sun flags on each house were fluttering in the morning breeze. There was a ceremony at school, which was held in Fukumitsu Lecture Hall. After we returned to our classroom, we wrote letters to sailors. I did as I always did. I tried as hard as I could to write letters that would make them happy. Today we even made envelopes, and we did all this together.[76]

On one occasion Nakane even "drew a comic book picture riddle" in one of her letters to a serviceman.[77] To heighten the "reality effect" of writing these letters, the children were even told where they would be sent: for example, Nakane's June 8 letter was going to "North China," her July 8 letter to "Central China," and her August 8 letter to "soldiers in hospitals."[78]

Their teachers also involved Nakane and her classmates in the war by having them take part in the send-off of conscripts. In her April 14, 1945, entry, Nakane wrote:

> Today I got up at 5:00 A.M.—someone in the Maeda house was going to the front, and we saw him off. The tips of our feet and hands were very cold. After a while, we shouted "Maeda banzai!" three times. He boarded the train. When that happened, the band started playing. It was very merry. We clapped our hands in time with the music, and before we knew it, the train had disappeared in the distance.[79]

As might be expected, the send-offs of their own teachers were deeply affecting. "It happened right during lunch today," wrote Nakane. "Saitō-sensei made an announcement. 'During lunch a conscription notice came for Ishida-sensei. He'll leave on August 11 and join the 136th Infantry Regiment.' When we heard this announcement, no one said a word. I thought to myself, 'Well, so Sensei is going off. Please be strong and go off in good spirits.'"[80]

Before they sent off Ishida-sensei, the children sent off Maeda-sensei:

> Today was the day to send off Maeda-sensei. In the morning we had the send-off ceremony in the No. 2 classroom. We prayed for his success in war and shouted banzai three times. After that, we opened

our umbrellas and went with him to the station. While we waited for the train, we sang war songs with great enthusiasm. Miyaji-sensei imitated university students and clapped his hands, "Ta-ta-ta." Then the train carrying Maeda-sensei disappeared from sight, leaving puffs of smoke floating in the air.[81]

Ishida-sensei's departure deeply affected Nakane and her classmates. In her July 19 entry, she described what the children did for him:

Today we made rice cakes for Ishida-sensei's celebration and had self-study in the morning. Tanaka and I together made things to give to Ishida-sensei. We'll give him a charm, two dolls, and a little of the "Ishida-sensei Diary" that I wrote. In the afternoon we had a send-off ceremony. Tokorozawa represented us and read things that were written on a piece of paper. I felt that today was far sadder than the send-offs I went to when I was in school in Tokyo, but I had happy feelings when I thought about Ishida-sensei's going to war for the sake of the country. Then we had a prayer service in front of the shrine just before dinner (*A very interesting diary* ["Ishida-sensei's Diary"]).[82]

Two days later, the day of Ishida-sensei's departure arrived, which Nakane described in her diary:

Today we were seeing off Ishida-sensei, so we got up early. We gathered at school and then went right away to the train station. It was drizzling, but we didn't open our umbrellas and went on to the station singing war songs we had learned from Ishida-sensei. There was still time until the train came, so we sang war songs while we waited. When we finished a song, we shouted, "Ishida-sensei banzai! Banzai! Banzai!" Those voices! Strong voices! Everyone sang as loudly as they could. After a short time the train arrived. Sensei boarded it, and we shouted banzai and kept clapping hard until he disappeared from sight. It felt as though the train Ishida-sensei boarded left faster than most.[83]

Because the children were away from home and their families, their teachers acted as their surrogate parents, and thus their departure was deeply affecting. This suggests that the Ministry of Education's vision of the evacuation making "school and family one" had been realized.[84]

The teachers also had the children participate in another local ritual: meeting the "spirits" of local men who died while serving in the military. The cremated remains of these men were returned to their home villages in beautiful wooden boxes that were brought by train. The same local officials, teachers, relatives, and friends who had sent them off to war met the train carrying their remains and then marched with them to the family home for the wake. On May 10, 1945, Nakane wrote, "In the afternoon we welcomed the spirits of departed heroes." In early July, she greeted more returning spirits: "We greeted the spirits of the war dead. I really feel grateful to them." Two weeks later: "In the afternoon we welcomed spirits of the dead, and people from both the Fukumitsu and Akamatsu schools joined in. It was a truly sad affair."[85] Nakane's diary reveals that she felt sadness and gratitude, which was what she was supposed to feel, and her sense of indebtedness implies that she would repay the soldiers in some way and at some time. The Japanese social mechanism of repaying debts (*on-gaeshi*) clearly served a useful function during the war, creating ever widening and deepening networks of indebtedness and encouraging the students to prepare to do everything they could for their country.

Outside class, most of what the teachers had the children do took the form of hikes or drills. After her group arrived in Fukumitsu, for instance, Nakane's first hike was to a small airfield about four and a half miles away.

Today we marched to the training site at Tatenogahara. The weather was very nice. After the morning assembly, we went off with our box lunches, and it was hot enough for us to perspire. The rice in the fields swayed like green waves. After a long time we arrived at an open field, but we rested at a better place. After we had been there for a while, the chief talked to us and showed the gliders.[86]

As time passed, the hikes got longer and more arduous. On one hike in late May 1945 the students climbed Mount Kuwayama. Another hike in late July was a two-hour march, and, as Nakane noted, "because we haven't marched recently, even this short hike somehow seemed long."[87]

The teachers designed the hikes to involve some kind of work. For example, the children often moved firewood. According to Nakane's May 1, 1945 entry: "We moved firewood all morning. The little second-graders moved firewood, too. We did this while it was raining, but when I thought of the soldiers, it was easy. I made three or four trips. It wasn't as far as it usually is, and the wood was very light."[88] Nakane's words "when I thought of the soldiers, it was easy" shows that the teachers militarized the work they asked the children to do in order to make it more bearable and to make them want to do it. Nakane's description of moving firewood on May 10 clearly reveals this:

Today fourth-graders and above moved firewood. When I had made my third trip to where Ishida-sensei was standing, he said, "Mmmm. What shall I call you? Let's see. 'Lance Corporal Nakane!'" I thought, I'll work even harder and ran to where the wood piles were. This time Nagino and I carried a big piece of firewood together. When we did this, Ishida-sensei asked, "Nakane, what were you?" When I said, "Lance corporal," he said, "Well, you're now a corporal!" I was so happy I couldn't stand it. In the end we rose to the rank of apprentice officers. I was very happy.[89]

More moving of firewood followed on June 29:

Today we moved firewood. The second- and third-graders picked bracken ferns. Today the people from the Fukumitsu School brought firewood. When we went to where the firewood was, the Fukumitsu School people already were there. We rested. In an instant, the logs were piled as high as a mountain, and there was firewood only at the bottom. We took our firewood and rested at a spot just in front of the shrine. The Fukumitsu School people carried lots of firewood on their backs, and what they carried looked heavy. Here's what I thought: "I was really grateful. They helped move our firewood, and they carried more than we did. If it had just been us, we would have had to make many, more trips. I am truly grateful! How happy I am!" After a time I plodded along, carrying firewood.[90]

At the end of July Nakane and her classmates gathered cranesbill grass "for burning."[91]

Their teachers also had the children forage for wild vegetables, no doubt to give them some exercise and fresh air and to find foods that could supplement their diminishing food rations. Nakane's first food-foraging expedition came on April 22, 1945:

Today is Sunday. After the morning assemble ended, we went to gather mugwort. We went to the Oyabe River embankment. . . . We split up and began to search for mugwort. Everyone was saying, "I wonder if this is mugwort. If we make a mistake and pick poisonous grass, it'll be terrible!" After we searched for a long time, Sensei said, "Stop!" We all put the mugwort we had collected in our hats into his big wrapping cloth.[92]

That day ended with the children making rice cakes and adding the newly gathered mugwort. Summer was the best time to gather *sansai*, "mountain vegetables." Weather permitting, Nakane and her classmates were sent out at least once a week, and sometimes twice a week, to gather wild vegetables.

May 7, 1945
Today we had a fun march. It was very good weather and felt good. . . . The fourth-graders and above . . . went to a place that was a little far away to pick bog rhubarb, bracken ferns, flowering ferns, and various other things.[93]

May 11, 1945
Today we had a fun march. It rained a little in the morning, so everyone talked about how we were going to have good weather. . . . Before long, it was good weather. I was very happy. Because of this, we got ready and went to school. Then we went to pick various things. It was lots and lots of fun. We picked mugwort, field horsetail shoots, yamaudo [wild *udo*], bog rhubarb, bracken ferns, flowering ferns, chives, and rocamble.[94]

May 24, 1945
Because the weather today was good, we went to pick bracken ferns at Tatenogahara. There were lots and lots of bracken ferns.[95]

May 28, 1945
Today we went to pick wild vegetables at Tatenogahara and took *bentō*. . . . We went farther in and picked lots of bracken ferns.[96]

June 1, 1945
Today we went toward Kanazawa to gather wild vegetables. There were very, very steep mountains. It was cloudy, but as we went farther and farther, the weather got much better. We ate our *bentō* in the mountains, and they were really, really delicious. Then we climbed a steep mountain and picked bracken ferns. There were some very long ones but not very many.[97]

June 10, 1945
Today it was National Time Day. Then we went to pick bracken ferns at Tatenogahara, and there were a lot.[98]

June 15, 1945
Today we went to Tatenogahara to pick bracken ferns. It was very hot. In our *bentō* were pickled onions and pickled radishes. Lots of big bracken ferns had sprouted in the shade of trees, and I intended to pick enough to fill up my bag. When I picked as many as I could, my bag was full.[99]

June 18, 1945
Today we went to Mount Kuwayama to pick wild vegetables. The second- and third-graders picked wild vegetables at the base of Kuwayama, and the fourth-graders and above climbed Kuwayama. It was very tiring. Ishida-sensei said, "There are ghosts at the top!" This made it really fun, and we completely forgot we were tired. The fourth-graders did not go to the top and, for a while, collected bog rhubarb below us.[100]

June 20, 1945
Today we went to pick wild vegetables. We were divided into two groups—the third- and fourth-graders formed one group, and the fifth- and sixth-graders the other—and we went to collect lots of dropwort. Our squad leader was Kimon-sensei. We walked along the embankment of the river just before Tatenogahara and picked dropwort. There was a lot of dropwort, but also a lot of buttercups, which were easy to mistake for parsley, so we had to pick carefully. . . . After we ate our *bentō*, we picked stone parsley, and although it was poisonous, I picked something that looked like it.[101]

June 29, 1945
Today we moved firewood. The second- and third-graders picked bracken ferns.[102]

These foraging expeditions offered opportunities for aerobic activity and helped their cooks, and they also were a form of "training."

In addition, the teachers had the children undergo what was euphemistically termed "spiritual training," the most rudimentary kind of military training. At first, it seemed to be a form of conditioning. On May 6, 1945, Nakane explained:

Today was Sunday, and the playing field was open, so the whole school had spiritual training there. For the first time in a long time, we took off our *monpe* and trained in white slips. It felt good to train while warm morning breezes were blowing. The first-, second-, and third-grade boys and the fourth- and fifth-grade girls. Our voices echoed clearly in the sky. There we were under the big sky—in undershirts, red sashes, and white skin. Strong voices, a breeze that felt good, a spring breeze. We perspired. Iwamaru-sensei's smiling face was glistening, and everyone's eyes glittered. After the calisthenics ended, we threw balls. The fourth graders were divided up into red and white teams. We tried throwing the balls under a very hot sun. Dear me! I hit someone—the strongest person on the white team, Hotta. We all raised a battle cry.[103]

Later that month, Nakane and her classmates had a "nighttime drill," which she described in detail:

In the afternoon we went to Tatenogahara for nighttime drills. We were going to leave at 1:30 P.M., but we were late and soon it was 2:30. We took firewood, rice paddles, ladles, pots, pans, and buckets as well as miso, dried tofu, onions, bentō, canteens, and side cups. We finally arrived at Tatenogahara. We rested for a short time, and then the fifth-graders and below collected firewood, and the sixth-graders and female and male teachers dug a hole and made a stove and cooked the meal. After a long while, it was time for dinner. In addition to our *bentō* and the pickled onions, there was a really, really delicious miso soup, which we heated with the firewood we collected. After the meal was finished, we practiced military songs. It was all really, really interesting. Then we played "Search for the Treasure." In the end, our group couldn't find even one "treasure." It was very disappointing but lots of fun. Then we had dried cuttlefish. The fifth graders found two bags of *tororo konbu* and five *onigiri*. And then we practiced walking quickly and striking the enemy. It was lots and lots of fun.[104]

There was "spiritual training" on June 3 and then another "nighttime drill" on June 4.

Evacuated children drilling with wooden swords. Undated. Photo courtesy of the *Mainichi shinbun*.

Today we had fun evening drills. We left here this afternoon at 2:00 P.M. We put on sedge hats and went off. It was very hot and seemed like summer. After some time, I could see Ishida-sensei strip down and put on a headband. We went there and rested for a while. Then we went to gather firewood. The third-section fifth-graders were already there. We gathered firewood for some time and then returned. After a while we had a meal. The miso soup had dried tofu, strips of dried gourd, and two rice cakes in it. It was really, really delicious. After the meal, we practiced singing war songs. Then we played "Search for the Treasure." The "treasure" turned out to be Kobayashi's apple, but because she wrote to please make it Hori-sensei's *omiyage*, it wasn't much fun for the rest of us. I searched as hard as I could, but finally we were ordered to assemble. In our group, it was Kobayashi alone. Then we were divided into attack and defense units and made war with each other.[105]

Two weeks later, Nakane and her classmates learned "hand-to-hand combat":

Today was a spiritual training day for the whole school, and we did something different—we did hand-to-hand combat. Iwamaru-sensei told us many different stories. Then we piggybacked the person across from us and ran and did other things. The next station was Akuzawa-sensei's hand grenade–throwing class. We used small balls for hand grenades and imagined that the large ball we used for the intergrade meet was the enemy's head and threw the small balls at it. We threw the hand grenades with all our might, but they didn't hit their target. Then we moved to Hachikuwa-sensei's station, where we practiced striking and killing with a wooden sword. We faked to the left and faked to the right. Then after a bit we went to Ishida-sensei's station. We took off our clothes and practiced spearing someone. We used our foreheads to butt the chest of the person in front of us, thrust our hands into that person's armpits, and pushed with our feet firmly planted on the ground. In the end, only one person was still thrusting. Then when that was done, we went to Yoshikado-sensei's station, where we practiced spearing. Yoshikado-sensei said, "They're still there. Spear them! Spear them!" and it was really fun. I was tired, but I realized that even one person can kill a lot of the enemy.[106]

There was "spiritual training" again on July 29 and a long early morning march that got the students up at 4:00 A.M.[107] The military training, nighttime drills, and long marches pointed ominously to the "decisive battle" expected to take place that fall when the Allies invaded the Japanese home islands. No doubt, Nakane's teachers understood that the purpose of these drills, hikes, and training was to prepare the children for what was coming, even if the children did not. For example, the teachers were learning to fly gliders that would be loaded with explosives and flown into the ships carrying Allied invaders.[108] This in fact was one of the reasons they hiked to Tatenogahara, which had an air strip and several gliders.

"Splendid Little Citizens"

Since its formation, the Ministry of Education had worked to mold the nation's children into "good Japanese" who would be of use to the country. This entailed writing ethics textbooks that would shape the children's character, values, and behavior and would encourage physical fitness and hygiene. Every new edition of the textbooks brought new content, refined the implicit rhetorical strategies and tactics, and changed the focus, in order to transform each student into a "splendid little citizen." Just as important as the ethics textbooks were the teachers who accompanied the children to their evacuation sites, aided by locals hired as teachers and "house mothers." Together with the school authorities who oversaw the evacuation from afar, these teachers and house mothers did everything they could to protect the children, to preserve their health, to involve them in the war effort, to have them participate in official events, and, if possible, to keep them happy. They now were responsible for not only teaching the children but also managing their lives from the moment they rose in the morning until they went to bed at night. Given these demands, it is hardly surprising that their responsibilities exhausted many of the teachers, especially the older ones. Most got sick, and a few had to return home.

The children did their best to become "splendid little citizens." They studied as hard as they could under trying circumstances. They endured their homesickness. They tried to stay fit and healthy. They foraged for food—chiefly wild vegetables and grasshoppers—and trekked to distribution sites to pick up food rations. In addition, they supported the war effort: they stood at attention and read the imperial declaration of war on the eighth of every month; they wrote "comfort letters" to servicemen overseas, urging them to fight hard; and they enthusiastically saw off local conscripts, were sad when their teachers were sent away, and met the spirits of "departed heroes." In the summer of 1945 they even learned to throw hand grenades at targets and went on long conditioning hikes, some even at night, so as to be ready for the "decisive battle" expected in the fall of 1945 when the Allies invaded the Japanese home islands.

4

Monitoring the Evacuated Children

Of the 1,303,200 children evacuated from Japanese cities to the safety of the countryside, 857,000 were sent by their families to live with relatives. The remaining 446,000 were moved by their schools in a collective evacuation (*shūdan sokai*) that posed huge logistical challenges for administrators and teachers. Finding suitable accommodations was the first challenge and required many trips to evacuation sites to vet the inns, schools, and Buddhist temples where the children were housed. Once the children had been moved, they were under the care of teachers from their home schools and local hires who did everything humanly possible to buoy the children's morale, to keep them healthy, and to encourage their support for the war.

Although the families' decision to send their children away under the care of their teachers could not have been easy, they did much to make the evacuation go smoothly. First, they visited the evacuation sites from time to time for "official interviews" with teachers and meetings with their children. Second, they regularly brought or sent their children scarce commodities and foods, a real feat in a time of rationing and shortages. Third, they helped them in many other, unexpected ways—for example, by teaching them things that urban children usually did not know, such as which wild plants and fruits were edible and how to trap and cook animals and insects.

The families also encouraged, and contributed to, the transformation of their evacuated sons and daughters into "splendid little citizens" (*rippana shōkokumin*). They did this mainly through the steady stream of letters and postcards they sent to their children

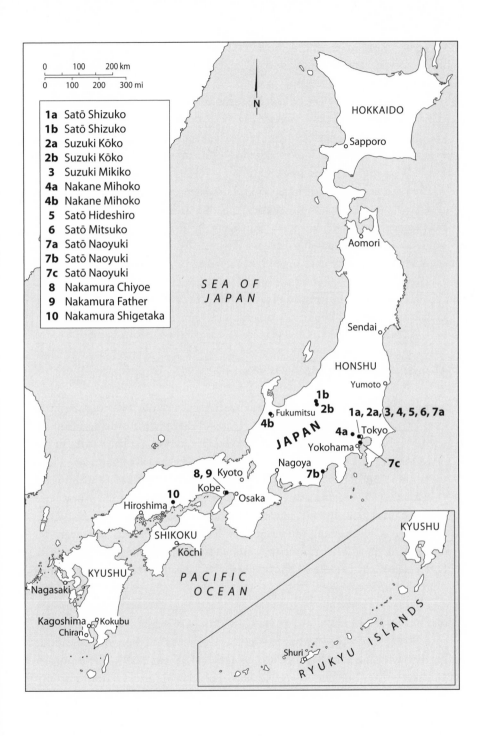

1a	Satō Shizuko
1b	Satō Shizuko
2a	Suzuki Kōko
2b	Suzuki Kōko
3	Suzuki Mikiko
4a	Nakane Mihoko
4b	Nakane Mihoko
5	Satō Hideshiro
6	Satō Mitsuko
7a	Satō Naoyuki
7b	Satō Naoyuki
7c	Satō Naoyuki
8	Nakamura Chiyoe
9	Nakamura Father
10	Nakamura Shigetaka

0 100 200 km
0 100 200 300 mi

N

HOKKAIDO

Sapporo

Aomori

SEA OF
JAPAN

Sendai

HONSHU

Yumoto

1b
Fukumitsu **2b**   **1a, 2a, 3, 4, 5, 6, 7a**
4b
JAPAN   **4a** Tokyo
Yokohama
Nagoya   **7c**
8, 9 Kyoto   **7b**
Kobe
10   Osaka
Hiroshima

KYUSHU

SHIKOKU

Kōchi

KYUSHU

PACIFIC
OCEAN

Nagasaki

Kagoshima   Kokubu
Chiran

Shuri   RYUKYU ISLANDS

and through their communications with the children's teachers. In fact, this three-way correspondence—among families, children, and teachers—was an important, and often overlooked, dimension of the wartime subjectification of Japanese children.

This is amply revealed in the correspondence of two families that sent their children to the countryside. The first is the Satō family, from Denen-chōfu, a Tokyo suburb, whose eleven-year-old daughter, Shizuko, was evacuated to Hirao village in Nagano Prefecture in August 1944. The Satō family's correspondence amounted to 232 letters and postcards: Shizuko's mother, Mitsuko, wrote 107; Shizuko herself wrote eighty-three; her older brother, Naoyuki, wrote thirty-four; and her father wrote eight. The second family, the Nakamuras, lived in Kobe, and their eleven-year-old son, Shigetaka, was evacuated to Ibara village in Okayama Prefecture. He and his parents faithfully exchanged letters during the six months (September 1944 to March 1945) that he was away from home. The correspondence of the Satōs and the Nakamuras reveals exactly how these two families helped transform their children into "splendid little citizens."

Monitoring the Children: Teachers

As I explained earlier, the children's instructors carefully followed the Ministry of Education's guidelines, teaching and doing what it prescribed. Accordingly, the teachers had the children keep diaries and submit them every seven to ten days for diary checks (*nikki kensa*), which allowed them to monitor the children's morale and to shape their behavior. Monitoring student morale became even more important as the dwindling food supplies meant drastically reduced food rations and as popular support for the war flagged on the home front in 1945. These diary checks thus were an efficient form of surveillance that enabled the teachers to discipline (in a Foucauldian sense) their students' internal lives and to transform them into "splendid little citizens."

This transformation is apparent in the diary of Nakane Mihoko, the nine-year-old girl evacuated from Tokyo to Fukumitsu in Toyama Prefecture. She clearly wrote for her teachers and often asked them directly about her behavior, and they nearly always responded. On May 1, for example, Nakane wrote "Starting today, it's May. This month, too, I want to do my best to become a splendid citizen."[1] Becoming a "splendid little citizen" was the goal of students like Nakane, and her teachers' comments in her diary show how they encouraged this. For example, after describing how she helped move firewood on June 29, Nakane declared, "Today was I a good child?"[2] The next day she wrote, "Today was the end of June. Was I able to be a good child in June? When I thought about that, I was embarrassed by the bad things I had done. I thought, I will be a good child for sure in July."[3] The teacher who reviewed her diary at the end of June commended Nakane for her thoughtful reflections on her behavior in June, writing: "Good self-reflections. In July, please become a better child."[4]

Several weeks later, Nakane was on her best behavior when Imperial Princess Kaya visited the Fukumitsu Girls High School, and she asked in that day's entry, "Was I able to be a good child all day today? Did I do anything bad? I must become an even better good child."[5] Two days later, July ended, prompting Nakane to write: "Today is the end of July. I wondered whether I was able to be a good child in July. In August I want to be a better, better child and make Sensei happy."[6] The censoring teacher crossed out "Sensei" (teacher) and wrote in "Father and Mother," reminding us of the place of the family in official wartime discourse.

On the first day of August, Nakane resolved to be "more of a better child than I was last month," adding, "During the morning assembly we had a ceremony to appoint squad leaders. I'm now becoming a squad leader. Because of this, I want all the more to be a good child and to act like a squad leader."[7] The effects of her teachers' diary checks are obvious: Nakane worked hard to become a "good child" and "splendid little citizen" and to act as she was supposed to.

For several reasons, the teachers also routinely read the postcards and letters the children sent home to their families. This allowed them, first, to monitor the children's morale; second, to quash any rumors; and, third, to reassure the children's families that their sons and daughters were well. Often the teachers wrote directly on the letters and postcards being sent home, describing the background of a child's remarks or explaining something that might be misunderstood.

The Satō family's correspondence is typical. Satō Shizuko's teachers who censored her correspondence always identified themselves.[8] The name of Fujimoto-sensei appears the most often, as either "Fujimoto" or just "Fuji." At the end of Shizuko's first letter home, for instance, he wrote, "Both the food and lodging are fine, and [Shizuko] is extremely energetic; as for food, we worry about [the children's] overeating and [so] have everything served. Don't worry. Fujimoto."[9] Five days later, he wrote on another of Shizuko's letters: "She is full of spirit every day. She does a good job of helping others and is doing well as a squad leader. She made a mistake about when [the letters] arrived. Fuji."[10] Five days after that, he added to Shizuko's September 7 letter: "She is, as always, doing everything with a lot of spirit. Please don't worry."[11] As it got colder, Shizuko's teachers were careful to reassure her parents that their daughter was in good health. "The temperature has fallen," one wrote, "but the children are well and responding to the cold. Shizuko-san is the picture of health and has not caught a single cold."[12]

Shizuko's teachers were fulsome in their praise. At the end of her October 11 letter, one of them wrote, "She is displaying a certain style as group leader, and doing a good job. There are moments when I am amazed by her spiritual power."[13] At the end of Shizuko's December 6 postcard to her mother, Fujimoto reported that "[she seems] extremely energetic. Please don't worry."[14] Three days later he added to a postcard, "Every day [she] is energetic and vigorously persevering."[15] At end of Shizuko's December 31 postcard, he thanked her family for the dried sweet potatoes and candy they brought and reported that "the children were very happy to get this."[16] At the end of Shizuko's January 24, 1945, postcard home, Fujimoto praised her, writing, "She has really improved in skiing and is progressing happily."[17] After Shizuko's mother visited, the teacher censoring the mail reassured her that all was still well: "Thank you for the various things [you brought] the other day. I hope you got back to Tokyo safely. Shizuko-san did not show any sadness about your leaving. She was as happy as she always is."[18] A week later, a teacher told her family that Shizuko was about to be given a leadership role: "We will have her work hard as the class leader for a term. Because she is relatively energetic, please don't worry."[19] This was followed by a report that "Shizu-chan has become class head and is full of pep. Yonekura."[20]

The children's families also found ways to use the censoring system. The Satō family, for example, used it to express their feelings, especially their gratitude, to their daughter's teachers. Shizuko's older brother and mother, for example, often included messages meant for her teachers. In his first letter to his sister, her brother commented, "Everyone probably wants to go home, but pull together and persevere. Give my best to your teachers."[21] In her September 8 letter to her daughter, Satō Mitsuko was careful to add, "Please say to your teacher(s), 'Thank you for worrying [about me]. There is nothing I can do except thank you. We are relieved that everything is going well.' Grandmother and Father send their greetings too."[22] What is interesting about this passage is that Shizuko's mother addressed her remarks to her daughter but knew that her daughter's teacher, Fujimoto-sensei, would read it; and we know he did because he signed off on the letter. Shizuko's mother ended her September 22 letter with "Please give my best to Fujimoto-sensei."[23] Inexplicably, in her March 3 postcard, she asked Shizuko to apologize to Fujimoto-sensei, and her orthography conveyed her sincerity: "Please say to Fujimoto-sensei, 'Forgive me for inquiring about Shizuko.'"[24]

Nakamura Shigetaka's family also used the censorship system to communicate with their son's teachers. His father closes his September 30, 1944, letter, written twelve days after Shigetaka left Kobe, by asking him "to please give my best to your teachers."[25] A week later he wrote again and closed his letter with "Give my best to your teachers, house mothers, and friends."[26] Three and a half weeks into his son's evacuation, he commended his son's teachers and the citizens of Ibara, his son's evacuation site.[27] Unlike Satō Shizuko's correspondence with her family, however, the names of the teachers censoring Nakamura Shigetaka's letters and postcards home do not appear.

Monitoring the Children: Family

Both Satō Shizuko and Nakamura Shigetaka were dutiful correspondents, sending home at least one postcard or letter a week and sometimes more. Although everyone in Shizuko's family—her father, mother, and teenaged brother—wrote to her, her mother wrote most often.[28] As expected, Shizuko's first postcards and letters home describe her life as an evacuated schoolgirl. She told her family what she ate, what she did every day, where she and her classmates hiked, what they foraged for (grasshoppers, chestnuts, firewood, flowering ferns, bracken ferns, wild grasses), what special events were held, what military drills and exercises they practiced, what official visitors they entertained, and how her classmates were getting along.[29] She also noted what food her classmates' families brought, how grateful she was for what her family sent her, that some of the tangerines that her family sent had not arrived, who wrote to her, and how she was feeling.[30]

Shigetaka's first letters home also describe his new life. He reported that he got up at 6:00 A.M.; roll was called; and the children faced the imperial palace, bowed to the emperor and empress, and said, "Good morning, Father and Mother."[31] This was followed by their doing radio calisthenics, rubbing themselves with towels (to warm up), washing their faces, cleaning their room, working in the garden, enjoying some free time before breakfast, and then eating breakfast. At 8:00 A.M., Shigetaka and his classmates left for Yoshi Primary School.[32] At 8:20 the morning assembly was convened and was followed by exercises. Shigetaka's group of evacuated children and the local children shared their assemblies and lessons.[33] At night, before the children went to bed, roll was called, and once again they bowed to the imperial palace before saying "good night" to their parents.[34]

Shigetaka wrote vivid descriptions of what he did every day. He worked in the garden and gathered nuts and mushrooms.[35] Like Satō Shizuko and Nakane Mihoko, he and his classmates took hikes, foraged for edible plants and insects, and picked up rations and firewood.[36] He and his classmates even harvested potato vines and helped the local farmers, who gave them food in return for their work.[37] Shigetaka always was careful to mention his participation in local war rituals, such as sending off conscripts and welcoming home the remains of men killed in war.[38] As was true with Nakane Mihoko, some of the hikes that Shigetaka and his classmates took were thinly disguised conditioning exercises. They not only picked up firewood but also had dedicated training runs.[39] "Beginning last Sunday," Shigetaka wrote proudly, "every morning we jog with no shirts past the front of the Jūrinin, turning at the corner of the Yamanari liquor store, and from the Tsuchihashi Bridge past the rice fields. It was cold and quite tiring, but when I thought 'this is training,' I was able to persevere." One of these jogs was a little more than seven miles.[40] Again like Satō Shizuko, Shigetaka and his classmates had a steady stream of visitors who exhorted them to support the war effort; they ranged from members of the local women's association, who brought snacks, to veterans and a *kami-shibai* performer.[41] But unlike Shizuko, Shigetaka rarely described what he ate, how his classmates were faring, or what he was feeling.

Their families' letters were always cheerful, positive, and encouraging, which is abundantly clear in the letters and postcards that Satō Shizuko's parents and her older brother Naoyuki sent to her. In Shizuko's first week away from home, her mother sent four letters and her brother two, which were very optimistic and asked about her life as an evacuated child. In her first letter to Shizuko, dated August 25, 1944, her mother wrote, "It was lucky, wasn't it, that you evacuated with lots of your friends, and last night was probably really fun and happy."[42] Her brother Naoyuki, a high school student mobilized for war work in Shizuoka Prefecture, sent a letter dated August 25 that simply rehearsed the official wartime discourse:

This is the first time you are on your own, and everyone, beginning with Father and Mother, is watching to see how well you fight. To fight means to do what your teachers tell you and to live happily with a strong spirit and a strong body. At present, Japan has truly risen up; Fuku-chan and other strong military units are attacking the enemy in force; and when they have driven away the American and English armies that are approaching Japan and the children of America have evacuated, all of you will bravely return home. Until that happens, keep in mind the important young bud of the great tree that will construct the Japan of the future and persevere.[43]

A day later, in another letter, Satō Mitsuko quoted part of what she said was Naoyuki's letter to Shizuko. It reads: "There was the following sentence from your brother: 'Shizuko, go off in good spirits! While you are there, Japan probably will begin to defeat the enemy. It will be the turn of American children to evacuate. Until that happens, persevere with a strong spirit! . . . And when you return to Tokyo, it will probably mean that Japan has [won] a great victory!'"[44] In the same letter, she asked her daughter about Nagano Prefecture and urged her to make the best of the evacuation:

This is your first time in Nagano; what kind of place is it? I bet it's nice. Please become a really good child who breathes the clean air, develops a strong body, and creates a sturdy spirit that can endure anything. When you return, you will have become a healthy child who looks different. Shizuko, give it your all! Your mother, too, will work at not being outdone by you. Give my best to your teachers and house mothers. And I will write (was the *bentō* all right?). Good-bye. (Be careful not to cut into your lips with the new toothbrush.)[45]

At first glance, these letters seem to show simply that Shizuko's family was worrying about her and wanting her to be happy. But in fact, much more was going on.

In their letters, Shizuko's family always apprised her of the situation in Tokyo. Many of her mother's letters simply describe the many things she was doing to contribute to the war effort, such as building a bomb shelter at home and doing her share as a member of her neighborhood association and the housewives association.[46] "I'm doing all I can because it's for the soldiers," she announced at one point.[47] She loaded luggage full of winter clothing for the children, sent off conscripts, greeted the "returning heroic spirits" of local men, joined air-defense drills, built air-raid shelters, picked up fruit, and went to get her allotment of charcoal.[48] In June 1945, however, the big news was their neighborhood association's war garden:

It was decided that our neighborhood association should plant a war garden. The . . . field is what is left of the Takei house, and it extends into the Umehara property. Each household has a ten-square-meter field. Four or five days ago I went to till the soil with the Matsui and Nakazawa mothers.

On a evacuated plot, I "talked and worked the soil with friends, and [we] planted eggplants and potatoes." Yesterday, because we were given twenty-four sweet potato shoots, we worked as hard as we could, and I hope we will be able to grow a lot and send you dried sweet potatoes. Please look forward to this.[49]

In subsequent letters, Satō Mitsuko always reported on whether what they had planted was growing and what was blooming in the garden: "The neighborhood association war garden is steadily showing real achievements: The usual grasses, Chinese cabbages, cucumbers, pumpkin squash, and Shizu-chan's favorite sweet potatoes (*satsuma imo*). I can't tell about the sweet potatoes without digging them up, but four pumpkin squash are appearing, and the cucumber flowers are in full bloom."[50]

Nakamura Shigetaka's parents also did their best to let him know what was happening in Kobe. In her letters, his mother described building an air-raid shelter with the Mizuno family from next door and raising silkworms as a housewives association project.[51] She also complained that her community council work was keeping her from finishing the pair of wool pants she was sewing for him.[52]

Shigetaka's parents wrote about their war garden as well. His mother reported that they had harvested all four of their sweet potatoes, which, his father said, weighed just over thirteen ounces. His father also reported that they had planted giant white radishes and transplanted chard and Chinese cabbage and that their chicken had begun to lay eggs, five so far.[53] In a letter dated December 12, Shigetaka's mother reported that "the 'peas' in the garden are developing nicely, and the fava beans are doing well too."[54] The war garden is mentioned only two or three times more, perhaps because the things they planted weren't growing well and their hen stopped laying eggs.[55]

Although the postcards and letters the Satō and Nakamura families sent to their children seem little more than accounts of what they were doing back home, they served to make the war and everything they were doing to support the war effort seem perfectly normal. "Yesterday morning we had an air-raid drill," Shizuko's mother wrote at one point. "Father read your letter during the drill and then read it again during a meal."[56] The implicit message was that Shizuko should do the same.

The two families' correspondence with their children served as well to naturalize the war and the strong feelings it generated. Many of the Naka-

A wartime garden in bombed-out Tokyo, January 1, 1945. Photo courtesy of the National Shōwa Memorial Museum, Tokyo.

mura family's letters, for example, focused on the latest war news. Shige-taka's father reported to his son on the war films he had seen. He saw *Ano hata o ute* (*Fire on That Flag: The End of Corregidor*) and recommended it, and he also saw *Nikudan teishintai* (*The Human Bullet Volunteer Corps*) but did not care for it.[57] In a letter dated October 6, Shigetaka responded to the news that Guam and Tinian had been lost to the enemy. "Everyone at Guam and Tinian died in battle, didn't they? While I was ready for this sort of thing, the soldiers who fought back were really pathetic."[58] His mother, in a letter written on the same day, shared a patriotic moment with her son:

> Beginning the day before yesterday, for the first time in a long while, I heard the "March of Battleships" . . . and was really thankful. The naval battles in the Taiwan Straits and the attacks of the army's "Thunder [units]" were brilliant, weren't they? It was music that came on after the seven o'clock news the day before yesterday—"The March in the Pacific," "The Sinking," and the "Tokkan"—and I sang along with the radio. I was really happy![59]

A week later, while visiting a niece in Kōchi, his father broached the war situation in a postcard to Shigetaka. "While I was at Sumae-san's house," he wrote, "I read in the newspaper about the attacks on Okinawa and Taiwan and the results. At long last, there is full-scale fighting, and your evacuation is coming to have real significance."[60] In a reply eleven days later Shigetaka wrote proudly about what the military authorities described as the Japanese forces' huge victories in the Taiwan area: "Apparently we launched a huge attack on Task Force 58, led by [Admiral Mark] Mitscher. On the nineteenth the battle results were announced, and we heard a talk from Sensei at school. Damaged and sunk: fifty-seven ships. Wow! That's amazing. But we lost 310 aircraft, and the pilots of our planes, who resolved not to return, pressed the enemy ships, and I think they were truly noble but sad."[61]

In a long letter to Shigetaka dated December 10, 1944, his father, too, discussed the "special attacks" then taking place: "The violent war in the Philippines continues day and night, and many brave special attack units are racking up impressive battle results. Is this something to be thankful for? I don't know. Doing everything we should do as best we can is the unique [distinctly Japanese] way of showing gratitude and service. Let's persevere energetically and happily."[62] His father's ambivalence about special attack tactics that the army and navy were using in the Philippines is surprising, however.

Several letters touched on the flashy new American bomber, the B-29, that had recently appeared in Japanese skies. In his November 26, 1944, letter, Shigetaka indicated that he had heard about the B-29 attacks on Tokyo. "We can no longer be negligent," he warned, "The reason for our evacuating has become apparent, and Japan's situation has begun to look perilous."[63] In her December 20 letter, his mother reiterated the official discourse about the Allied bombing raids and closed with the words, "From now on we will probably have frequent air raids and there probably will be damage, but I'm sure you expected that."[64]

Some members of the Nakamura family were even entranced by the B-29. Apparently Shigetaka's father and a neighbor saw a formation of nine B-29s and called them "splendid." His younger brother Tatsuyo was pleased that he had gotten a look at the B-29 and fancied himself something of an expert. "He looks at the sky through the telescope he made himself," wrote their mother, "and stands at the entrance to the children's air-raid shelter, explaining various things [about the B-29]."[65] The spell did not last, however. In his January 7, 1945, letter to his son, Shigetaka's father, tiring of the nightly air-raid alerts, exclaimed, "The absolutely hateful enemy aircraft! Oh, how much I want to win!!! I want to win!!!"[66]

The two families also naturalized the war by sharing bad news with their children, such as the impact of the enemy air raids. Satō Mitsuko mentioned the big air-raid drill on October 24, "which included lectures about incendiary bombs and how to fight the fires they start."[67] She described as well the many air-raid alerts and warnings and wrote how glad she and her husband were that "we made you evacuate. Even though it was a horrifying thought, we did it, even though it was unpleasant. It would have been terrible if we had made all of you, who carry the future of the country on your backs, put yourselves in harm's way."[68] Anticipating Shizuko's fears, Satō Mitsuko assured her that her parents "did not want to die a dog's death."[69] She continued:

> Whenever there is an air-raid warning and alert, we do our best and resolve not to die, and this for the sake of our two children. Please do not worry about your family: when the siren starts to sound, we always are surprised but when we remember that "we have two children and we must be strong . . ." we calm down. So Shizuko, please do not worry and be strong.[70]

After the devastating March 9 and 10 firebombing of central Tokyo reduced a densely populated thirteen-square-mile area of the city to ash and killed close to ninety thousand people, Shizuko's mother reassured her: "Luckily, the area near our house was OK. I don't know about tonight, but please don't worry."[71] Later that month, she wrote, "Please take care of yourself; there is nothing for you to worry about at home. Even if we are hit, it will be for the sake of the country, so don't regret or be sad about it."[72]

At around the same time, Shizuko's brother Naoyuki wrote to her, commenting on the growing intensity of the Allied bombing of Japanese cities:

The bombing attacks of enemy aircraft are gradually getting fiercer and fiercer, but Shizuoka [where he was working] has not had anything. So Shizuko, please just promise that it'll be fine even if our house is destroyed. Your older brother has resolved to do this. Because this great war finds us fighting the Americans and British, you probably realize that victory will not be easy. But Japan's winning is a sure thing. Universities and high schools throughout the country will not have classes starting in April, [because] everyone will have more important things to do for the country.[73]

Early in April, Shizuko's mother told her that she would be evacuating to nearby Ibaraki Prefecture to live with "Grandma."[74] "It will most certainly be inconvenient for Father," she wrote, "and I would rather not go away, but this is the [kind of] perseverance we must have until we win the war. Let's do our very best."[75] Her brother's April 19 postcard describes the impact of the April 13 B-29 raid on the Mejiro and Ikebukuro areas of Tokyo, not far from the family home, and notes that the western half of the No. 5 National Citizens School burned down.[76] In his April 20 postcard to Shizuko, her father reported that the air raid the day before "was a pretty big raid, but our house and everyone in the neighborhood association was unharmed."[77] Then, in an April 30 postcard to Shizuko, Satō Mitsuko reported very, very bad news: her daughter's journal—"Excerpts for Shizuko"—had been burned, and she added, "I would like you to accept this because this is war. If you return in one piece, let's have another one made. Let's pray for success in war."[78]

Then in the spring and summer of 1945 the Satō and Nakamura families prepared their evacuated children for the worst. Satō Mitsuko's letters to her daughter report more houses destroyed in the air raids,[79] and by the end of May she even seemed resigned to losing their house as well and tried to convey these feelings to her daughter:

Shizuko, from now on I think things will get much, much worse. But please don't worry. We have made doubly sure that the house is ready, so if there is an air raid, please think of the house as gone. The reason, as I told you before, is that "it's strange that the house has not burned down." We are ashamed that we are not one of those who have been bombed. Because we absolutely don't want fires to start at our house, we will work as hard as we can to prevent them.[80]

"Think of the house as gone" reveals just how sure Satō Mitsuko was that the bombing would claim their residence. In his June 8 letter, Naoyuki urged Shizuko to strengthen her resolve. "Even if the house burns down," he wrote, "don't lose heart; from now on strengthen your resolve! No matter how many houses are destroyed, it will be fine if we win. Shizuko and your classmates must hold brightly to your hearts until 'the day of victory' and study hard."[81]

A month later, her brother shared some very sad news: one of their teachers, Fukujirō-sensei (Fuku-chan), had died in a special attack, but, he added, Sensei had taken time to write to them before he took off on his final flight: "Even though it was just a few hours before the attack from which he would not return, he kindly wrote you a last letter, and we should be thankful for this, shouldn't we? . . . 'Persevere until we win.' Let's persevere in that way."[82] In a July 9 letter, Shizuko's mother also related the news about Fukujirō-sensei:

I read Fukujirō-sensei's last postcard, thankfully and happily. I feel nothing but gratitude. In the few hours he had left, he did not forget you, and I am full of gratitude for the letter he sent you.

As for his really and truly giving this to you, when we think about his feelings, let's give our all for our country, shall we? I think the name of his unit—"Barbarian Quelling Unit"—soon will be made public, so let's [be sure to] notice it on the radio and in the newspaper.[83]

A week later, her mother closed with a comment about Utsunomiya, the capital of Tochigi Prefecture: "A lot of Utsunomiya also burned, didn't it? In everything we do, let's keep going for the sake of the war."[84] In her August 11 letter she reported that Fukui, on the west coast, had been heavily bombed by the Americans and added, "It's the hateful B-29s."[85]

Subjectifying the Children: Family

The Satō and Nakamura families' correspondence also shows how they participated in the subjectification of their children from the moment they sent them away. Early in September 1945, when Satō Shizuko's brother heard that she had been made a squad leader, he wrote, "Congratulations! You should know that becoming the leader of others has few pleasures and many hardships, so be strong!"[86] Eight days later he wrote again, this time closing with "Let's both persevere until we win the war."[87] Three weeks later he described his own spartan living conditions and reported that he had pulled a cart filled with firewood several miles. "It was a very demanding task," he remembered, "but we thought of the Japanese servicemen who had had glorious deaths, following the example of the brave warriors of Tinian and Guam, and we were able to keep going." His letter closed with an exhortation to Shizuko to become "a splendid little citizen."[88]

Her parents did exactly the same thing. In her October 18 letter Shizuko's mother commended both Japan's military forces and her daughter's teachers when she wrote, "Thanks to the great military achievements of the imperial forces, I think the teachers have power, and let's both do our best together and pray for military success."[89] A week later Shizuko replied, "As I was writing this letter, wonderful war news was announced. Mother probably stopped her kitchen work and listened to the radio. At long last the great decisive battle. Japan will persevere."[90] Naoyuki did the same as well. In his October 27 letter to his sister, he observed that "recently there have been great military achievements, and it feels good."[91] Two weeks later, Shizuko's father wrote in a postcard: "Father will really persevere. Even if enemy planes come, it'll be fine, so don't worry."[92] In late November, Satō Mitsuko visited her daughter's evacuation site, and after her return to Tokyo she commented on everything her daughter was doing as an evacuee:

I was really glad to hear your pleasant and proud stories of gathering firewood and washing daikon, and not being outdone by your friends, and managing to do everything. I will share with the family your happy stories of doing things every day that you once could not do, doing them without complaint, and doing them so you are not beaten by friends and proudly managing to do hard things. No matter what, if you give your all, you can do it, can't you? Be confident and be steadfast. The truth is your mother did not imagine that Shizuko could do what you're doing. . . .

I understand that because it's you, you have not shown a defeatist attitude. I wondered how much you would be able to do, and I'm really happy that you are doing even more than I expected. Even with the many difficult things you will be asked to do, I believe that if others can do them, you can too. I know that each difficult thing you overcome will make you a strong child. Don't forget that correctly living the evacuated life is your most important service to your country, Japan.[93]

In a letter dated November 29, her brother likewise reminded Shizuko that "your being strong and living an evacuation life is your task as a child of the state."[94] The phrase "your task as a child of the state" is revealing. A few days later, Shizuko replied as she was supposed to: "No matter how difficult things get, I will be able to do them. I've become a much stronger child than I was in Tokyo, haven't I?"[95] She, like Nakane Mihoko, was doing her best to become "a splendid little citizen," and she wanted, and needed, affirmation of her behavior from everyone around her, both her family and her teachers, and they responded as she hoped they would.

Nakamura Shigetaka's parents, too, encouraged his subjectification from the moment he left Kobe. At the end of her first letter to her son, dated September 19, 1944, Nakamura Chiyoe wrote: "Well, let's [all of us]—Father, you, Tatsuyo, and me—fight as hard as we can in our different locations."[96] Nine days later she urged Shigetaka "to pass each day in a manly way" and "to please persevere."[97] Shigetaka made the same exhortations to his parents, urging them "to please persevere."[98]

By January 1945, though, both families recognized that the war was not going well for their country. Satō Mitsuko urged her daughter to bear up in these difficult times. "Let's both do our very best in 1945," she began. "Don't do anything you will regret. Please take good care of yourself. It will mean patiently waiting until we win the war. Keep your spirits up."[99] Shizuko embraced the model offered by her parents. "Because Father and Mother are ready to grab the enemy's incendiary bombs," she wrote, "I, too, am inspired and naturally will be able to become a splendid child. Thank you, Father and Mother."[100]

A week later, Shizuko even invoked the self-sacrificing discourse of the special attack pilots:

. . . the scattering cherry blossoms (war buddies scattered as special attack units)
the remaining cherry blossoms (left behind in the home islands)
scattering cherry blossoms (we too will scatter for sure)[101]

The last line, "scattering cherry blossoms (we too will scatter for sure)," reminds us that the children were being prepared for the Allied invasion of Japan expected that fall. Shizuko's brother Naoyuki reminded her that her teachers, friends, and relatives all were "in good spirits and doing their best."[102] His message is clear: you should do the same, too.

The new year brought an intensification of the Allied bombing of the Japanese home islands and even more talk of a "decisive battle." In his New Year's greeting to his parents, Shigetaka wrote: "Father and Mother, Happy New Year (*omedetō gozaimasu*). This is the year of decisive battles. Let's keep our bodies healthy, stand up straight, and live."[103] He also described a special New Year's program in Ibara that included watching *kami-shibai* entitled "My Beloved Aircraft Flies to the South" and "After I Lost Father." He and his classmates, he admitted, "were deeply moved, to tears."[104] His mother responded on January 5, reporting that "Koiso-san" [the prime minister] had announced, "'This is the year I would like to make the year of certain victory.' Let's give it our best shot. Both Dad and Mom will give it their all and endure any hardships. . . . Let's keep going."[105] Then, in his February 4 letter to his parents, Shigetaka reported that he and his classmates had begun shouting, "We are students of the imperial country" as they jogged around town, alternately singing "The Clouds Divide, the Clouds Divide," which contained the following stanza:

> The sacred war to drive out the demons
> The imperial country takes up the swords with righteousness
> Ah! We now will attack
> Never look back
> The imperial flag of the sun fluttering, the jewel will shatter.[106]

On February 14 Shigetaka visited a local family, the Otas, and he reported that "even people living in lonely places deep in the mountains have strong feelings about the war." He quoted Mr. Ota, who said, "Today I paid a visit to the Hachiman [Shrine] and asked Hachiman to see that we win this war." Shigetaka concluded that "it is because of people like this . . . that Japan will win."[107]

But by the spring of 1945, the Satō family sensed what was coming and what sacrifices would be necessary. In a long letter to her daughter, dated March 5, Satō Mitsuko's writing moved into a different register as she elevated the country over her own family:

> At the moment I have no regrets, because when our country is completely victorious, it will be good. As much as possible, I think I want to keep on living and serve my country. I hate to keep repeating this,

but don't worry about your family. Because taking good care of your-self and studying is the best way to serve the country.[108]

After visiting her daughter in late March Satō Mitsuko reaffirmed her behavior:

I think it was good that I received special permission from your teach-ers to meet you freely. No matter what happens, you mother won't worry and will be able to be of service to the country. Just by seeing the color in your face, what good shape you're in, it goes without say-ing that your perfect evacuation life is the reason for your good phys-ical condition. And I am relieved that your daily life is being observed by Sensei. So from now on, please give it your all.[109]

Her father chimed in, closing an April 20 postcard to his daughter with "Shizuko-san, please persevere in Nagano. It will be all right: victory will be with Japan."[110]

Shizuko responded in a May 2 letter after she heard about the last big air raid on Tokyo. "[After reading] Mother's letter, I really understood the situ-ation with the air raid. It was terrible, wasn't it? It's not surprising that my favorite things burned up. Thinking about Mother's words—"it's because this is war"—helped me bear the sadness. I also heard from Tanaka-sensei about "Excerpts for Shizuko" burning up. I'm even more determined to destroy the enemy."[111] Shizuko's mother wrote back saying, "Because of the war, all sorts of difficult and sad things are happening. This is when we have to be patient. If we are defeated by America, it will be truly regretta-ble, so let's work hard."[112] Three and a half weeks later her mother wrote, "Shizuko, be strong and let's keep going. If we don't push the enemy back, the brave warriors who carried out the special attacks will have died for nothing . . . take good care of yourself. Taking good care of yourself is a form of imperial service for the country."[113] Shizuko responded enthusi-astically: "My will has become firmer and firmer, and I have renewed my determination."[114] Her mother closed a letter sent in June with the words "until we win, think carefully about a future Japan in the distance."[115]

A few weeks later, Shizuko received Fukujirō-sensei's last letter and quoted from it in her July 4 letter home: "Shizu-chan, this probably will be the last letter. The day of our long-awaited attack has come. In a few hours, I will fly into a huge aircraft carrier near Kerama Atoll. This isn't much, but [two poems follow]."[116] The reason for his writing to Shizuko is clear: he was going to follow orders and to die, and the authorities wanted her to do the same. In his July 4 letter to his daughter, Shizuko's father invoked the official discourse even as he broached the possibility of defeat:

> Much of Tokyo has burned up. Even in Ginza, one can't buy anything. The Matsuzakaya, Matsuya, and Mitsukoshi department stores all have burned down. The same is true of Shinjuku. Here and there everything is completely burned down. That our Mejiro house has survived is rather surprising. This is war. Being weak-willed is not good. Winning or losing now [will be decided]. Will we lose? We will win for sure. When all of us pull together with one heart, it will be fine. Let's get down to business.[117]

It is telling that in the end, it was Shizuko, in an August 9 postcard, who commended her parents' behavior. She began, "Mother is always thinking about Shizuko—thank you." She continued, "I am the happiest and will never forget the mother I love." With impressive prescience, Shizuko added, "Tokyo for sure is probably having a hard time [with the air raids and attacks]. My living comfortably here seems like a waste. But this is for the sake of the country."[118] Shizuko's message is both revealing and unexpected, as she was now sustaining her parents and encouraging their subjectification.

In the letters they exchanged, Nakamura Shigetaka and his parents often imagined what the other was doing. In his October 29, 1944, letter home, for example, Shigetaka imagined what his family was doing in Kobe and what they must have been thinking.

> On the way back [from a nearby shrine], I heard an air-raid alert and warning. Apparently B-29s have come to parts of Kyushu and Saishū-jima. At this moment in Kobe, the strange sirens are sounding; you, Mother, are changing into your monpe, and while you push on a [water] pump, you are probably talking about us with Mizuno-san's aunt. You're imagining that Tokuda-kun and Nagano-san are ordering us at school to put on our air-raid hoods and it's getting chaotic.[119]

He did the same thing in a letter dated December 10, 1944: "Recently the air-raid warnings are issued often, and are you, Mother, getting along all right at home? Floating up in my eyes is your stern figure putting on your *monpe* when the air-raid warning is issued and holding your bucket and fire broom."[120] Nakamura Chiyoe also tried to imagine what her son was doing. In December, after hearing that he was jogging without a shirt early in the morning, she praised him, "You're great." When he described carrying so much firewood that he was on the verge of crying, she said she could envision his doing this and added, "None of this could be done in Kobe. It's all good practice, isn't it?"[121] Interestingly, it was Shigetaka, the oldest son, who took the initiative and urged his parents to be unflagging in their support of the war. Just as Shigetaka's family had once encouraged him to become a "splendid little citizen," he now exhorted them to be patriotic and useful citizens.

When Nakamura Shigetaka and his parents were imagining what the other was doing to support the war effort, and even what they were thinking, they were affirming the prescribed behaviors and values of the official wartime discourse. Imagining what the other was doing and thinking was informed by a kind of empathy that engendered a subtle, and perhaps unintended, form of mutual surveillance and subjectification.

The Success of the Evacuation

In retrospect, the collective evacuation went surprisingly well. This was the result of the meticulous preparation of government and school officials, the efforts of the teachers who moved to the evacuation sites, and also the cooperation and support of the children's families. After all, it was their parents who allowed them to join the collective evacuation and who actively encouraged their transformation into "splendid little citizens."

They did this in a number of ways. First, they urged their children to behave and do everything that was asked of them. The evacuation that took them from their homes to strange new towns and villages was necessary, they explained, so they should endure until Japan "wins the war." Above all, they should not worry about home. They reminded them, as well, that taking good care of themselves was "a form of imperial service."

Second, the families worked surprisingly closely with their children's teachers. They tolerated the censoring of their correspondence with their children and even found ways to use it to let the teachers know that they wholeheartedly approved of what the teachers were doing and to thank them profusely. Knowing that the teachers would be reading their correspondence allowed families to ask after their children's health, studies, and morale, and to let their teachers know what worried them and what issues might need attention.

Through the postcards and letters they sent to their children, the families did much to naturalize the war for their children, which was the third way that they facilitated the subjectification of their children. Their detailed descriptions of everything they were doing at home to support the war effort offered their children a model of patriotic behavior, with the implicit message to do just what they were doing. They shared news of recent battles, the latest developments in the war, new strategies and tactics, and new weapons such as the B-29. They also normalized the war by conveying bad news and reporting whose houses had burned down and who had given their lives for the country. Then, when the Allied bombing of Japanese cities intensified in the winter of 1944–1945, they reminded their children that this was why they had been sent away to the safety of the countryside.

The letters and postcards that families exchanged in 1945 rehearsed the darkening official discourse, with its call for the "Suicide of the One Hundred Million" and its talk of the coming "decisive battle." That spring, when the Allies' carpet-bombing tactics began to destroy Japanese cities, parents announced to their children that they were ready, if necessary, to lose their homes, all their possessions, and even their lives. They said that in the end, supporting the war effort was a way of expressing their gratitude to their teachers and repaying the huge debt they owed all those brave and selfless citizens who had given their lives to defeat the enemy. In their responses, their children announced their willingness to do everything possible to bring about the victory and to embrace the fierce, self-annihilatory discourse.

Nonetheless, not all of this is what, at first glance, it seems to be. The families' correspondence with their children cannot be taken at face value. As long as the teachers were reading the postcards and letters that the families exchanged, they could hardly be regarded as private documents. In fact, they were public documents that occupied not the private space that Japanese call *uchi*, or "inside," but the public space called *soto*, "outside." Thus, the letters and postcards cannot be read as expressing the families' sincere and honest thoughts about the war, government policies, Japan's military, and the huge impact that the war was having on the home-front population. How could they? They were being censored. The fact that the words "Suicide of the One Hundred Million" do not appear in the correspondence suggests that we would do well to see their letters and postcards as another form of surveillance and control, a well-designed method of ensuring that families censored their own writing about the war.

5

The "Food Problem" of Evacuated Children
in Wartime Japan

Several formidable problems faced the teachers who accompanied the 446,200 students moved by their schools to the countryside beginning in the summer of 1944.[1] Along with the administrative and pedagogical challenges of moving so many children from the cities to rural villages and continuing their instructional program were the predictable problem of homesickness and the unexpected problem of the older children bullying the younger ones. But by far the most daunting problem that school officials and teachers had to resolve was ensuring that the children had enough to eat. Although all the schools had brought food with them, once it ran out the evacuees depended on the allotment of rationed food, what could be procured locally, and what their families brought or sent. Indeed, one commentator wrote that the "problem of the evacuated children was, in a certain sense, a food problem."[2]

In this chapter, I examine the food situation of the evacuated children during the last year of the Pacific War (1944–1945), using both wartime diaries and postwar memoirs to catalog the responses of school administrators, teachers, dorm mothers, local farmers, parents, and the children themselves to this "food problem."

The Food Situation

The evacuees' first meal in their new homes was often a special and memorably good one. White rice or red-bean rice was served at some sites, and the evacuees recalled that "it was far more delicious than Tokyo food." In other sites, the featured dish of their

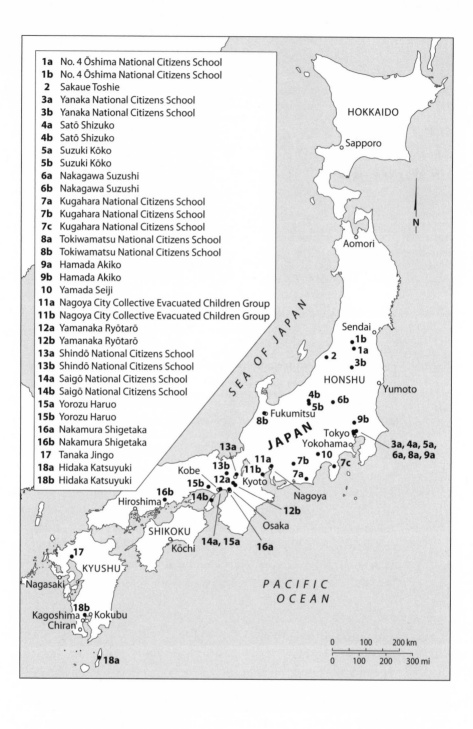

1a	No. 4 Ōshima National Citizens School
1b	No. 4 Ōshima National Citizens School
2	Sakaue Toshie
3a	Yanaka National Citizens School
3b	Yanaka National Citizens School
4a	Satō Shizuko
4b	Satō Shizuko
5a	Suzuki Kōko
5b	Suzuki Kōko
6a	Nakagawa Suzushi
6b	Nakagawa Suzushi
7a	Kugahara National Citizens School
7b	Kugahara National Citizens School
7c	Kugahara National Citizens School
8a	Tokiwamatsu National Citizens School
8b	Tokiwamatsu National Citizens School
9a	Hamada Akiko
9b	Hamada Akiko
10	Yamada Seiji
11a	Nagoya City Collective Evacuated Children Group
11b	Nagoya City Collective Evacuated Children Group
12a	Yamanaka Ryōtarō
12b	Yamanaka Ryōtarō
13a	Shindō National Citizens School
13b	Shindō National Citizens School
14a	Saigō National Citizens School
14b	Saigō National Citizens School
15a	Yorozu Haruo
15b	Yorozu Haruo
16a	Nakamura Shigetaka
16b	Nakamura Shigetaka
17	Tanaka Jingo
18a	Hidaka Katsuyuki
18b	Hidaka Katsuyuki

Table 5.1. Meals Offered to Pupils of Yanaka Primary School, November 1, 1944

Breakfast	Lunch	Snack	Dinner
Miso soup with daikon and potatoes	Daikon and potatoes	Persimmons and sugar	Miso soup with Chinese cabbage
Dried sardines	Pickled Chinese cabbage		Potatoes mixed with beef and onions
Pickled Chinese cabbage	Barley mixed with potatoes		Pickles made with miso
Barley mixed with potatoes			Barley mixed with rice

Source: Ikeda Kiyoko, *Higashiyama sokai gakudō no nikki* (Tokyo: Tōkyō-to taitō-kuritsu yanaka shōgakkō, 1995), 25.

first meal was "soybean rice" (*mame gohan*), which one evacuee remembered as "extremely delicious."[3] But not all first meals were memorably good: a group from Osaka had "four pieces of bread" for their first dinner at their evacuation site.[4]

The surviving documentary record reveals that these first meals were not typical of what was served to the children during their evacuation. Since each group brought their food coupons with them, the expectation was that the children would have enough. Indeed, this was the official line presented in the media and by officials,[5] and early on, the meals were better than they were later.[6] Table 5.1 above shows what the children from Yanaka Primary School in Tokyo's Taitō Ward, who were sent to Higashiyama in northern Aizu, ate on November 1, 1944.

Table 5.2 shows what the same group ate just over a month later, on December 12, 1944.

A month later, the Yanaka group was served what is shown in table 5.3.

The children's meals clearly began containing less and less protein and were becoming much more monotonous, although as might be expected, those evacuated to villages near the ocean, lakes, or rivers had more fresh fish. For example, the group evacuated from Kobe to Awaji Island in the Inland Sea had lots of fresh fish,[7] but a group from the same school evacuated to a mountain village in Izushi-gun had only dried sardines and occasionally "canned salmon on *sōmen* [noodles]," and even this was regarded as a "special meal."[8] Conversely, those in the mountain villages had foods not found

Table 5.2. Meals Offered to Pupils of Yanaka Primary School, December 12, 1944

Breakfast	Lunch	Snack	Dinner
Miso soup with Chinese cabbage	Soup with green onions and taro	Bread	Sardines
Barley	Barley		Miso soup with Japanese radish
Sesame salt	Pickles		Barley
Bread			Pickles
Pickles			

Source: Ikeda Kiyoko, *Higashiyama sokai gakudō no nikki* (Tokyo: Tōkyō-to taitō-kuritsu yanaka shōgakkō, 1995), 42.

Table 5.3. Meals Offered to Pupils of Yanaka Primary School, January 11, 1945

Breakfast	Lunch	Snack	Dinner
Miso soup with eggplant	Simmered Chinese cabbage	Bread	Miso soup with Japanese radish
Seaweed topping (*furikake nori*)	Pickles		Simmered taro and potatoes
Pickles			Pickles

Source: Ikeda Kiyoko, *Higashiyama sokai gakudō no nikki* (Tokyo: Tōkyō-to taitō-kuritsu yanaka shōgakkō, 1995), 54.

near the sea. Ōmura Izō, a third-grader evacuated from Tokyo to Yonezawa in northern Japan, had happy memories of gathering chestnuts and roasting sweet potatoes not long after he arrived.[9] The arrival of Kimura Mitsuko and her classmates coincided with the autumn bamboo shoot season. "Those of us raised in the city," she wrote, "were surprised to learn that bamboo shoots were dug up from the ground. . . . We enjoyed hunting for them and enjoyed bamboo shoot cuisine." Bamboo shoots were included in rice or miso soup or as a vegetable side dish.[10] Bog rhubarb (*fuki*) also grew in abundance in the mountains and was served at nearly every meal.[11]

The portions of food served to the children were not large. At the beginning of the evacuation, the daily ration per child was 19.2 ounces—roughly two and a half cups—and was mostly vegetables. *Okara* began to be added to rice, and then soybeans were added to the children's rice porridge (*okayu*)

Evacuated children eating a meal, June 1945. Photo courtesy of the *Mainichi shinbun*.

or rice gruel (*zōsui*).[12] Then on June 1, 1945, the daily ration per child was cut to 14.4 ounces, or less than two cups.[13] At that point, the portions were drastically reduced, and soybeans or sweet potatoes started to be served at breakfast. By the very end of the war, when food became even more scarce, the soybeans and rice were prepared as a porridge to which dandelion greens and sweet potato vines were added.[14]

It is hardly surprising, therefore, that the children's lasting and most powerful memory of their evacuation is hunger. One former evacuee remembered that "every day our stomachs were empty"; another wrote that their stomachs were "habitually empty"; and a third spoke of persistent "pangs of hunger."[15] Many years later, one former evacuee reported that "all we thought about was eating; all we talked about was what we ate in the past and what we wanted to eat to fill our stomachs. Just that."[16] Hashimoto Kumiko, who had been evacuated to a farm, tried to mitigate her hunger by imagining what she would eat after the war ended.

Day after day we ate watery gruel in the cottage of the farmhouse to which we had been evacuated. Things got even worse, and our daily chore was to gather field grasses. One day, I came across a book of

Western cooking among the few remaining items on the bookshelf. I turned the pages to shiny photographs of roast beef, Spanish omelets, Scotch eggs. It became my secret pastime to stare at the beautifully taken photos and read the book over and over. I didn't care what the outcome of the war might be. I swore in my heart that when the war was over, I would eat all these dishes. Looking back on that time now, I smile ruefully that I was a hungry maiden with a big appetite.[17]

Hashimoto's dreams were just one of the many ways that the children dealt with their hunger.

The Children's Responses

The oldest boys—usually sixth-graders—often bullied the younger children, forcing them to give up what little food they had. After telling them to "hand it over," the food would be passed from student to student under the table.[18] Not surprisingly, "the third-grade boys seemed pitiful and pathetic," according to one former evacuee.[19] The children also learned to eat more quickly and efficiently and even devised strategies that allowed them to eat more. For example, one group of evacuees realized that when the dumplings called *suiton* were served, they should hurry to dinner because the dumplings floated, and once they had consumed the dumplings, they could eat the porridge and *udon* noodles more slowly because they sank to the bottom of the bowl.[20] Some children even resorted to eating in the toilet, one of the few places where they could escape the jealous gaze of more senior boys.[21]

The teachers and dorm mothers were sympathetic to the children's plight. The dorm mothers did what they could to allay the children's hunger, such as secretly cooking what the children brought them, including the grasshoppers the children caught, "an amazing delicacy."[22] They even cooked what the children acquired by less acceptable means. In one such incident, Wataumi Kikuo remembered that the children who helped with the delivery of rationed rice were given rice in cloth bags sewn by the dorm mothers, who then cooked the rice and made rice balls for them. But when the teachers discovered this, they punished the children by depriving them of their meals for a time.[23] Occasionally the dorm mothers invited the children to their homes for snacks.[24]

Local officials and organizations also did what they could for the children. In the village of Tsuda-machi in Kitakawachi-gun in Osaka Prefecture, the evacuated Osaka children took a short hike into the surrounding countryside a month into their stay, and when they rested at one point, the women of the local housewives association treated them to "a repast of boiled soybeans."[25] On October 19, 1944, the children participated in the village's autumn festival and were rewarded with two rice cakes for lunch. The "children's faces were [described as] radiant."[26] Five weeks later, eight women from the local community council's Young Women's Collective came to the children's dorms, washed their clothes, and handed out *da-izu-iri* (a dish made with soybeans) and steamed sweet potatoes.[27]

No one, however, worked harder to ensure that all the children had enough to eat than their teachers, who saw them every day and were acutely aware of their hunger. Some teachers organized "buying units" and set off with a borrowed cart and several students with knapsacks on their backs. They all would hike to the closest black market and buy daikon, onions, potatoes, and sweet potatoes. Other teachers made trips to the seashore, where they fished or bought fish from local fishermen.[28] Then when the food supplies began to run out, many teachers visited nearby relatives and came back with food. Early in the evacuation, Takai Toshio, a teacher at an evacuation site in Mie Prefecture, visited his in-laws in nearby Gifu Prefecture and brought back *matsutake* mushrooms, a rare and special delicacy.[29] Takai also hunted. As he explained, "One day an air gun came into my possession, and I shot sparrows and fed them to the evacuated children. As long as I had shot, I walked around the prefecture and continued to shoot sparrows."[30] One young teacher periodically treated her students to curry *udon* at the local noodle shop.[31]

The children's postwar memoirs reveal other ways in which they alleviated their hunger. The parents or older siblings of many of the children brought them food from the cities, which was difficult, given the food shortages there as well. Ōmura Izō remembers that his mother would bring both news and sweets. Takeda Masako, a fourth-grader in the same group, described her parents' visits as the "happiest things" in her life.[32] But unless enough food was brought for everyone, the teachers discouraged such gifts.[33] In the late summer and fall of 1944, those who visited the children from the Hōbayashi National Citizens School in Tokyo, who had been evacuated to Satsute-machi in Saitama Prefecture, always brought enough to be shared: apples, bread, candy, doughnuts, wild rice, chestnuts, homemade jam, and rice cakes.[34] The father of one child evacuated to Yokkaichi in Mie Prefecture was a butcher and he brought meat, which was cut into "tiny portions for each child."[35] Takeda Masako's father brought candy, "enough to share with everyone," and this, too, was distributed.[36] These gifts were especially welcomed when food supplies were running low. The dorm mothers always "cooked whatever parents brought . . . no matter whether the food could be added to the gruel or not," and apparently the "results were meaningless and indescribable dishes."[37]

Secret gifts, however, were strictly prohibited, and if discovered, they were shared with the other children. As a result, visitors learned to ask to take their children or siblings on an outing, during which they gave the contraband—usually homemade sweets, dumplings, or filled buns—to the children, away from the watchful eyes of the teachers and other evacuees, and often what was brought was consumed on the spot or hidden.[38] The contraband had to be hidden because whenever possible, the children stole one another's food, even the valuable cache of sweets carried from the cities. One parent, the father of Sasaki Setsuko, a third-grader evacuated to Yonezawa, even visited local farmers to implore them "to fill the stomachs of the evacuated children" and "to give them several pieces of cut rice cakes for emergency use when enemy planes attacked."[39]

Local families, too, tried to address the children's "food problem." Although largely self-sufficient, most farmers found that the wartime government's system of food requisitioning often took most of what they produced. Shimizu village in Ashigarakami-gun in Kanagawa Prefecture, for example, could keep only a third of what it produced for its own needs, with the government taking the other two-thirds.[40] Farmers in Yokkaichi had to send off all the rice and sweet potatoes they grew as well as all the firewood they collected, and they survived only by using every piece of land that could be cultivated: traditional Japanese gardens, sides of roads, and so forth.[41]

Local farmers helped the evacuated children as much as they could, bringing vegetables and other things to the students' dorms,[42] because, as one elderly man in Toyama Prefecture put it, "it was painful to see the students get thinner by the day."[43] Itō Shizuko and Katsuyama Fumiko, who cooked for the children in Yokkaichi, remembered that "we received rice, soy sauce, and miso from the cities, but no one expected these supplies to suffice. The village people would say, 'We must make the evacuees eat,' and they would bring us cartloads of assorted vegetables and potatoes. We made dishes that combined these vegetables and potatoes in various ways."[44] Itō Hisakazu, a local farmer who raised cows in front of one of the temples housing evacuated children, "would pour milk that he had just squeezed into copper tubes and would deliver them to . . . [the teachers and students], saying 'Drink up.' Everyone was overjoyed, and both the teachers and children would drink one mouthful each."[45] In a mountain village in Izushi-gun near Osaka, farmers gave the children sweet potatoes and persimmons.[46] Since the children were not supposed to accept gifts of any kind, the farmers often left food for them to find. Itō Takashi remembered receiving a secret gift when he went to take a bath at a Yokkaichi residence. "While we were in the bath," he recalled, "the women of the house left sweet potatoes just outside the door. That was happiness, sheer happiness, and as we came out of the bath, we took the potatoes and flew back [to our dorm]."[47]

Farmers helped the evacuated children in another, highly inventive way. They hired them to help with simple chores such as weeding, cutting grass or wheat, planting rice, harvesting sweet potatoes, or even milking cows. This was called "eating to work."[48] Suzuki Haruo pointed out that farmers did this so they could feed the children. "From time to time," he recalled, "we would be asked by the residents of farmhouses to help them clear fallow land or to help in the fields, and off we went. After the work was done, the families gave us food. It seems that this work was an excuse to give the children food as compensation."[49] In return for their labor, the children received persimmons, rice cakes, roasted or steamed sweet potatoes, boiled soybeans, milk, and, occasionally, *onigiri* made with "white rice" as well as uncooked rice.[50] Suzuki Takako, a teacher at the Yokkaichi site, reports that the farmers would even "kill a chicken for us in return." "When that happened," she recalled, "we cooked rice. We added minced chicken and cooked it, making a one-pot dish (*kama-age*). Though one calls it a one-pot dish, it was close to gruel, and each person's portion was quite meager. But the unexpected pieces of meat were exceedingly delicious."[51] One group of children, evacuated from Tokyo to Gunma Prefecture, were even invited to the village festival on December 1, 1944, and were sent in pairs to local farmhouses, where they ate their fill of soup with rice cakes and were given dried persimmons and dried chestnuts to take home.[52] Sometimes the children were sent to local farms simply to have a real meal, the kind of meal the children dreamed of having.[53] Sasaki Setsuko, a third grader evacuated to Yonezawa in northern Japan, recounted the indescribable pleasure of having "a warm tofu dish under the broad beams of a farmhouse."[54] Even farm families in villages that did not have evacuees from the cities shared their resources. The families in one such area, Kanazaki, provided rice, wheat, and canned goods at low prices.[55] Naturally, there was nothing that the children looked forward to more than visits to local farms.

Their hunger made the children active hunters and gatherers, and table 5.4 shows some of what they collected and ate on their own.

Table 5.4. Food Gathered by Children on Their Own Initiative

Fruits	Vegetables	Nuts	Other
Akebi	Bamboo shoots	Chestnuts	Freshwater shrimp
Apples	Bog rhubarb	Hedama (not identified)	Frogs
Mulberries	Bracken	Walnuts	Grasshoppers
Pears	Chickweed		Ground beetles
Persimmons	Chinese chives		Loaches
	Dandelions		Pigeons
	Fiddlehead ferns		Snails
	Knotweed		
	Mugwort		
	Rocamble		
	Water dropwort		

Sources: Aoki Kiminao, *Kōbe Saigō kokumin gakkō no baai*, vol. 2 of *Gakudō shūdan sokai no kiroku* (Kobe: Aoki Kiminao, 1991–1992), 125, 139, 144; Nakagawa Suzushi, *Tokyo-to Itabashi dai-go kokumin gakkō gakudō sokai "kaizō-ryō" no kiroku* (Urawa: Kaizōji-kai, 1995), 10–13; Kyoto zeminaru hausu, ed., *Yamabōshi: Kita kuwata no gakudō sokai kiroku-shū* (Kyoto: Kita kuwata, 1996), 57.

The children gathered fruits, vegetables, nuts, and herbs in season, including *akebi*, bamboo shoots, bog rhubarb, bracken, chestnuts, chickweed, Chinese chives, cock sorrel, dandelions, fiddlehead ferns, knotweed, mugwort, mulberries, rocamble, walnuts, and water dropwort. Yorozu Haruo also remembers gathering tiny little black beans that they called "crow's beans" (*karasu mame*), which they roasted and ate.[56]

The children fished local rivers and streams for freshwater shrimp, wild goldfish, and loaches and often exchanged the shrimp with local farmers for eggs.[57] The children also hunted for snakes, which they learned to skin and roast.[58] Nakagawa Susumu, evacuated from Tokyo to Gunma Prefecture, learned how to do this from his father. "When my father came to visit," he recalled, "he caught a snake, skinned it, cut it into pieces, roasted it, and had us eat it." Apparently Nakagawa and his classmates liked roasted snake because "whenever we found a snake, we competed to catch it, and everyone ate it."[59] Teacher Suzuki Takako was given some roasted snake by a dorm mother and remembers that it was "really delicious."[60] Roasted snake reminded Yorozu Haruo of *hatahata*, a kind of sandfish caught in the waters off northern Japan.[61] The students did the same with frogs.[62] Nakagawa remembered that when he and his classmates discovered a frog hole, they "reached in, pulled out dozens of them, pulled off their skins, roasted, and ate them."[63]

Grasshoppers were another important supplementary food. The children were sent into the fields of ripening rice "to protect the 'rice that was important to soldiers'" by catching grasshoppers.[64] Some students were so hungry that they ate the grasshoppers raw. Others skewered them on bamboo sticks and took them back to their dorms, where they basted them with soy sauce, roasted them, and ate them.[65] Grasshoppers were said to taste like grilled shrimp.[66] Not all students ate them, however. Kanamori Junko "really hated things fried in butter" and could not bring herself to eat grasshoppers, so when roasted grasshoppers were served, she let her classmates happily divide up her share.[67]

The younger and more timid boys and girls who were less inclined to hunt or fish found other ways to suppress their hunger. Many swept through the sweet potato fields, eating what had been overlooked or left behind. Others picked and ate the still unharvested heads of wheat or sucked on green plums, which caused diarrhea.[68] Some children collected the grasses that grew along the sides of roads and sucked on them to suppress their hunger.[69] Malnutrition even drove many children to lick the sores on their own bodies.[70]

Finally, some of the bolder and more desperate children resorted to thievery to staunch their hunger. Itō Katsunari, a Yokkaichi evacuee, remembered that when he and other boys were asked to help transport delivered rice, daikon, pumpkin squash, or cucumbers, they "secretly took some of what we were carrying and ate it raw."[71] Other children had less success. A boy at a Gunma Prefecture site stole a sweet potato from the dorm kitchen and roasted it on the foot warmer (*kotatsu*) in his dorm room, but the fragrant odor of the newly roasted potato gave him away: "The teachers got very angry at the boy, and he shouted 'Mother' and started to cry. The crying spread, and soon all the children were weeping. The teachers and dorm mothers were caught off guard and ended up distributing popped beans to the children, which calmed them down."[72]

Many children took full advantage of what the evacuation sites offered. They sneaked out in the night to steal persimmons and pears when they were in season and did the same with sweet potatoes and daikon, often eating them raw on the spot.[73] They also stole beans and soybeans, which they boiled or roasted before eating.[74] But some of these thieves were caught or forced to turn themselves in when the thefts were reported by local farmers. Hayashi Hisao, evacuated from Osaka to a village in Izushi-gun in Osaka Prefecture, described how he was caught stealing sweet potatoes:

I heard that sweet potatoes were planted in a field [nearby]. On the way back from the public bath, I invited a friend to break from the line. On the way back, there was a river, and we didn't cross over on the bridge, but by walking along the road that ran along the river, we came to the place. At the bottom, where one area was surrounded by a three- to four-meter-high mud wall, a few sweet potato shoots had emerged. We went in and dug up the potatoes, cramming them into our air-raid hoods. In the darkness we could see that someone was standing in the distance. Perhaps the house mother with a female evacuee, we thought. "This is not good. We've been discovered. Let's go back." Excited, we circled back and returned to the temple. We divided up the potatoes and ate them. We ate them without washing them and just dropping the dirt.

The next day there was a call for "everyone to assemble," and we were made to sit in front of the main hall. Hayashi-sensei spoke: "Someone stole potato seedlings yesterday. [The farmers] prepared these buds and planted them. They did something really important. Who took them?" No one said a word. Sensei spoke again, shouting "This traitor . . ." and fuming. As a result, the children sitting in front ran off, and next everyone ran off in all directions. The amazing utterance of the word "traitor" and Sensei's anger, together with friends fleeing, left a deep impression on me.[75]

On another occasion, Hayashi and his classmates had better luck stealing soybean meal. He described what happened:

Every day or perhaps every other day, I don't remember, all the evacuees went from Hachijōji to the public bath. Along the way from the temple to the bath, there was a horse named Ōyama-go, which might have been famous. It was a splendid creature in whose stable we heard there was soybean meal. So I invited a friend to enter the stable on the way back from the bath to take some soybean meal. On the way back from the bath, the two of us broke from the line and stole into the stable. In front of the big horse was a feedbag, and inside it was the soybean meal. We filled the air-raid hood that usually hung from our shoulders and quickly left the stable. The big horse's face was frightening. We went back to the temple and divided up the meal and ate it. I thought it was delicious and thought that the horse was eating something truly extravagant.[76]

Table 5.5. Meals Offered to Pupils of Yanaka Primary School, August 1, 1945

Breakfast	Lunch	Snack	Dinner
Miso soup with seaweed (*wakame*)	Simmered soybeans and kelp (*kobu*)		Cucumber hash
Soybeans	Rice		Miso soup with green onions
Pickles	Pickles		Rice
			Pickles

Source: Kurosawa Yoshiko, *Watakushi-tachi no gojūnen: yanaka shōgakkō de mananda (Shōwa nijūnen-sotsu) shōjo tachi no kiroku-shū-Higashiyama sokai gakudō no nikki* (Tokyo: Tōkyō-to Taitō-kuritsu Yanaka chū-shōgakkō "Yanaka-shō de manada [Shōwa nijūichi-nen sotsu] shōjotachi no kirokushū" henshū iinkai, 1995), 42, 54, 60.

Stolen soybean meal offered only a temporary respite. The "food problem" was never solved satisfactorily, despite the best efforts of school administrators, teachers, dorm mothers, local farmers, and even the children themselves.

Finally, on August 1, 1945, the evacuees from Yanaka Primary School were served the following, as shown in table 5.5.

This completely vegetarian menu was typical. By this time, according to one medical report, the children were consuming roughly one thousand calories of food a day, much less than the normal daily requirement.[77] Had the war continued through the fall of 1945 and beyond, the health of the evacuated children would have become a profoundly serious problem. Fortunately, the war ended on August 15, 1945.

The End of the Food Problem

The children were not able to return to their homes for a long time, and many no longer even had a home. Allied bombers had reduced all the major cities and industrial towns to what the Japanese termed "plains of ash" (*yakenohara*), and many children had lost their parents and siblings to the bombing as well. Although the evacuation ended officially on December 20, 1945, some children already had returned home, including a group from Yanaka National Citizens School.[78] Most, however, returned the following year, although some did not return until 1949.

After the surrender, the food served to the children improved. The administrators and teachers had been hoarding supplies of rice and other foodstuffs, preparing for the "decisive battle" expected when the Allies invaded the Japanese home islands. One evacuee remembered that "on the second day after the war ended, Nakagawa, the dorm mother, said that beginning tomorrow we would have delicious rice for breakfast. It really appeared! It was delicious, delicious, and we ate it as though in a dream."[79] The children's last meal before they returned home also was memorably good, just as their first meal had been. Iwasaki Kimiko, a fifth-grader returning to Tokyo from Shiobara in Ibaraki Prefecture, recalled that "when the war ended, and it was decided that the evacuation site would be emptied, the sensei used the rice they had hoarded and made big, triangular and pure white rice balls as a snack. I have never forgotten the deliciousness of that moment."[80] Many years later, Murase Yoshie, a third-grader returning to Tokyo, still could describe the white rice balls they were served on the day she and her classmates returned home. "Inside the pure white rice," she wrote, "was a pickled apricot (umeboshi), and the triangular rice ball was wrapped in a big piece of nori."[81] In addition, the children were warned that "when you return to Tokyo, you won't be able to eat [things like white rice]," and this turned out to be true.[82]

What is most remarkable about the evacuation is, first, that it actually was carried out, moving 1,303,200 children from their urban homes to designated sites in the countryside; second, that the administrators, teachers, dorm mothers, and children fared as well as they did under very difficult circumstances; and third, that relatively few children died. Of the 1,303,200 children evacuated from the cities to the countryside, between 330 and 360 died.[83] Moreover, the teachers and administrators who accompanied the children and the local communities that hosted them were able to find ways to make do with what little they had. Finally, the children themselves deserve credit, for both doing what they believed was right and devising a variety of methods—some brutal and others ingenious—to survive.

PART 3

The Last Resort

6

Learning How to Die

Americans have long been fascinated by the Japanese pilots who flew off on one-way missions in the last ten months of the Pacific War. In fact, the word *kamikaze* is now part of American popular culture and has given us, among other things, the name of a cocktail, a computer game, and a heavy metal band; *kamikaze* even is used as an adjective to mean "a person or thing that behaves in a wildly reckless or destructive manner." Clearly, the fascination with the kamikaze phenomenon is also a fascination with death.

Japanese continue to be interested in what they call the "special attack," or *tokkō*, phenomenon but for very different reasons.[1] Those whose fathers, sons, brothers, nephews, friends, and classmates died in these attacks have not forgotten their losses. Many still grieve, none more than those who were scheduled to go off on special attacks but never did. Indeed, many Japanese who lost loved ones in this way believe that they still exist in spiritual form. My agent discovered this when she communicated with a woman whose brother had died in a special attack and had left a diary that I translated into English and wanted to publish. "Yasuo will be pleased," she told my agent, "when he hears that his diary will be published in English." As far as she was concerned, her brother Yasuo was still alive.[2]

Those who commanded these pilots never forgot what they asked of them, and at the end of the war, many went off on special attack missions of their own. Admiral Ōnishi Takijirō, who formed the first navy special attack unit in October 1944, committed *seppuku* two days after Japan surrendered to the Allies.[3]

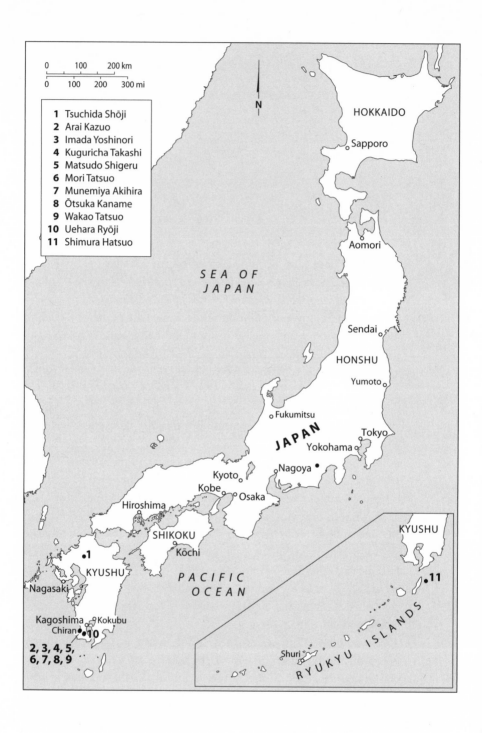

0 100 200 km
0 100 200 300 mi

1 Tsuchida Shōji
2 Arai Kazuo
3 Imada Yoshinori
4 Kuguricha Takashi
5 Matsudo Shigeru
6 Mori Tatsuo
7 Munemiya Akihira
8 Ōtsuka Kaname
9 Wakao Tatsuo
10 Uehara Ryōji
11 Shimura Hatsuo

N

HOKKAIDO

Sapporo

Aomori

SEA OF
JAPAN

Sendai

HONSHU

Yumoto

Fukumitsu

JAPAN

Tokyo
Yokohama

Nagoya

Kyoto
Kobe
Osaka

Hiroshima

SHIKOKU

Kōchi

1

KYUSHU

Nagasaki

PACIFIC
OCEAN

KYUSHU

11

Kagoshima Kokubu
Chiran 10

2, 3, 4, 5,
6, 7, 8, 9

Shuri

RYUKYU ISLANDS

Conservatives, nationalists, and rightists still remember the special attack pilots as heroes and continue to venerate them.

Scholars, however, have been slow to write about these pilots, and the first accounts of the special attackers were written by veterans. An early example is the short history of the navy special attackers written by two officers involved in forming the first navy units, which was translated into English as *The Divine Wind: Japan's Kamikaze Force in World War II*.[4] Journalists and amateur historians also have written about the special attack units, but the quality of their accounts varies considerably. The shortcomings of studies of the special attackers written by Western journalists who neither speak nor read Japanese are too obvious to warrant comment. Not until the first decade of this century did we have the first real scholarly studies written in English. An example is anthropologist Emiko Ohnuki-Tierney's *Kamikaze, Cherry Blossoms and Nationalisms: The Militarization of Aesthetics in Japanese History* and *Kamikaze Diaries: Reflections of Japanese Student Soldiers*.[5] In addition, the historian Yuki Tanaka, well known for his important studies of wartime Japanese atrocities and the "comfort women," has begun to write in English about the special attack phenomenon, as he did in his article "Japan's Kamikaze Pilots and Contemporary Suicide Bombers: War and Terror."[6] But we still need someone to explore the special attack phenomenon in the way that historian Omer Bartov wrote about Germany's Wehrmacht on the Eastern Front.

Japan's Special Attack Units

In this chapter I focus on an important aspect of the special attack phenomenon: how the Imperial Japanese Army trained pilots for their one-way flights. My analysis is based on twenty-four diaries kept by army pilots, several of which are complete, and twenty-five "last letters." All my sources have been published. Despite the abundance of unpublished materials, most are not accessible to foreign scholars. I learned this in 1998 when I traveled to a special attack pilot museum in Chiran, Kyushu, in order to examine the diaries and correspondence in its collection. Although I was initially told that I would be able to see, and even copy, these materials, when I got there I was informed that they were "sacred documents" and thus could not be shown to me. Someday, though, scholars will have access to the reams of unpublished materials that survive, which will enable us to write, and perhaps better understand, the special attack phenomenon.[7]

Formation of the Special Attack Units

The first special attack units were formally organized in the fall of 1944, although "special attack" tactics were discussed as early as 1943 when the superiority of Allied aircraft and aircraft production first became apparent in the Asia-Pacific Theater.[8] Captain Shiro Eiichirō, an aide-de-camp to the emperor, suggested using "human-bullet attacks" (*nikudan kōgeki*) in June 1943 in conversations with Ōnishi.[9] This discussion intensified early in 1944 after Japan lost first the Marshall Islands and then the Mariana Islands to Allied forces, and it became clear that the Japanese would not be able to maintain the defensive perimeter in the Pacific that they had established in September 1943.[10] There already had been much talk in both navy and army circles of using "body-crashing" (*tai-atari*) tactics.[11] Navy policymakers saw this tactic as a way to compensate for the inferiority of the once dominant Mitsubishi A6M Zero to the new American aircraft that appeared in 1943, the F4U Hellcat and the P-38 Lightning,[12] whereas army policymakers were aware of several documented instances when body-crashing tactics had been successful.[13]

The army and navy adopted special attack tactics for other reasons as well. Earlier, when the army had tried to teach its pilots techniques for attacking ships with bombs and torpedoes, it was not successful. The program thus was terminated in the belief that it taught army pilots too much, too late, and the army's adoption of special attack tactics was an admission of this. Nonetheless, the army authorities still assumed that even a pilot with limited training could crash his aircraft into a target. The navy, in contrast, had the more immediate problem of not being able to meet the logistical challenges posed by the massive Allied task force gathering in Leyte Gulf in the Philippines in September 1944. This was simply a matter of numbers: at the beginning of September 1944, Japan's First Air Fleet, based in the Philippines, had 280 aircraft, but by September 22 it had only sixty-five; and by October 20 the army and navy had a total of seventy aircraft.[14] The historian Mark Peattie, who studied the Japanese navy and naval air corps, believed that by the summer of 1944 it was clear that Admiral Yamamoto Isoroku's strategy of using island air bases as "unsinkable carriers" had not worked, and the navy had fewer air bases and more shortages of supplies, ordnance, and, above all, aviation fuel. Moreover, the pilots and ground crews were poorly trained and inexperienced.[15]

The decision to create special attack units came only after lengthy discussions in both the army and navy, first at the highest levels, then in both services' general staffs, and finally among those in command positions.

The decision was made in 1944, as early as the spring for the army and in late summer or early fall for the navy.[16] In just two or three days, the navy formed the first special attack unit in mid-October at Malabacat Air Base in the Philippines. Vice Admiral Ōnishi Takijirō, the newly appointed commander of the 201st Air Wing based at Malabacat, flew there from Tokyo and presented the proposal to form special attack units to Commander Tamai Asaichi, the air wing's executive officer. Tamai discussed the proposal with each of his squadron leaders in turn and finally with his enlisted men. We are told that the last group's response was universally positive: Tamai remembered that "in a frenzy of emotion and joy, the arms of every pilot in the meeting went up in a gesture of complete accord."[17] It is important to note that the men in the 201st were regular navy pilots and many had graduated from the naval academy and thus were among the best pilots in the country. The army formed its special attack units around the same time. Army aircraft are reported to have used "body-crashing" tactics between October 24 and 26, 1944, and many more army special attacks followed in November.[18] By the end of the war, nine and a half months later, 3,843 men had perished in special attacks: 2,514 navy pilots and 1,329 army pilots.[19]

The decision to use pilots in this way raises a number of questions: What did the army and navy general staffs hope to achieve with the special attacks? How did the army and navy pilots react to the decision to use special attacks? As the special attacks continued from the fall of 1944 into 1945, did pilots still volunteer for them, as was the case early on, or were they coerced? Finally, how did the army and navy train the pilots for special attacks? Answering these questions would require a careful reading of the documents that survive but are not open to scholars. Therefore, I will try to answer the last question and to focus on the methods used to teach these pilots how to die and their responses.

Teaching Pilots How to Die

Japanese pilots' training was comparable to that of their American, British, and German counterparts. At that time, pilots in all modern air forces underwent a two-stage training program of, first, basic flight training and then advanced flight training. Between 1935 and 1940, U.S. Navy pilots received six months of basic flight training and five and a half months of advanced training.[20] German pilots underwent nine months of basic flight training and four months of advanced flight instruction before they were sent into combat.[21] As the war continued and pilots were lost, the demand for new pilots led to a shortening of this training, in Japan as well as in the United States, Britain, and Germany. Accordingly, in July 1943, the Japanese army cut its basic flight training to four months.[22]

All the special attack pilots first underwent basic military training, which lasted from ten to twenty-four months.[23] Then they began flight training, which lasted for nearly a year. (In his autobiography, the Imperial Japanese Navy ace Sakai Saburō writes that he underwent ten months of basic flight training.[24]) After finishing their flight training, the new trainees began advanced flight training, which lasted for three to four months. At this stage, they learned to fly in formation and to execute aerial combat maneuvers. At the end of this stage of flight training, the pilots were promoted and posted to combat units, where they had two more months of training.[25]

Despite these similarities, the training of Japanese army and navy pilots differed from that of their Western counterparts in three respects. First, it was unimaginably brutal, which was true of Japanese military training in general and not just that of the army and navy air forces. Recruits were beaten with wooden bats, punched, and hit in the face with the soles of hobnailed shoes, blows that often broke cheekbones or noses. In fact, all recruits seemed to sustain injuries of one kind of another during their training, sometimes even requiring hospitalization. Deaths or suicides in basic training were not uncommon.[26]

The training of Japanese pilots was distinctive in a second way. During the war—especially after 1943—not only was their training shorter, but, owing to dwindling fuel supplies, they also had less flying time before going into combat. One army pilot, who later died in a special attack, had had fewer than one hundred hours of flying time before he was sent to a frontline unit, and in his diary he makes clear his nervousness about flying.[27]

Japanese pilots were taught as well that "spirit" (*seishin*) mattered more than anything else, even technical competence, and that spirit could, and would, prevail over matter. Japanese pilots thus were taught to cultivate their spirit, which added another performative dimension to their training.[28] That is, they were expected not only to be good servicemen and to learn how to fly military aircraft but also to have cultivated themselves spiritually, which, it was believed, would enable them to defend the emperor and protect their homeland.

As part of their spiritual training, the pilots were taught to reflect on themselves and so were required to keep "diaries of self-reflection" (*hansei nikki*), in which, at the end of each day, they recorded what they had learned that day, what they had done either well or poorly, and how they felt about this. This diary of self-reflection was one of three diaries the pilots kept. The second was a pilot's diary (*sōju nisshi*), which the trainees were "obliged to keep and to present to the flight leader at the school every week," and the third was a record of their superiors' lectures on "spirit." Then once every seven to ten days, they submitted these diaries to their superiors for diary checks, and their superiors added their own comments, observations, criticisms, and encouragement.[29] Once they completed their flight training, the pilots stopped keeping the pilot's diary. (This practice of keeping a diary for instructional purposes was universal in Japan during the war. Teenagers mobilized for war work and city children evacuated to the countryside also had to keep diaries and to submit them for diary checks, which allowed their superiors and teachers to monitor their morale.)

The special attack pilots' diaries of self-reflection are extremely valuable sources of information about their training. One such diary was kept by an army pilot named Tsuchida Shōji, who entered a school for army aviation cadets when he was fifteen. What makes Tsuchida's diary especially important is that it is complete. He started writing his diary of self-reflection on October 12, 1942, the day he entered the Tokyo Army Cadet Aviation School, and continued adding to it through August 22, 1945. Among other things, his diary reveals exactly how he was taught to cultivate himself spiritually.

A close reading of Tsuchida's diary reveals, first, that he was taught by repetition, as is evident in the key words, concepts, and practices mentioned over and over again in his journal.[30] For example, "self-reflection" is, understandably, the term most often used in his diary. It first appears in the entry he wrote on his second day as a recruit and continues to appear well into entries from the spring of 1945, in nearly four hundred diary entries written between October 15, 1942, and May 26, 1945. Self-reflection was a form of self-policing, or what Michel Foucault would call "self-subjectification," the process by which one makes oneself into a subject. Foucault would have been fascinated by Tsuchida's diary of self-reflection as a kind of internal Panopticon.

To illustrate how this process of self-policing worked, consider the following: After "self-reflection," the word that appears most often in Tsuchida's diary is "spirit" (*seishin*), found in almost two hundred diary entries. This, too, is not surprising, given the spiritual dimension of Japanese pilots' training. Tsuchida's very first diary entry, dated October 12, 1942, closes with, "After we entered this unit, we were given a copy of the principal's instructions, which spelled out clearly the frame of mind and resolve expected of us in the future."³¹ Although Tsuchida used the terms "frame of mind" (*kokorogamae*) and "resolve" (*kakugo*) instead of "spirit," that soon changed. During his eleven months at the Tokyo Army Cadet Aviation School, he learned a lot about "spirit," a word that appears with increasing frequency in his diary. In fact, many of his days began with his superiors' "spirit lectures" (*seishin kunwa*), which were both hortatory and admonitory, and inevitably about spirit.³²

During his training, Tsuchida also was introduced to the "airborne worker's spirit,"³³ the "serviceman's spirit,"³⁴ and the "attack spirit."³⁵ Drummed into him as well was the idea that "spiritual focus" mattered and that spiritual deficiencies led to mistakes, oversights, and failings; spiritual focus affected even the condition of his shoes.³⁶ Apparently Tsuchida believed this, as he wrote over and over again, "When one's spirit lacks tension, lots of things are lost."³⁷

Tsuchida's diary reveals, too, the importance of the *practical* dimension of his training. This is apparent in the emphasis on "effort" (*doryoku*), a word that appears well over a hundred times in his diary. Tsuchida learned that "effort is important for all things," that a person's life is the crystallization of effort, and that "without effort one cannot hope to succeed."³⁸ He even was taught that "effort trumps brilliance" (*doryoku wa tensai ni masaru*), which he mentioned four times in his diary.³⁹ In the final stages of his training, he was told that "the final victory is in effort" and "to win, there is only effort."⁴⁰ The verbs "do" and "act" are used early in Tsuchida's diary but later are replaced with the more technical "to carry out" (*jikkō*) and the more official "to execute" (*jisshi*).⁴¹ For example, his October 6, 1943, entry closes with "In the future, I will make an effort not to err in carrying out orders," a passage in which both "effort" and "carry out" appear.⁴² Nearly two months later, he wrote:

> When I think every day about that day's affairs, I seem to manage them perfectly in the course of that day and to make them my own. But in daily life, things do not always go as expected, and various things occur. There are duties and jobs. How should one overcome these and achieve what one has planned? It is simply a matter of effort: one should silently carry them out without fear or hesitation. The battlefield demands that things be carried out.⁴³

In his May 11, 1944, entry Tsuchida berated himself for not "carrying out" something: "Because I have not caused a single accident, am I someone who is ignorant of the outcome [of such an accident]? Why am I unable to carry out something I say? I'm a fool! I'm asleep." A week later, he continued his self-criticism: "For two or three days, I have been reflecting deeply after I go to bed. At the moment I have not progressed spiritually one iota, and it is because I am not making an effort to cultivate myself. Although I have various ideals in mind, I am weak-willed when it comes to carrying them out."[44] Tsuchida believed that his inability to carry out certain ideals was due to his not cultivating himself spiritually.

"Self-cultivation" (shūyō) and its cognates began to appear in Tsuchida's diary after he started flight training at the Kumagaya Army Flight School on September 25, 1943, and occur 150 times. He used "self-cultivation" for the first time on October 12, 1943: "With respect to the points about which I was cautioned, there is nothing to be ashamed of. By quickly correcting myself, I should offer something for the resources of cultivation and strive untiringly [to fulfill] the essential duty of a student." The woodenness of this passage suggests that he had learned the word "cultivation" but had not begun to practice using it. A little more than a week later, he wrote: "Today we had the scheduled one-item inspection. The order of the inside of my desk and the order of my shelf. Generally, my things are without order and still inadequate. I feel the truth of my squad leader's words 'Embellish not the exterior but the interior.' An air cadet should first order his interior and, after that, the exterior."

Gradually Tsuchida came to understand what self-cultivation entailed and its centrality in his training, as is suggested by his writing, on November 2, 1943, that "advancing on the path of cultivation each and every day is what should be called the life of the serviceman." His superiors compared self-cultivation to keeping a sword sharp: "One cannot neglect cultivation even for a moment," Tsuchida wrote on January 15, 1944,[45] and just over two weeks later, after hearing about the collective suicide of the Japanese army units on Attu in the Aleutian Island chain: "We heard about the gyokusai of the brave warriors on Attu. This was truly the glory of Japan's way of the warrior. I will cultivate myself so that in the future I will value this view of life and death and my honor. Afterward, 'find a good place to die' was stressed, the essence was to scatter purely when one should scatter."[46] The reference to "scattering" (chiru) was a harbinger of what was coming.

After Tsuchida completed his basic flight training at Kumagaya Army Flight School in March 1944 and started advanced flight training, "self-cultivation" and its cognates appear more often in his diary than do "carry out" and "execute." The first type of cognates includes "cultivate" (osameru, *yashinau*) and "nurture" (*yōsei*) and is explicitly spiritual;[47] the second type, represented by the word "studies" (*shūgaku*), refers to study and mastery;[48] and the words "rectification" (*shūsei*) and "improvement" (*kaishū*) point to the third type, the need for correction and revision.[49] In fact, not long after Tsuchida started advanced flight training in late March 1944, he took to heart something he was told by his superiors: "The education at this school is an education for the cultivation of both spirit and skill . . . do not take any pride in your previous academic achievements. This is the greatest danger." The idea that spirit mattered was pounded into Tsuchida, and he began to rehearse this language, as he did on May 28, 1944, writing, "Piloting [an aircraft] is not a skill; it is spirit." Three weeks later, he quoted his superiors admonishing the trainees: "You guys are still cowards! Piloting [an aircraft] is spirit! Do it with your moral energy!"[50]

Tsuchida's diary also shows us how he was taught to die. As is well known, sacrificing oneself for the emperor and country was an idée fixe in wartime Japanese discourse. It was codified in the *Senjinkun* (*Field Service Code*), the handbook issued to every army recruit beginning in January 1941. The relevant passage reads: "The destiny of the Empire rests upon victory or defeat in battle. Do not give up under any circumstances, keeping in mind your responsibility not to tarnish the glorious history of the Imperial Army with its tradition of invincibility."[51]

This message was communicated to Tsuchida as soon as he entered the Tokyo Army Cadet Aviation School in October 1942. Accordingly, he reported in his second diary entry, dated October 13, that his platoon commander defined a "student's duty" as "understanding the essence of the *kokutai*, finding pleasure in revering the emperor and loving the country, sacrificing the self and serving the larger good, transcending death and life, and existing in the Great Righteousness."[52] In his November 14 entry, his use of the phrases "sacrificing the self and serving the larger good" and "transcending death and life" shows that he had internalized the idea of sacrificing oneself for the emperor and country. The entry was written after he heard about a relative's death and reads:

> Received letter today. From my older brother. News that a relative [Bunji] has died. Telling me to send condolences. When I left, this sick person seemed well. Seems it was just five or six days ago I remembered him sending me off to become a splendid soldier. After twenty years in this life, he has left this world. He departed this world without leaving a thing to later generations. I feel the evanescence of human life. Above and beyond placing ourselves under the command of the

military, we will die splendid deaths for the sake of the Great Ruler. We should always be attentive to our health.[53]

A month later, he announced, "I have become a serviceman who, as an army aviation cadet of our imperial country, will die smiling for the Great Ruler in the future."[54]

Tsuchida often quoted from the eighteenth-century warrior classic *Hagakure* (In hidden leaves), as he did on October 2, 1943: "One has to be able to die at any time and to have prepared one's spirit [to do this]."[55] Four months later the collective suicide of the Imperial Japanese Army men on Attu reminded Tsuchida and his fellow pilots that they were, as the *Hagakure* suggested, "to find a good place to die."[56]

Four months after that, in his May 23, 1944, entry, Tsuchida borrowed another concept from the *Hagakure*, the idea of the "frenzied death" (*shinigurui*): "When one can die in a fit of madness, nothing is impossible."[57] The news of Japan's loss of Saipan was presented as an example of a "struggle to the death."[58] Interestingly, these references to death and self-sacrifice were not major themes in the early stages of Tsuchida's training and even disappear for a time from his diary, replaced by simple injunctions to work hard.

Once Tsuchida began advanced flight training in March 1944, however, he began to refer to death more often. This may have been the result of several things. First, he had witnessed death by this time. A number of his fellow pilots, and even his instructors, had died in flight accidents, which were common in flight training during World War II. Second, Japan had suffered huge setbacks by the spring and summer of 1944, with the loss of Saipan being the most momentous. Third, the army's advanced flight training pedagogy appears to have featured what might be called a "discourse of death and self-sacrifice."

Evidence of the change is hard to miss. Tsuchida began using the new vocabulary in his diary. The word "sacrifice" (*gisei*), for example, appears in several diary entries each week. The words "spirit of sacrifice" (*gisei no seishin*) appear in his March 28, 1944, diary entry, his first after he began advanced flight training. Both terms were used by his superior: "The commander of the education unit's instructions: first, become a person who does not spout theory but does everything with a sincere heart; second, become someone who advances and brings to any difficulty the spirit of sacrifice."[59] Clearly, Tsuchida rehearsed what he was being told, as the words "spirit of sacrifice" appear in his April 8, 14, 21, and May 12 entries,[60] and "world of sacrifice" (*gisei no sekai*) appears twice in May and June.[61] In all these cases, Tsuchida spoke of "being ready" or "determined" to sacrifice himself.

An even more ominous word begins to appear in his diary at this point: *shashin* (literally, "discarding the self"), which I translate as "sacrificing the self" or simply "self-sacrifice." Tsuchida uses the words *shashin no kōgeki* ("an attack in which one sacrifices the self") and *shashin no senpō* ("the military tactic of sacrificing the self"). At the end of his second day of advanced flight training, for example, he recorded his commander's words:

The instructions of the commander of the education unit:

1. Youth is life, and youth is honesty, energy, passion, and responsibility.
2. Refine the spirit of self-sacrifice.
3. Devote training to prevail over the enemy.
4. Overcome the deficiencies of the aircraft and the environment.[62]

Apparently, the words "attack of self-sacrifice" were posted somewhere on the base, because four days later Tsuchida wrote in his diary that the officer on duty had told them, "Every time you see 'attack of self-sacrifice' at the entrance, you should pledge in your heart to rise up, face adversity, and to refine yourself."[63] "Self-sacrifice" became Tsuchida's mantra, one he recorded in his diary once a week all through April:

Without relying on others, one will advance and sacrifice one's self. That conception is necessary (April 8, 1944).[64]

We live, having resolved to die. The time from the present to death is special, and to fulfill one's soldierly duties, one needs quick action, inner strictness, and the spirit of self-sacrifice (April 14, 1944).[65]

Extolling the spirit of self-sacrifice. There is still individualism within me (April 21, 1944).[66]

Today, listening to the unit commander's points of instruction, I was able to grasp them deeply: our mission as young army air cadets is a matter of great concern and magnitude, and we must truly cultivate ourselves for the attack of self-sacrifice (April 29, 1944).[67]

Tsuchida continued to use this discourse of death and self-sacrifice from May 1944 through August 1945 as he prepared to die in a special attack.

Army Special Attack Pilots and the Discourse of Death and Self-Sacrifice

Many of the army pilots who died in special attacks in 1945 were stationed in Manchuria.[68] They first flew south to bases in Korea and then to bases in the Japanese home islands. At each base they were celebrated and given rousing send-offs attended by the top brass, officers, fellow pilots, and local schoolgirls. Once they arrived at bases on the southernmost island of Kyushu, they were given a crash course on how best to attack ships.[69] They also practiced night flights, since many of the army special attacks took place in the early evening.[70] Typically the army pilots sortied for their special attacks from Chiran, Kikajima, Bansei, Tachiarai, and other bases on Kyushu. A few sortied from an airfield on Tokunoshima, which was 264 miles south of Kyushu and 54 miles north of Okinawa. No matter where they originated, the army special attackers always were sent off in grand fashion, and most sortied in April, May, and June 1945.[71]

Given Japan's worsening military situation and the special attack pilots' ultimate mission, it is hardly surprising that the discourse of death and self-sacrifice appeared in their diaries and letters. But did the pilots really accept it? Even a cursory reading of their diaries reveals that they all used many of the same words and concepts that Tsuchida used in his diary. For example, the term "sky worker" recurs with some regularity.[72] Similarly, the same belief in the value of self-reflection, the same emphasis on practice, and the same preoccupation with spirit can be found in their diaries.

Moreover, army pilots like Tsuchida invoked *bushidō* and its celebration of Japanese masculinity, as well as Motoori Norinaga's famous poem and their pledge to give everything—even their lives—for the emperor and the nation. Motoori was an eighteenth-century scholar of national learning (*kokugaku*) who, late in his life, composed the following poem:

Shikishima no	If someone asks about the
yamatogokoro o hito towaba	Yamato spirit of Japan,
asahi ni niou	it is mountain cherry blossoms
Yamazakura-bana	fragrant in the morning sun.

This poem became an iconic representation of the special attack spirit, with the pilots likened to cherry blossoms, a famously short-lived flower.[73]

The pilots' preoccupation with spirit and their fervent belief in the efficacy of self-cultivation is unmistakable. In February 1945 Wakao Tatsuo

Army special attackers departing Chiran Air Base, Kyushu, April 1945. Photo courtesy of the *Mainichi shinbun*.

wrote admiringly of his colleagues who had gone off on special attack missions: "We have been sending off as human bombs pilots who, with their mastery of combat tactics and advanced spiritual state, are national treasures." Wakao also recognized how much further he had to go before he, too, could become a "national treasure." "My spiritual training is still deficient," he wrote. "I believe one must improve one's skill and work at spiritual cultivation for the goal of body crashing."[74] Like Tsuchida Shōji, the pilots attributed their shortcomings and failures to their spiritual deficiencies. When Kuguricha Takashi committed an unspecified blunder, he blamed it on his "inadequate self-cultivation."[75] Arai Kazuo complained about his subordinates' spiritual deficiencies: "As far as bombing ships goes, the fliers under my supervision all lack spirit and don't have enough of the one-attack, certain-death spirit, and this is truly regrettable. What would

be good to do? Flying scared is not acceptable. The spirit of body crashing is absolutely necessary: one should enter the tiger's cave and grab the tiger cubs."[76] Arai's belief that self-cultivation was the solution was widely shared by other pilots.

Yet even the pilots who believed that self-cultivation enabled decisive action admitted that acting decisively was harder than just talking about it. In fact, they all rehearsed the adage that "saying something is one thing, but doing it is another." On February 3, 1945, Shimura Hatsuo put it exactly that way in his diary: "Acting is more difficult than speaking, and one is unable to act." On March 28, 1945, Ōtsuka Kaname, an officer, echoed Shimura in his diary when he observed that "thinking, speaking and writing are easy. Actually performing is hard. This is where self-cultivation becomes necessary." In addition, Lieutenant Ōtsuka found inspiration in his pride as a

Japanese man: "I believe that Japanese men will not lose to the frivolous Yankee youth," he wrote in the same diary entry. Two weeks later, he declared, "I am an officer of the imperial country—this is the basic nature of a man." Less than a month later, he gushed, "For a man, a Japanese man, what greater joy could there be than dying for the emperor?"[77]

Other pilots were not sure they could live up to the vaunted ideal of Japanese masculinity. Munemiya Akihira put it this way on April 10, 1945: "When a Japanese man is preoccupied with personal matters and is unable to find a place to scatter, he will not be able to face his ancestors' mortuary tablets." Three weeks later, he was even blunter: "Handling myself as a man is, in fact, quite difficult: I am neither a rock nor a tree and find it hard to sever my ties of love and desire." Not surprisingly, some pilots even ran away, including a certain Itagaki who landed his aircraft on a racetrack in the Isesaki area and fled.[78]

To raise the pilots' sagging spirits, their superiors encouraged them to identify with venerated Japanese warriors and the fabled warrior tradition. Writing on March 8, 1945, Matsudo Shigeru found comfort in his commander's words: "The way of the warrior is the discovery of death."[79] The concept of "finding a place to die" is, again, a reference to *Hagakure*. Indeed, Lieutenant Ōtsuka repeatedly invoked the warrior tradition in his diary. On April 5 he wrote, "Become a warrior loyal to a lord," and two weeks later, "Single-mindedly and only single-mindedly scatter with the humble shield of our lord." Continuing this theme, he added two days later, "Barbarian ships break apart and sink to the ocean floor. With the ruler's right-hand man, I will scatter happily."[80]

The object of these assertions of loyalty was the emperor. Only a few days after he enlisted, young Tsuchida recorded in his diary what he had just been taught: "I have become a serviceman who . . . will die smiling in the future for the Great Ruler."[81] He frequently reaffirmed in his diary this goal of dying for the emperor, referring to the "Great Ruler" and stating his "loyalty to the lord."[82] Wakao Tatsuo summed it up this way: "Our duty clearly is to gladly offer our lives for the One Person Up Above."[83]

In the last month or two before their final flights, many of the army special attackers waxed philosophical and religious. Two things may explain this. First, they were facing death and had to deal with the prospect of dying. Second, their instructors introduced them to concepts that might help them accept the imminence of their deaths. For example, Lieutenant Ōtsuka invoked a famous Daoist text in his January 25, 1945, diary entry: "Whether or not I should aspire to the special attack units does not depend on arguments. I exist because my country exists; without a country, I would have no family. If there is life, there is death. Joining a special attack unit and 'shattering the jewel' is, to me, the highest site of death."[84]

Ōtsuka's diary entry echoes the following passage in "The Great and Venerable Teacher" chapter of the Daoist classic the *Zhuangzi*:

Nanbo Zikui said to the Woman Crookback, "You are old in years and yet your complexion is that of a child. Why is this?"

"I have heard the Way!"

"Can the Way be learned?" asked Nanbo Zikui.

"Goodness, how could that be? Anyway, you aren't the man to do it. Now there's Buliang Yi—he has the talent of a sage but not the Way of a sage, whereas I have the Way of a sage but not the talent of a sage. I thought I would try to reach him and see if I could get anywhere near to making him a sage. It's easier to explain the Way of a sage to someone who has the talent of a sage, you know. So I began explaining and kept at him for three days, and after that he was able to put the world outside himself. When he had put the world outside himself, I kept at him for seven days more, and after that he was able to put things outside himself. When he had put things outside himself, I kept at him for nine days more, and after that he was able to put life outside himself. After he had put life outside himself, he was able to achieve the brightness of dawn, and when he had achieved the brightness of dawn, he could see his own aloneness. After he had managed to see his own aloneness, he could do away with past and present, and after he had done away with past and present, he was able to enter where there is no life and death. That which kills life does not die; that which gives life to life does not live. This is the kind of thing it is: there's nothing it doesn't send off, nothing it doesn't welcome, nothing it doesn't destroy, nothing it doesn't complete. Its name is Peace-in-Strife. After the strife, it attains completion."[85]

Two weeks later, Ōtsuka again invoked Daoism when he wrote, "Sergeant Ogawa will depart as a member of a special unit. Are those around me going? I too will go. [My] view of death and life is that if there is life, there will be death. The living always perish." Munemiya Akihira, writing on April 10, 1945, stated: "What is there to be hesitant about? Death and life are fated. There is nothing to discuss. Those who die die, those who live live."[86] Clearly, Munemiya too was using the vulgarized form of Daoism that his superiors taught him.

The pilots were introduced to Zen Buddhism as well, no doubt to calm themselves in the weeks and days before their final flights. They were told, for example, that they should "transcend life and death." Shimura Hatsuo took this advice to heart and wrote on February 3, 1945, that he hoped "to achieve a noble character and a full awareness of death and life."[87] The pilots were even taught Zen Buddhist meditation techniques and encouraged to seek *satori*, "enlightenment" and the advanced spiritual state Zen Buddhists call "death in life."[88] Lieutenant Ōtsuka wrote in his diary on February 6 that he was willing to try meditation but admitted that he "did not expect to achieve *satori*."[89]

Like Lieutenant Ōtsuka, Wakao Tatsuo was still based in Manchuria and had not had much training in attacking ships. Understandably, he wondered whether he had the ability to crash his aircraft into an enemy ship or aircraft. On February 4, 1945, he wrote:

I know that Corporal Sasaki already has attained a glorious end as a member of the Banda Special Attack Unit and that now our former squad leader, Katsumata, and a sergeant in Manchuria have scattered with the Kyōkō Unit. "Special attack unit"—that is something only we can join. Once one boards the aircraft, it is decided that one will not return. Who but a Japanese could perform this wonderful task? This is a new weapon that transcends science, transcends materiality, and should be feared. It surely will be seen as a shooting-star bomb that has a will and eyes. Let's consider whether or not I can join a special attack unit right at this moment. For starters, from the standpoint of [my] skill at present, with around a hundred hours of flying time, I still am not confident that I could most effectively hit an enemy ship or a B-29. One speaks simply of body-crashing into enemy aircraft, but I hear that it is quite difficult. Up to now, special attack units have been sending off as human bombs pilots who, owing to their mastery of all combat tactics and their advanced spiritual state, are national treasures. Until one says, "Hit," one cannot say that it is fine just because the pilots can simply pilot a plane. Viewed spiritually, many difficult thoughts arise. My harboring some strange feelings when I think about the moment when I will hit [a target] is probably because my spiritual training is deficient. My scattering as a human bomb in the enemy fleet and not being able to know the military results is a regret. When one has transcended life and death and given one's all to complete one's duties, no matter what happens, nothing is impossible.[90]

Three months later, Wakao appears to have attained his goal. On May 2, 1945, he wrote:

The basic function of the special attack groups is to transcend life and death, and with their truly selfless and destructive spirit and their superior military tactics, to display their distinctive fighting force. [That function] exists in dashing and crashing into enemy warships, ships, and boats on the open ocean or in their berths, decisively sinking them and frustrating the enemy's plans, and opening the way to a total military victory.[91]

Wakao's unit left Manchuria on May 6, and he sortied on a special attack from Bansei Air Base in Kyushu on May 28, perishing in the seas off Okinawa.

One of the most fascinating accounts of the special attack pilots' spiritual quest is Lieutenant Ōtsuka's survey of Daoist, Buddhist, Christian, and Shintō views of death that appear in a long February 6, 1945, entry:

[My] view of death and life is that if there is life, there will be death; the living always perish. I am an ordinary person, and as I think about death and life, there is much that I don't understand. The path that one follows [after] dying can be described in Buddhist terms. Paradise and hell are what Christianity mentions. [Others] speak of the heavenly country, gods, and evil spirits, but I don't know, a living being can't know, what follows after death. If Japanese die, they become gods; if a soldier dies, he becomes a god at Yasukuni [Shrine]. After dying, one becomes an eternal god; one becomes a god of that divine country that prospers and is coeval with heaven and earth—this is what I believe.[92]

The last sentence suggests that Ōtsuka accepted the Shintō view of death—or at least the official wartime version of it—which is confirmed in his next diary entry, dated February 7: "I think of friends who were made to die and how we now live in separate worlds. I think of friends who were young and died without knowing the great imperial age. I think of my father. I think of my cousins. All watch over me in heaven. The point is that Ōtsukas are living on in this way in this place."[93] Ōtsuka found comfort in the Shintō belief in an afterlife.

Belief in an afterlife was reassuring to the pilots. As Arai Kazuo wrote on March 24, "I absolutely believe that I will continue to exist." On the day

Army special attack pilots from the Jinbu Unit donning headbands, April 1945.
Photo courtesy of the *Mainichi shinbun*.

of his special attack, Mori Tatsuo wrote a message in his diary addressed to
his parents: "I'm finally taking off, Father and Mother. Take care, OK? I'll
return home at 7:30. I sortie at 5:00 P.M. and will arrive at my target in two
and a half hours. I promise to sink a ship."⁹⁴ Of course, when Mori wrote,
"I'll return home at 7:30," he assumed that he would be "returning home"
in spiritual form. Since his family would not receive his diary for some time,
it is clear that he was being encouraged to think and write in this way to
prepare himself for his final flight and to ensure that he would follow orders
and do his best to crash his plane into an enemy ship. This was an intensification of the subjectification process that the pilots underwent from outset.
In this instance, the intended effect of the discourse on death and self-sacrifice is clear. The presence of Shintō beliefs in these diaries is not surprising,
since Shintō was the national religion and an important part of the Japanese
ideology during the wartime years.

Despite his thoughtful survey of different religions' views of death,
Lieutenant Ōtsuka could not stop thinking and writing about death. On

April 18, 1945, he wrote, "The ideal of a single attack and a sure kill is the spirit of a serviceman. We cannot but act according to this ideal." On May 9, his unit left Manchuria and arrived in Seoul. An old friend visited him while he was there, and they "talked about death." Their conversation led Ōtsuka to write in his diary, "What is this thing called 'death'? We must die. Our dying has been decided."[95] The passage continues:

> To us, death and life are not problems. Those who are members of special attack units and those who are not differ not at all. It was always painful to receive special treatment just because I was a member of a special attack group. Aren't servicemen—no matter who—the same? Orders, duties. It's just that. Death is easy, death is liberating, death is nothingness. When there is no self, what will there be?[96]

Ōtsuka's ruminations continued: "May 11. One month has passed since it was decided that I would become a member of a special attack unit. Have I progressed? Until he dies, a human being should cultivate himself." Then twelve days later he invoked the Zen Buddhist notion of "death in life": "May 23. . . . Tomorrow is one day for a body to die, but I already have died. Tomorrow what will hit an enemy ship is my spirit."[97] Ōtsuka flew to his death in the Okinawa area on May 25, 1945.[98]

Tsuchida Shōji and the Discourse of Death and Self-Sacrifice

What about Tsuchida Shōji, the young army pilot? Did he embrace the discourse of death and self-sacrifice? His diary reveals that he continued to do everything he had been taught. For example, in his April 15, 1945, diary entry he reflected on his development as a pilot, noting his technical and spiritual strengths and weaknesses.

> No matter what environment I find myself in, I must not lose my fundamental heart. I must not stray from the path on which I should progress. I should think about the position of my person and act accordingly. At this point, my achievements and so forth are not a problem, but I should realize that since [my days in the] Nitta Instructional Corps, my actual power has clearly declined, and my position has sunk quite a lot. I should honestly record that it is because my self-awareness and real power are not in agreement.[99]

Sensing that something dramatic was afoot, Tsuchida rehearsed in his diary on April 16 everything he had learned to date:

In any case, my life will not be long, and thus doing untoward things is something those unable to cultivate themselves should discuss. The shorter life is, the more one needs to make the best effort. One does not stop making an effort even for a moment: it is something one has to do all through one's life. If one discusses things in this way, there is much for an individual to reflect on.[100]

Eight days later, on April 24, he continued in the same vein: "6:30. Got up. Had feelings. If my spirit is pure, my skill, naturally, will be pure. Increasing and improving on days of night flights, I am truly and unbearably happy."[101]

Then on May 5, his officers began to pressure Tsuchida and his fellow pilots to join special attack units. That day he wrote in his diary: "For some time, there has been pressure to form special attack units. With my nineteen-year-old body, I will embellish with flowers the end of the beginning of the way of flying cultivated up to now. Ah! This is the basic nature of a man! If we are able to die, we will be able to rescue the state! . . . We will attack!"[102] The next day Tsuchida learned that he had been chosen for a special attack unit. He closed that day's entry with, "Until the moment of death I will give it my all."[103]

Not surprisingly, death began to suffuse his diary. Eighteen days later, the prospect of dying was brought home to Tsuchida when five of his fellow pilots were killed in a freak accident. That night he wrote in his diary: "I will call the fifth volume of my self-reflection diary 'Friends of Memory.' It will be different from the earlier volumes of my diary. Because I have entered the life of a special attack unit, self-reflection and self-cultivation must rule my life. At this juncture, it is not the season of self-cultivation but the moment to display the fruits of my cultivation to date."[104]

Interestingly, Tsuchida sees his final flight as an opportunity to "display the fruits" of his spiritual cultivation and does not mention death or dying. Three weeks later, however, the farewell party held for him and others joining special attack units reminded him of the imminence of his death. That night he wrote in his diary:

A "farewell party" is a moment that will not come again, and it is hardly a pleasant or a happy one. The more serious this moment is, the closer is the step-by-step approach on the path leading to the land of death. Yet this does not mean I fear death. Just because we are a special attack unit, we want to be treated like other servicemen. We should truly mourn for the country and face this crisis that is hard to describe in words.[105]

Three days later the imminence of death was brought home even more powerfully when two fellow pilots were killed in ship-attacking drills. Their deaths prompted Tsuchida to write: "These deaths were absolutely not fated. Nor could they have been avoided with spiritual cultivation. After all, human life cannot be measured. Even though this body has not died yet, it will in a few days. I should be thinking about steadily carrying out my preparations for death."[106] There was no escaping the prospect of death.

At the end of June, Tsuchida got word that he would be transferred to Yōkaichi, home of the 303rd Jinbu Special Attack Unit, and he busied himself with preparations. His diary entries tell the story:

June 24, Sunday, clear
Order given to advance to base airport. Immediately commenced preparations. Am busy taking care of my private belongings and writing a last letter. I'm in a swivet and realize that my view of death and life is not completely firm, and feel shame. I remembered Lieutenant Yoshitani's doctrine of fate, [and] there is room for further self-cultivation.

June 25, Monday
Test flight of beloved plane. Spent the whole day on maintenance and preparations for departure.

June 26, Tuesday
Departure is set for the twenty-seventh. Wrote last letter to younger brothers and sisters. Packed personal belongings in a trunk and have no regrets about anything. Received various words of encouragement from my mentors. I was deeply moved.

June 27, Wednesday, cloudy
Rose at three o'clock, made departure preparations right away, and by six o'clock all the aircraft were lined up in front of hangar. Received farewells from the company commander on down, and I cannot thank them enough. Major Tōgō, Captain Ishida, Captain Fujita, warrant officers, instructors, and fellow pilot Nishimoto, tears, tears, and tears.

A moment of gratitude. At nine o'clock the formation grandly left for Yōkaichi Airport. Three thousand meters, the Japan Alps below. Now I am alone in flight; isn't it wonderful to embark on this enterprise. Thought of my deceased parents and my younger brothers and sisters far away back home. Good-bye, good-bye. . . .

Arrived in no time at familiar Yōkaichi and had no problems on the way. Two sister aircraft of the 303rd sustained considerable damage on landing.[107]

These four entries reveal how Tsuchida was encouraged to die and what enabled him to accept his fate. In these entries, he located himself in two distinct communities: first, his unit and second, his family. He is linked to the people in these communities by his gratitude for what they have done for him and his anticipated repayment of what he owes them. Tsuchida also worried about his spiritual state, writing: "I am not calm and realize that my view of death and life is not completely firm, making me feel shame . . . there is room for further self-cultivation."[108] His chief worry was that he would not be able to repay the debts he owed his family and his unit.[109]

The 303rd Jinbu Special Attack Unit had dispatched many special attackers up to that point. The plan was for Tsuchida to fly on to the army air base at Tachiarai in Kyushu, which was closer to the battle raging in and around Okinawa. Although his flight was scheduled for June 28, it was canceled when his aircraft's right engine malfunctioned. Other pilots from his unit left as scheduled, and Tsuchida was distraught.[110] The malfunctioning engine was replaced, and Tsuchida took off on July 1, but then the other engine malfunctioned, forcing him to return to Yōkaichi. While he was in the air, the effigy of the guardian deity from Taga Shrine that hung in his cockpit suddenly fell, prompting him to conclude that "it was as though it ordered me to land. I am truly grateful for the divine protection of the gods." Tsuchida took off twice more—on July 2 and 3—but both times had to return to the base.[111] Finally, on July 4, he took off and arrived safely at Tachiarai Air Base. He was one step closer to his final attack.

At Tachiarai, though, things did not go as Tsuchida hoped they would. He was frustrated by his inability to perform as expected despite the increasing frequency of drills on how best to attack ships and the late-dusk drills. It also was the rainy season, and spells of bad weather kept postponing his special attack. "I want to die but can't," he wrote in his diary on July 19. "On what day will my life be extinguished?" Attacks by Allied aircraft compounded Tsuchida's misery. On July 22, B-29s and carrier-based fighters attacked Tachiarai. "Spent the whole day in fear and trembling. Couldn't get any work done," he wrote in his diary that night. The enemy attacked again and again, damaging not only the air base but also nearby communities.[112]

On July 30, Tsuchida was transferred to the north side of the Tachiarai Air Base, where the Sixty-Sixth Combat Squadron was housed. Then on July 31, two aircraft in his unit collided during a drill, leaving the pilots badly injured.[113] The Sixty-Sixth had already sent off five special attackers—three on May 4 and two on May 25.[114] On August 1, Tsuchida steeled himself for what was coming. He read Miyamoto Musashi's *Book of Five Rings*, a sixteenth-century warrior classic, and wrote that he saw Miyamoto as a "model of dignity and nobility." As expected, on August 2, he received orders to prepare for a special attack. "Am extremely busy with personal arrangements and do not expect to leave anything out from the personal effects I send home."[115] That same day Tsuchida received a letter from his younger sister reporting that Major Tōgō had sent his family ¥50. "I bow my head in gratitude," Tsuchida wrote in his diary. He continued: "How should I repay the debt?" and answered, "I will simply offer this body to the Great Ruler and achieve brilliant military results."[116] The farewell party for Tsuchida's group of special attackers was held on August 3:

Last night, a last attack farewell party was held at the headquarters residence. Major Yamazaki, commander of the Sixty-Sixth Air Group, was invited. Farewell salutations for us, together with the 304th Squadron, and it was an exceedingly solemn scene. Because I realized this might be the final banquet, it was very moving. Gradually the party came to an end, and I will show my long-cherished skill.

Everyone's morale was extremely high, and both the squadron commander and squad leader seemed satisfied. I was overcome by emotion, thought of my younger brother and sister back home, and my awareness of my coming attack was lost in my cups, and I could not exist just for that. The party ended at eleven o'clock, and I moved to the air group headquarters, staggering into my new quarters.

Today I drank too much and, overcome with grief, could not sleep.[117]

Tsuchida was coming closer to realizing his ambition.

On August 4 he was told that special attack pilots on standby could not leave the base. Squadron Commander Higashiyama announced to them: "Once you take off, you absolutely will not return. Even if your engine malfunctions, you should not return to the base. Realize that you should be satisfied with crashing into the sea or into the mountains." Tsuchida added, "This is the highest resolve of a warrior. I have no objection."[118] He was ready and willing to die. He wrote in his diary the next morning:

At long last greeted the day of August 5. The life I have this morning, will I have it at dusk? When I think about it, it is truly mystical. Although I received a death declaration several days earlier, nothing has changed spiritually, and my calmly living my life is because, first, we have died and are gods, and if I die for the sake of Correct Righteousness, a hundred million comrades will greet the happiness!

The imperial country has enjoyed a 3,000-year history. Because of this history, I am pleased that my five-limbed body will accompany my beloved aircraft and my fate. Just before death, this self that is now displayed in the present should truly know the revered spirit of the Yamato [Japanese] people, who have no equals in the world.[119]

The next day Tsuchida discussed his family's financial situation with Higashiyama, who promised to send condolence money.[120] On August 7, Tsuchida wrote in his diary:

Not having died yet, today, too, I see the sun. . . . For a second, I feel as though I'm dreaming of peace. But in my heart, having already committed my life for six days, the tension continues.

A cow exists. Cute calves play. No, they still have life. Somehow living in this world is shameful. The feeling that I am seeking death has finally emerged. Entering a temple gate, I become a Buddha, and I will coexist with my parents and my older brother, and I yearn to be filial in that world.[121]

As Tsuchida waited for his final flight, the Soviet Union declared war on Japan and invaded Manchuria.

The Importance of the Discourse of Death and Self-Sacrifice

The discourse of death and self-sacrifice that appears in the diaries of special attack pilots was important for four reasons. First, it reveals how the special attack pilots learned to die. Once their advanced flight training began, this discourse was drummed into them, perhaps even beaten into them. They heard it in the morning, in the afternoon, and in the evening. The gist of what they heard was always the same: you have the honor of flying off to die a brilliant death for your emperor and the nation, so don't dishonor yourself, your superiors, your comrades, your family, or your hometown and country.

Second, the pilots also learned variations of this discourse cast in different philosophical and religious languages: Confucian, Buddhist, Daoist, and Shintō. Loyalty was a cardinal Confucian virtue, and loyalty to the emperor even superseded other Confucian virtues, such as filial piety. In fact, dying for the emperor, the pilots were taught, was a way of being filial to their parents, a recurring refrain in their last letters to their families. The pilots were introduced as well to Zen Buddhist notions of "transcending life and death" or "achieving death while alive" and were even taught to practice Zen Buddhist meditation. The special attack pilots were reminded that after their deaths they would survive in spiritual form and would meet their deceased relatives and friends, and even the surviving members of their families. These beliefs originated in Shintō, Japan's indigenous religion. Believing that they would survive in spiritual form, many special attack pilots asked their families to visit the Yasukuni Shrine, the shrine for soldiers and sailors in Upper Kudan in Tokyo, where, they said, they would be waiting. These Confucian, Buddhist, and Shintō terms and practices explain the vocabulary of the discourse of death and self-sacrifice that was taught to special attack pilots in the months before their final flights.

Of course, the simple recurrence of this discourse in the special attack pilots' diaries does not tell us exactly what they felt about their one-way missions. After all, the pilots' diaries may not have been completely private journals; that is, they may have been read by their superiors. In fact, the recurring vocabulary of death and self-sacrifice in the pilots' diaries may reveal both the continuing presence of their commanders, as actual or possible readers, and the self-subjectifying process encouraged by "self-reflection," an important third point that should not be overlooked. In contrast, the diaries of the navy special attack pilots reveal less evidence of their superiors' presence and less self-subjectification. Perhaps because of this, many of the navy pilots seem to have been at loose ends before their special attacks. The difference between the diaries of the army and navy special attackers may reflect something else as well. Most of the navy diaries that have survived and been published are the work of university graduates drafted after 1942, when the deferments of everyone but science students ended. University students in prewar Japan were a highly educated and elite group; they were well versed in history, literature, philosophy, and Western culture, and they may even have known more about German philosophy than about their own religious tradition. Yet the diaries of the career navy pilots who became special attackers are more like the army diaries in their use of the discourse of death and self-sacrifice. They seem less troubled by the prospect of death and seem more willing to accept the inevitability and imminence of their deaths. This was the case, for example, with navy pilot Itabashi Yasuo, who simply longed to fly off on a special attack to join his deceased buddies.[122] This is not so surprising; military historians tell us that loyalty to one's unit is universal in all modern armies and a powerful motivator.[123]

Finally, the presence of the discourse of death and self-sacrifice in the special attack pilots' diaries is important for a fourth reason. It resonated with home-front propaganda in the last year of the war, when this same discourse began appearing in the government-controlled mass media directed at the population of the home islands and the colonies. Early in January 1945, Japanese newspapers carried articles that described the "special attack spirit" (*tokkōshin*), and apparently, every day it "was being stressed over and over again in the newspapers and on the radio." In February 1945, in a national radio broadcast, a Lieutenant General Nakai Ryōtarō called for the *gyokusai* of the entire Japanese population.[124] The fact that the discourse of death and self-sacrifice taught to the special attack pilots was also being used on the home front reveals something observed by historians studying German propaganda during World War II. These wartime military and civilian discourses often overlapped and coincided, creating what one historian called an "inter-discourse." In turn, the operation of this inter-discourse may explain why both the home-front civilians and the special attack pilots were encouraged even by their own families, relatives, teachers, classmates, and friends to sacrifice themselves for the emperor and nation.

7

Popular Resistance to the Wartime Government and Its Policies

In the summer of 1944, someone in Shizuoka Prefecture, in central Japan, began writing angry letters to Tōjō Hideki, the prime minister; his wife; General Hata Shunroku, commander of the Second General Army based in Hiroshima; the prefectural governor; the head of the Greater Japan National Defense Women's Association; the head of the Patriotic Women's Association; and others. The unsigned letters implored their recipients to "please stop the war as soon as possible," declared that "Japan will lose this war for certain," and asked, "Aren't you aware of how difficult the lives of Japanese have been?" The letter writer carefully posted the letters from different mailboxes throughout the prefecture to avoid being tracked down, and this tactic worked for several months. But finally, on February 7, 1945, the police arrested the person they believed was writing and sending the letters. It was a fifty-three-year-old widow whose son had been drafted and killed in the South Pacific and whose teenaged daughter had been mobilized for war work. At the time of her arrest the woman denied writing the letters, but after she tried to commit suicide the police felt sure they had arrested the right person. In the end, she confessed and apologized.[1]

This incident led me to wonder how typical this woman's reaction was to the war and to the policies of the wartime government. Was there popular resistance to the wartime government and its policies? And if so, what forms did it take? These are important questions, for two reasons: first, wartime American propaganda suggested that "popular resistance" was

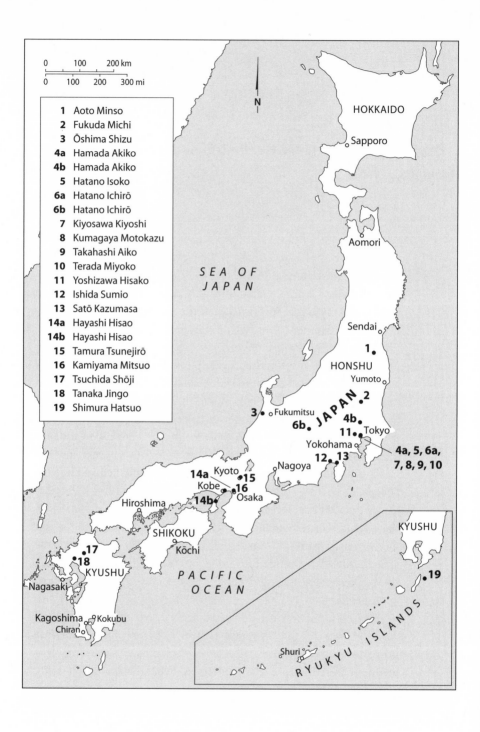

1	Aoto Minso
2	Fukuda Michi
3	Ōshima Shizu
4a	Hamada Akiko
4b	Hamada Akiko
5	Hatano Isoko
6a	Hatano Ichirō
6b	Hatano Ichirō
7	Kiyosawa Kiyoshi
8	Kumagaya Motokazu
9	Takahashi Aiko
10	Terada Miyoko
11	Yoshizawa Hisako
12	Ishida Sumio
13	Satō Kazumasa
14a	Hayashi Hisao
14b	Hayashi Hisao
15	Tamura Tsunejirō
16	Kamiyama Mitsuo
17	Tsuchida Shōji
18	Tanaka Jingo
19	Shimura Hatsuo

0   100   200 km
0   100   200   300 mi

N

HOKKAIDO

Sapporo

Aomori

SEA OF JAPAN

Sendai

HONSHU

Yumoto

1.

JAPAN

3. Fukumitsu

6b.   4b.

2

11. Tokyo

Yokohama

4a, 5, 6a, 7, 8, 9, 10

12. 13

Nagoya

Kyoto

14a   15

Kobe   16

Hiroshima   14b   Osaka

SHIKOKU

Kōchi

KYUSHU

17

18

KYUSHU

PACIFIC OCEAN

Nagasaki

19

Kagoshima   Kokubu

Chiran

Shuri

RYUKYU ISLANDS

impossible, even inconceivable, because the Japanese were so servile and such obedient subjects of the emperor. They were "prints off the same negative," as the filmmaker Frank Capra described them in his documentary *Know Your Enemy Japan.*

Second, after Japan was defeated in 1945, the Cold War required that the general population not be held responsible for what happened during the war. The reason was quite simple: once the Communists prevailed over Nationalist forces in China, the hated enemy Japan became an important ally of the United States. The American Occupation forces, who carefully censored everything published in postwar Japan until 1952, endorsed the following statement, which appeared in the first postwar Japanese history textbook (*Kuni no ayumi,* "The progress of the country") issued by the Ministry of Education in 1946: "The Japanese people suffered terribly from the long war. Military leaders suppressed the people, launched a stupid war, and caused this disaster."[2] This statement presents the "Japanese people" as victims of their wartime leaders, and it became the official Japanese view. But as a historian I questioned this characterization of them as victims and as "suppressed" by their leaders. No group, much less an entire nation, could be summed up so easily and neatly. Historian Carol Gluck put it this way:

> It is not possible to wage a total war with 28, 280, or even 28,000 people and the responsibility for war lies far more broadly in society than was earlier believed, or hoped. Just as in Europe, where it is no longer possible to explain such things solely in terms of Hitler, Mussolini, or Pétain, the ways in which the vast numbers of ordinary people were entwined in the complex mesh of war must be counted. Even those who did not actually march or collaborate are now judged as participants. It takes both states and societies—which is to say the individuals who comprise [*sic*] them—to make a total war.[3]

The wartime diaries and letters of ordinary Japanese confirm my suspicion: they were neither the dumb servile creatures featured in Capra's documentary nor simply "victims." Instead, most Japanese struggled with the wartime government and its policies, actively resisted the powers that the government exercised over their daily lives, and devised strategies and tactics to thwart the small army of officials and police enforcing laws and regulations. What follows is a catalog and description of the many instances and varieties of this resistance.

Resistance to the Wartime Government and Its Policies

In Japan, as in Germany, many individuals and groups plotted to kill the head of the government—in this case the prime minister, Tōjō Hideki. In Japan the plotters were members of extreme right-wing groups that, since the 1930s, had been assassinating government and military leaders who did not share their extremist vision of Japan and the world. Prime Minister Tōjō was only one of their targets. Accordingly, in June 1943, members of a right-wing group, the Takudaishō, plotted to assassinate the prime minister but were arrested before they could carry out their plan. In September of that same year, members of a second right-wing group, the Imperial Way Youth Assistance Alliance (Kōdō yokusan seinen dōmei), were arrested for concocting similar plans, and in December, eighteen members of a third right-wing group were arrested for planning something even bigger: a coup d'état. All the members of the three groups were civilians.

But military men, too, plotted to assassinate the prime minister. In July 1944, a group of officers devised a plan to kill the prime minister but were arrested before they could carry it out.[4] Two months later, Major Tsunoda Tomoshige was arrested by the military police for conspiring to assassinate the prime minister.[5] Such plots were clearly a form of resistance and a response to what was regarded as Tōjō's abuse of his power: in October 1941 he had assumed the posts of both prime minister and minister of war, and in February 1944 he also became the army chief of staff.[6]

Many other groups opposed the wartime government and its policies, though none more vigorously than organized labor. In 1943, for example, 417 labor disputes involving 14,791 workers were recorded; in 1944, 296 incidents involving 10,026 workers; and in 1945, 13 disputes involving 382 workers.[7] Workers also formed what they called "poetry clubs," whose functions were less literary than political. Farmers, too, opposed the government and its policies. In 1941 the number of landlord–tenant disputes was 3,308; in 1942 it was 2,756; in 1943, 17,738 farmers participated in 2,424 disputes; and in the following year, 8,213 farmers were involved in 2,160 landlord-tenant disputes. This pattern continued until the end of the war.[8] These incidents may have been directed, however, more at landlords than at the state and its policies.

In addition, large numbers of leftists, pacifists, and Christians actively opposed the government's policies, and these are the best-known cases of antigovernment resistance. In contrast, most intellectuals chose to affect a posture of what they termed "passive resistance," but even so, many were arrested and interrogated, and some were murdered; others simply took to the hills and spent the war in hiding; and a few even collaborated with the Allies.[9] A small number of draft resisters refused to bear arms, many of whom were Christians, but a surprisingly large number of servicemen either defected to the enemy or deserted.

	Defectors	Deserters
1939	669 (combined number of defectors and deserters)	
1943	20	1,023
1944	40	1,085[10]

These figures are far below the forty thousand Americans and more than 100,000 British servicemen who deserted during World War II.

Popular Resistance: Breaking the Rules

Popular resistance took many forms. Following Michel Foucault, I am defining "resistance" as opposition to the forms and techniques of the wartime Japanese state, and "popular resistance" as the resistance of ordinary people.[11] Even a cursory reading of the wartime diaries of ordinary Japanese reveals much evidence of popular resistance, dating from the start of the Sino-Japanese War in July 1937 and continuing until the end of the war. Individuals and groups throughout the country—in cities, provincial towns, and rural communities—found ways to resist their government's wartime policies and its regime of rules, rationing, rituals, and forced labor. Although most did this with impunity, a few were caught and punished. Popular resistance to the wartime government, its policies, and its agents assumed five forms that I have identified.

The first is what I am calling "calculated resistance." The best example is the premeditated violation of government rules and regulations, which was surprisingly common during the war. Most frequently, this type of resistance took the form of shopping on the black market. Many tens of thousands of Japanese citizens routinely defied the government regulations that prohibited them from buying scarce foods or commodities on the black market, where anything and everything was available, but at a price. Even generally law-abiding citizens were driven to buy food on the black market. Ōshima Shizu, a housewife in Kanazawa in western Japan, who was under some pressure to obey the law because her daughter was a live-in teacher for the emperor's children, was one of these usually law-abiding shoppers driven to shop on the black market or to buy directly from farmers.[12] Although Japanese also were discouraged from buying food directly from farmers, on any given day in 1943 and 1944, extraordinarily large numbers of Tokyoites traveled to the farming communities on the outskirts of the city to buy directly from farmers or to barter with them. For example, on September 12, 1943, a Sunday, sixteen thousand Tokyoites did this, as eight to twenty thousand did on nearly every day in 1944.[13]

These acts of calculated resistance tell us that despite the government's rationing program, which began in 1940, food was in such short supply that by 1942 most Japanese living in the big cities spent a good part of each day searching for food. Already in 1942 a family of five in Tokyo spent an average of four and a half hours a day standing in line for food, and one student in Tokyo wrote home that it took her three and a half hours to buy just one daikon.[14] Those with the means and time would go quite far to get the food they needed. One Kyoto resident traveled by train to Tokyo—a distance of about 1,600 miles—to buy bags of sweet potatoes for her family of six.[15]

Likewise, the farmers were not supposed to sell their produce directly to the buyers, but many did. Indeed, the fact that so many farmers defied the government is surprising, since rural communities were generally the most supportive of the war effort and supplied the largest number of recruits for the military. But many farmers resented the government's crop-requisitioning program, which took more and more of their crops at a time when it was harder to farm because they had less fertilizer and fewer hands to help with planting and harvesting.[16] This resistance appeared as early as the late 1930s, when Japanese forces invaded China. In 1940 Aoto Minso, the wife of a farmer, declared, "The state is like a selfish, unreasonable brat. We don't even have socks for our feet, but they demand 'more work, more work.' And we have to do it. There are higher taxes, higher this and that. Farmers can't take it anymore. It's all because of the war. Even if we lose, I just want them to end it quickly."[17] Tanaka Jingo, a farmer in Kyushu, complained often about the government and its policies.[18] Yet that same farmer and his fellow village headmen also enjoyed hard-to-get fish such as sea bream, as well as saké, whenever they gathered for their monthly meetings, thereby making their refusal to obey the government's policies a kind of resistance.

In the big cities, those with the means to do so still managed to buy foods and beverages that were in short supply. Well-to-do Tokyoites often had special occasion dinners at which they served white (polished) rice, chicken, and even chocolate, as well as liquor. At New Year's these families enjoyed the traditional array of dishes, whereas many urban families struggled to serve even one or two of them. High-ranking military men, members of the aristocracy, and those who traveled to the provinces on government business also enjoyed fine dining while their countrymen in the big cities were beginning to suffer the effects of malnutrition. Even family dogs were requisitioned for their fur and meat.[19] All this took place after the government declared that "luxury was the enemy."

In the summer and fall of 1944, when the government was expecting the Allies to start bombing Japan, more than a million children between the ages of nine and eleven were evacuated from the major Japanese cities. The systematic bombing of Japanese cities and towns began in November 1944 and continued until the war ended. The children were evacuated to rural towns and villages and usually were housed in inns, temples, and schools. Although their first meal in their new homes was almost always a splendid one that often included white rice, a scarce commodity during the war, they later were gradually fed less and less.

When parents heard about their evacuated children's hunger, they brought food to them. This was acceptable to the teachers and dorm mothers responsible for the children as long as what they brought was shared with the other children. Though equitable, this policy was not realistic, given the worsening food shortages in the big cities. So when parents visited, they often asked to take their children on an outing, during which they gave them the contraband food they had brought from the city. Usually the food was consumed on the spot or hidden. Of course, this violated the rule that anything given to one child had to be shared with all, which meant that both the parents and their children had to conspire to get around the rules. One evacuated schoolboy remembered the "silent understanding" that the rules could be violated if "the parents brought a certain 'snack'" for their child's friends.[20]

Many other government rules were routinely broken as well. The wartime government attempted to expunge all traces of American popular culture from daily life. As noted in chapter 1, the terminology of that great American sport, baseball, was changed, with Japanese words being devised for "strike," "ball," and "hit-and-run." The other great American cultural artifact, jazz, was banned as well, but jazz aficionados met secretly at one another's homes to listen to their favorite records. Other premeditated acts of resistance were little more than expressions of anger and resentment. Fukuda Michi, an army nurse at a military hospital in Utsunomiya, just outside Tokyo, quickly learned how enlisted men got back at their superiors: Those working in the hospital cafeteria would routinely shake their dandruff into the rice they served to their commanding officer and squad leaders. The dish was called "dandruff rice."[21]

Popular Resistance: Thievery

Thievery was the second type of popular resistance and, given the increasing scarcity of food and other commodities in the cities, is not surprising. In 1943 Kiyosawa Kiyoshi, the journalist based in Tokyo, cataloged the stolen articles, which included money and basic commodities like vegetables, fruit, shoes, straw mats and straw rope, and clothes.[22] Also stolen were luxury items with resale value. For example, thieves stole Kiyosawa's golf clubs and golf shoes, a cigarette lighter, a hat he had hung on a coat rack at a restaurant, and a cane that he had carefully slid under his seat at a kabuki performance and that someone sitting behind him had just as carefully pulled out from under his seat.[23] Kiyosawa lamented that even the night soil collector stole ginger and persimmons.[24]

In 1944 the thievery became more desperate. Kiyosawa reported that his daughter's classmates stopped heating up their lunches at school because they were often stolen then. He also heard of people stealing food through an open window while it was being cooked, keys or doorknobs disappearing from Japanese inns, and the leather upholstery in trains being cut out and removed. Kiyosawa's hat was stolen at a Ginza restaurant by "a man with the look of a gentleman." Even bars of soap, brought to the public bath, were stolen while the bather was lathering his or her hair.[25]

The thieves were utterly shameless. Kiyosawa heard the following story: "At the home of a certain farmer, two youths riding bicycles came by and said that because they had an acquaintance who was ill, he should sell them potatoes. When he brought out about 60 pounds, they asked him for still more. When he put a ladder down into the basement storeroom to get more, the youths pulled up the ladder from above and fled."[26] Even vegetables from carefully tended neighborhood association war gardens were taken.[27]

In the countryside, the thieves often were conscripts from nearby military bases or teenagers mobilized for war work.[28] In April 1944 one thief—a teenager—was caught after he broke into the summer house of one of Kiyosawa's friends. Here's what happened next:

> "Forgive me," he said and hid his face. When he was forced to show his face, he turned out to be a youth of nineteen. The master of the house felt sorry for him and had him stay over that evening and even take a bath. When the master tried questioning him, the boy said he was a draft laborer, but with the wages he received, he could not eat.

He was not turned over to the police, and now he is employed in a factory that is managed by the master of the house.[29]

Conscripts assigned to the food detail routinely stole food as they served it.[30] So severe was the thievery problem that Kiyosawa wrote in his diary, "Thievery is in vogue, and farmers are being raided. Japan will have the honor of being called the 'Foremost Thief Nation in the Whole World.'"[31]

When the Allied bombing of the Japanese home islands intensified in 1945, the thieves became even more desperate. Yoshizawa Hisako, a single working woman in Tokyo, met someone at the local post office who told her the following story:

A relative's father died recently, and because there were no coffins, they had to do something—after all, it was Father, they said—and so for the wake, they put him into the best wicker basket they could find. Then there was an air raid, and thinking that it would be too bad if they burned up together with Father, they loaded the basket onto a cart and started out. But in the confusion of the moment, someone stole the cart. Even though the family reported the theft to the police, the cart still hasn't been found.[32]

Indeed, coffins were in such short supply that they could no longer be bought but only rented and returned for reuse.[33]

In his August 3, 1945, diary entry, Kawamoto Michiji, a farmer in Osaka, wrote about a case of thievery reported in the local newspaper.

Four or five days ago, there was [an article] in the newspapers about a former Osaka University professor arrested for stealing tomatoes from a vegetable field. Some probably say that if people with PhDs are stealing, how low have we sunk? This does not mean that out of every ten people, ten people are stealing. At present to procure something, it is usually rations, and if one talks about things other than rations, no one is selling at the public prices [but at] the higher black market prices. . . . Even the professor, with the value of our currency falling, found his daily resources less than what a female day laborer makes. But food controls the life of a family. One can imagine that the professor's family was resigned to a life of abject poverty, but pressed by food problems, he probably ignored his reputation and stole.[34]

The *Asahi shimbun* reported that the judges who heard this case declared, "For households everywhere, putting up with an impoverished existence is the obligation of citizens during a war," and sentenced the hungry professor to five years in prison.[35] This was only one of several cases that attracted attention because they involved faculty at national universities.

Popular Resistance: Spontaneous Acts

The break-ins and thefts often were not premeditated but spontaneous, and were a third type of resistance. Many were committed by children. Nakamura Kyōko was eight years old when the following incident took place at her school's morning assembly:

> One day during morning assembly, when all students were lined up at attention, the principal asked, "Let's say that an American flag is placed here. You all are walking toward it. What would you do?" Everyone shouted in concert, "Trample on it as we pass by." This was an era when everywhere we looked we saw the demonic caricatures of Churchill and Roosevelt. Of the 1,500 pupils, just one, Arita Suzuko, a girl in my class, replied, "Bow deeply as I pass by." A thunderous roar of denunciation flooded the schoolyard. Word spread quickly as a swift wind from one child to another. Her mother was immediately called to the principal's office and cautioned severely about what should be taught at home. Suzuko was a tomboy with many siblings, and her father was a doctor. I often admired the originality of her way of thinking and her way of responding. I bow with admiration for the courage required in that period for her mother to instill a sense of respect for a national flag, even the enemy's. It was a symbol of that nation and should be bowed to. And I also admire the courage that it took Suzuko to be the only one to raise her hand and say what she did.[36]

Nakamura closed her account by noting that Arita Suzuko was "a girl who liked to study" and "she must now be making her mark somewhere as a doctor."

Another example of spontaneous resistance took place in a rural community in northern Hyōgo Prefecture in central Japan, recounted earlier, in chapter 5. Hayashi Hisao was a Kobe schoolboy evacuated to a rural community in northern Hyōgo, who, with a friend, stole sweet potatoes from a field on their way back from the public bath, they were seen, and the next day there was a call for "everyone to assemble"; when Hayashi's sensei condemned the thieves, calling them "traitors," the children sitting in the front immediately got up and ran off, as did all the other students.[37] Although Hayashi's theft was clearly premeditated, the children's rushing from the assembly and from their raging teacher was not.

One more example involved a schoolboy evacuated from Tokyo to Fukumitsu in Toyama Prefecture. His April 30, 1945, diary entry reads: "This morning we had class. In the afternoon we wrote postcards. Everyone wrote down everything: meals are skimpy, we want to drown ourselves, and things are pretty tough here." That evening the writer heard that some fifth-graders were scolded by their teacher for writing what they did in their postcards.[38] Many more instances of this sort of resistance can be found in the last year of the war.

Public vandalism also was rampant and possibly the spontaneous response of ordinary citizens to one or another aggravation. The ever observant and thoughtful Kiyosawa offered an explanation for public vandalism. "The trains are breaking down into total wrecks," he wrote in January 1945. "The windows are intentionally smashed by the passengers, and they are stealing the upholstery. I understand that if it announced that a train will be late, there is destruction on the grounds that the trains are late for other reasons. Anger against the enemy is first of all directed inward."

Popular Resistance: Acts of Nonconformity

Sometimes people simply refused to do what the government ordered them to do, making these acts of nonconformity the fourth type of resistance. Resisting in this way was risky, though, because it could result in their not receiving the scarce commodities and food distributed by their neighborhood associations. Apparently this happened often. A number of neighborhood associations withheld food to punish uncooperative members, and the home ministry had to tell these neighborhood leaders that they could not do this. One of those who frequently refused to participate in the activities of his neighborhood association was Tamura Tsunejirō, who, when his grandson was leaving to go off to war, chose not to attend the boy's send-off and had one of his daughters represent the family.[39] In this instance, Tamura was resisting the most immediate manifestations of state power: the orders transmitted from the home ministry to the community councils and then to his eight-family neighborhood association, orders that required that one family member be present at the send-offs of local men.

Mobilized teenagers outside their factory. Photo courtesy of the National Shōwa
Memorial Museum, Tokyo.

Another common form of nonconformity was tardiness or absenteeism.[40] For instance, teenagers mobilized for war work frequently showed
up late at the factories to which they had been assigned, or they did not
show up at all.[41] Terada Miyoko was a student at Japan Women's University
when she was mobilized for war work in September 1944 and sent to a munitions factory in Kamata, in southern Tokyo. She hated factory work and
so despised her supervisors that she delighted in recording in her diary how
many of her classmates were late for work and how many stayed home.
She reported that on December 16, 1944, two of the seventeen members
of her work group stayed home; on January 13, 1945, five stayed home; and
on February 9, 1945, twelve stayed home. Then when the firebombing of
Tokyo began, many of her classmates left the city for their hometowns.[42]
Moreover, many mobilized teenagers did not take their war work seriously

and spent much of their day at their factories "playing," as one of their comrades complained in his diary.[43]

Popular Resistance: Private Resistance

The last type of resistance was more subtle and less visible, what might be called "private resistance," and it abounds in the diaries of home-front adults. Expressions of private resistance were almost always directed at government regulations that constricted the diarists' behavior and daily lives. For example, seventy-five-year-old Tamura Tsunejirō resented the impact that government restrictions were having on his diet, especially his supply of the rare and expensive *matsutake* mushrooms, normally sent to him in the fall.[44] Takahashi Aiko, the wife of a Tokyo doctor, also missed *matsutake* mushrooms: "We had a letter from Yanagii, who normally sends us *matsutake* mushrooms in the fall," she wrote. "He said that he was just going to send us some mushrooms, but the post office turned him away, explaining that they no longer handled such small packages."[45]

Private resistance was often directed at the local officials who enforced and monitored compliance with government regulations. The septuagenarian Tamura fumed in his diary when he was humiliated by an air-raid warden who noticed a light showing at his residence and confronted and belittled him, calling him "a senile old guy."[46] Takahashi Aiko was furious as well, as she absolutely could not stand the local officials who carried out the periodic inspections of her neighborhood. She didn't like the way they talked and strutted about, with "their pompous clothes and pompous faces."[47] Because the war had strained class relations, Takahashi's contempt for these officials may have had more to do with her sense of her superiority as a doctor's wife and less to do with government policy.[48]

Often the resistance was directed at those in the family who represented the official voice. Hamada Akiko, a young teacher who had evacuated to Saitama with her students, slept through an air-raid warning on a trip back to Tokyo.

I was sleepy, sleepy and could not get up, . . . the bombs were dropped nearby; we heard [them] near the Matsuzakaya [Department Store] in Ueno. Although we heard all that, getting up in the middle of the night was hard, and we cried out, "It would be OK to die in the end" and stayed in bed. In the morning when it got light, Mom scolded us and we were laughed at.[49]

Neighborhood association fire drill, July 1943. Photo courtesy of the *Mainichi shinbun*.

Takahashi and other women, especially those who were mothers, had doubts about the war for another reason: they had teenaged sons who might soon be drafted. As early as June 1943, Takahashi was depressed when she saw young men going off to war:

Today a procession of soldiers being sent off to war came up the hill in front of our house heading toward the train station. At the start of the war, these processions were accompanied by a band and waves of fluttering flags, and continued for one or two blocks. But now as the war intensifies day by day, our daily lives are more and more constrained, and we have fewer hands. In the processions that pass now, there still are people holding the well-used flags but also some not holding flags; the war songs lack power; and those seeing off the troops are relatives and neighborhood association people who had to show up. The processions have become rather pathetic affairs. They pass often because our house is close to the station. As I look at them, I have the wrenching thought that today once again, a funeral of living people is passing, and youngsters with their sleeves rolled up are being sent off to die.[50]

Hatano Isoko, a social psychologist who also had a teenaged son, cried when she saw the young recruits going off to war.

> When I caught sight of those young men, it made me very sad to see them so full of enthusiasm. Each one of them has a mother who has gone through untold pain in trying to bring up her children well. These women must now witness without protest their sons being led off to war. When I thought of the sorrow of these women, I could not hold back my tears.[51]

Interestingly, Hatano's teenaged son scolded her for this display of emotion.

Some mothers were distraught and some broke down when their sons were drafted right out of college, because they were sure that they would not be coming back (and they usually were right). When Kiyosawa Kiyoshi was visited by some old friends, the Obamas, he wrote in his diary: "Obama and his wife came to tea. He said Masa . . . [his son] had gone off to war and his wife cries every day."[52] And when the inevitable happened—when a son was killed—the mothers often were furious. When one grieving mother was told that she should visit the spirit of her deceased son at the Yasukuni Shrine for soldiers and sailors, she screamed, "When those who have lost a precious child go to the Yasukuni Shrine, they are made to squat on the white sand like beggars, and they have to bow their heads. I will never go to that stupid place!"[53]

Not surprisingly, the word "defeat" appears often in these women's diaries and is the most blatant expression of their reservations about the war and their government's policies. Takahashi first broached the subject of "defeat" after Japan's ally Italy surrendered in September 1943. Then in July 1944, when the Japanese lost the island of Saipan in the Mariana Islands, she wrote: "Hearing about our troops' collective suicide on Saipan makes us angry. We should have the courage, come hell or high water, to give up the fight."[54] Three months later, she admitted that the "specter of Japan's imminent defeat has appeared before our eyes!"[55] Yoshizawa Hisako mentioned Japan's defeat six times in her diary beginning in January 1945.[56]

The authorities took all reported rumors seriously.[57] In May 1944, Watanabe Tetsuyō, an economics professor at Tokyo University, got into trouble for saying, "Even in the announcements of the Imperial [Army] Headquarters, there are mistakes, and they speak of the ruin of the enemy but publish little or nothing about the injury inflicted on them." He even went on to predict that Germany would be defeated. For making these statements in public, Watanabe was convicted and sentenced to one year of penal servitude.[58] A year later, in the spring of 1945, schoolgirl Ariyama Sachi's father was taken into custody, questioned, and held for fourteen hours. After his release, he explained that "someone in our neighborhood had informed on him. Father had said that Saipan had fallen to the American forces, so things were serious. He had mentioned this in conversation at a farewell party for a soldier being sent to the front."[59] He was released after writing a long explanation, but the family was closely watched by the military police for the rest of the war.

The subject of defeat was even broached in rural communities.[60] In his January 1, 1945, diary entry, Tanaka Jingo recounted a conversation with fellow farmers that began with a discussion about black market prices and then turned to the war:

"How will it [the war] turn out?"
"I suspect that we won't be defeated."
"Will we be defeated? After our persevering and putting up with inconveniences in order to win?"
"But with the Tōjō cabinet resigning and Saipan being taken last July, it looks like we're giving up."

Five days later, after B-29s bombed nearby Saga city, Tanaka wrote in his diary, "America has aircraft this big! How can Japan win?" In March, he recorded a conversation he had had with his brother about trying to meet the government's production quotas. When his brother asked, "With the farm labor to cultivate the fields disappearing, what are people with fields to do?" Tanaka replied: "Ain't that the case? At the moment we're at war, and there is no fertilizer, no resources, no harvesting of rice, but the government is still a stickler about deliveries. Even if we cultivate our fields, we can't meet the quotas, simply because we lack the labor. When the war is brought to an end, and the world calms down, we will be able to cultivate our fields."[61]

Two and a half weeks later, at their Itsukai meeting, Tanaka and his cronies had the following conversation:

"The Koiso cabinet probably resigned because with the taking of Okinawa, the war will become a huge problem."
"If Okinawa is taken, it's all over."[62]

All the talk about defeat is telling, and it also was dangerous, since writing about "defeat," even in one's own diary, could result in imprisonment.[63]

Sometimes "private resistance" became quite public. This happened when a detachment of military men was sent to remove some of the eighty-four thousand bodies left in the wake of a devastating Allied firebombing raid on Tokyo on the evening of March 10, 1945. They were confronted by a woman who shouted: "You there, soldiers, how do you feel about all these people? Can you look at them?" Another woman had a brief exchange with an officer touring a burned-out area of Tokyo: "This all happened because of you military men! What's the point of your coming here to look at this?"[64] These public expressions of powerful private feelings, uttered at some personal risk, were clearly spontaneous and might be regarded as examples of "spontaneous acts of resistance." In any case, the anger of these two women helps us understand the letters that the widow in Shizuoka sent to the prime minister and others.

Did Resistance Make a Difference?

Popular resistance clearly existed in wartime Japan. Most ordinary Japanese had reservations about their government's policies, and many actively resisted the power that government agencies exercised over their daily lives and devised tactics to thwart the small army of officials and police. Their resistance assumed different forms. First, it expressed itself as visceral, and often violent, reactions to the rules and regulations that affected them. Those offended reacted to the rules and regulations that deprived them of small pleasures: cigarettes, saké, seasonal delicacies such as *matsutake* mushrooms, and sweetfish. They resisted their neighborhood associations' demands that they see off conscripts from their communities, that they line up for the distribution of food and other commodities, that they rehearse fire drills, and so forth. And they complained constantly about the ever-dwindling supplies of food. Popular resistance also assumed the form of heartfelt concerns about government policy and military strategy, concerns that became huge anxieties after Italy and Germany surrendered. Resistance also came in the form of hopes that "defeat" or even "surrender" would bring an end to the privations, suffering, and carnage. Finally, popular resistance also assumed the form of strong emotional reactions to war news like the reports of the collective suicides of Japanese troops at Attu, Saipan, Iwo Jima, and other battle sites and, in the last year of the war, to the news of the "special attacks" by navy and army pilots flying into enemy ships.

In the end, however, most Japanese did what their government urged them to do; namely, to prepare for the "decisive battle" that would take place when the enemy invaded the Japanese home islands in the fall of 1945. Most realized that this might mean the end, their end, and they made the necessary arrangements, telling each member of the family what he or she was to do when the Allies invaded. This usually involved fathers breaking the news to their sons that father would take care of their mother and sisters but that they would be on their own. Most Japanese were willing and ready to defend their homeland against the invaders: village women practiced with bamboo spears; teenaged girls pledged to kill at least one of the enemy before they died; children practiced throwing balls at targets in preparation for the day when they would be lobbing hand grenades at the enemy; male teachers in the provinces learned to fly explosive-laden gliders into the enemy invasion force. And most Japanese—or at least the adults—understood that they would probably die in the process and become part of the "Grand Suicide of the One Hundred Million," which army men had been talking about as early as January 1945. In the end, therefore, most Japanese, despite their resistance to the wartime government, its agents, and its policies, accepted their fate.

8

The "Jeweled Sound"

The war ended as dramatically as it began. On Tuesday, August 14, 1945, a radio broadcast informed the country of "an important announcement at noon tomorrow." At dawn on Wednesday, August 15, 118 American carrier–based aircraft launched a final series of attacks, triggering air-raid warnings in the Tokyo area.[1] At 7:21 A.M., the Japanese were told that the emperor himself would make a special announcement at noon.[2] Most were sure he would talk about the war, but many expected him to ask them to redouble their efforts until "the war was won." One Tokyo grandmother was overheard promising her grandchildren that "if the war ends, I'll make you bean-covered rice cakes with real, sweet sugar."[3] But a few did know ahead of time what the emperor was going to say.

Shortly before noon, Japanese gathered around their radios. Takahashi Aiko's family had lunch early and then gathered in the living room of their Tokyo home. Her brother-in-law "Mr. Iwase, who worked at the neighborhood bank, came over during his lunch break because he wanted to hear the broadcast on our radio," Takahashi remembered.[4] Yoshizawa Hisako went outside onto the street fifteen minutes before noon to hear the broadcast on the neighborhood's public address system. "I went out," she wrote in her diary that night, "because I wanted to hear the emperor's broadcast in the street. Half the crowd seemed to understand what was about to happen, [and] half had puzzled looks on their faces, looks that said they expected the worst."[5]

Since many rural communities had only one radio, it was placed in a central spot, and the villagers sat or knelt in a circle around it. Ōmori Takuji was an eighteen-year-old who had been mobilized

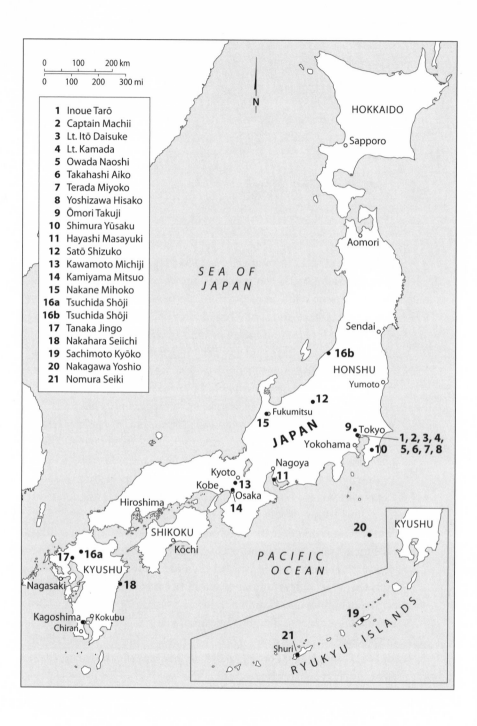

1	Inoue Tarō
2	Captain Machii
3	Lt. Itō Daisuke
4	Lt. Kamada
5	Owada Naoshi
6	Takahashi Aiko
7	Terada Miyoko
8	Yoshizawa Hisako
9	Ōmori Takuji
10	Shimura Yūsaku
11	Hayashi Masayuki
12	Satō Shizuko
13	Kawamoto Michiji
14	Kamiyama Mitsuo
15	Nakane Mihoko
16a	Tsuchida Shōji
16b	Tsuchida Shōji
17	Tanaka Jingo
18	Nakahara Seiichi
19	Sachimoto Kyōko
20	Nakagawa Yoshio
21	Nomura Seiki

0 100 200 km
0 100 200 300 mi

N

HOKKAIDO

Sapporo

Aomori

SEA OF
JAPAN

SENDAI

16b

HONSHU

Yumoto

12

Fukumitsu

15

JAPAN

9 Tokyo

Yokohama

10

1, 2, 3, 4,
5, 6, 7, 8

Nagoya

Kyoto

11

Kobe

13

Osaka

14

Hiroshima

SHIKOKU

Kōchi

20

KYUSHU

17 16a

KYUSHU

PACIFIC
OCEAN

Nagasaki

18

Kagoshima Kokubu
Chiran

19

21

Shuri

RYUKYU ISLANDS

for work at a munitions factory in Saitama Prefecture, just north of Tokyo. He and other student workers were informed shortly before the broadcast, and "an old radio, the only one in the unit," he remembered, "was placed at the center of an open space."[6] Kawamoto Michiji, a farmer, was doing war work at a site in Takatsuki, southwest of Kyoto, when he was told "to gather in open area in front of headquarters. At noon there will be an imperial broadcast."[7] That night he wrote in his diary: "We wondered what kind of important broadcast it would be. In England the king makes frequent broadcasts, but this was unprecedented in our country. I thought it would be a rescript declaring war on the Soviet Union. But unconditional surrender—I thought no one should have imagined that. At 11:30 we climbed a knoll and assembled in front of the main building."[8]

Kyushu farmer Tanaka Jingo wrote in his diary the night before the surrender: "I wondered what kind of broadcast it would be and couldn't help feeling uneasy." He described the hours before the broadcast:

Today, too, the weather has been fine since morning. I was irrigating the terraced fields when [I ran into] my friend Mazaki Kyōichi, who was returning from his fields. "Hey, Jingo," he said, with a worried look on his face, "they say there'll be an important broadcast at noon today. What sort of broadcast do you suppose it will be? I wonder if, by chance, it will say that we have surrendered."

"I'm thinking that, too, because right now Japan can't advance against the Americans. Maybe they surrendered, I don't know." Muttering, "This is worrisome," we parted.

At Sachio's house to the east of us, they were having Carpenter Shigekazu use the concrete fence posts in the small garden to strengthen the air-raid shelter.

Yonekichi from next door also was also worried about today's serious broadcast and said that the special announcement from Imperial Headquarters at eleven o'clock simply repeated: "Today at noon there will be an important broadcast. Because it will be a broadcast of the Jeweled Sound of His Imperial Highness, all citizens must listen to it."

When Sachiko asked, "What sort of broadcast will it be? Our radio has poor reception, so maybe I'll go to Kayo-san's across the street to listen to it?" Kayo-san graciously said, "Sure, that's fine. Everyone, please come to listen [on our radio]." When we got there, Heitarō, Father, and the children, after a hurried lunch, had come to hear the broadcast. We sat in a circle in front of the radio, impatient for the noon hour. Right at the stroke of twelve, there was an announcement.[9]

Most Japanese had never heard the emperor's voice—the "jeweled sound" (*gyokuon*)—until that moment.

Takahashi Aiko remembered: "Noon arrived. I don't remember who got up first, but everyone rose to their feet in front of the radio. The emperor read the surrender proclamation without feeling, gravely and in a trembling voice. As each word and phrase was etched on my heart, my eyes got quite warm, tears welled up, and I had to wipe them with a handkerchief."[10]

Yoshizawa Hisako described the minutes leading up to the broadcast and then the broadcast itself:

Five minutes before the broadcast, then four, and as the noon hour approached, people gathered. They paid their respects to the emperor, removed their hats, and said, "Please let us hear . . ."

A siren went off, and we heard the emperor's voice. People silently bowed their heads, and in an instant, the streets were dead quiet, and various thoughts ran through my head.

Word by word, the emperor's voice reached us, and tears ran down our cheeks. My only thought was that from now on we would have to work as hard as we could so that our fellow Japanese would not fight among themselves.[11]

Terada Miyoko, a Japan Women's University student who had been mobilized for war work and had been sent first to a factory on the outskirts of Tokyo and then to the Imperial Headquarters in central Tokyo, recounted what happened next:

At long last, the great announcement that the war has ended was issued. Today at noon the emperor broadcast it in his own voice to our 100 million countrymen. It was awe-inspiring. It was the first time in the eternal, 3,000-year history of the country [that we had heard our emperor speak]. On August 6 the enemy dropped an atomic bomb on the city of Hiroshima. I understand that the magnitude of the damage pained His Majesty. The military war has ended, but the next war has begun. This time, we [students] will become the warriors and will have to fight. Hearing the Great Announcement at noon, we were moved to tears by the pain of it all and by His Majesty's compassion. I just cried.[12]

Like Terada, Inoue Tarō was a teenager who had been mobilized for war work, and he was at home in central Tokyo when, at nine in the evening on August 14, he heard there would be a broadcast at noon. The tenseness in

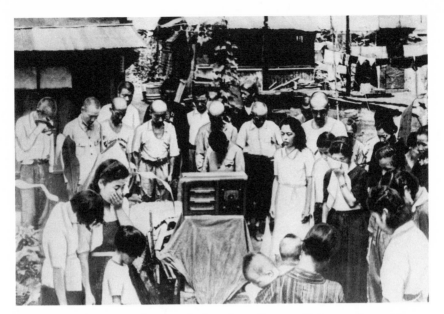

Listening to the emperor's surrender broadcast, Yotsuya, Tokyo, on August 15, 1945. Photo courtesy of the *Mainichi shinbun*.

the announcer's voice said it would be important. He remembered thinking it would be about the end of the war. "Ah! It's all over," he wrote in his diary on the day of the surrender announcement. "But the less visible war, the fight to rebuild the ancestral country has only just begun. Cry! Let's cry until we can't any longer. Later we'll probably see the outpouring of a new power."[13]

Kamiyama Mitsuo, who worked in the Munitions Planning Department Office in Osaka, remembered, "At noon, because there was going to be an important radio broadcast, we were ordered to assemble in the hall on the eighth floor of Mitsukoshi [Department Store]. His Majesty, with his jeweled sound, honored us with an imperial rescript announcing that Japan had surrendered unconditionally to the United States and England."[14]

Outside the major cities, the reception of the broadcast was poor, full of static. Hayashi Masayuki, a teacher from Nagoya who was living with fifty-four third-grade boys in a temple in Minami Kasuya on the Chita Peninsula in central Japan, described the day of the surrender:

By August 15 we were nearly at the limit of our endurance. We had no idea when the war would end. It was a hot day. I heard the Imperial Rescript on the ending of the war in a scratchy radio broadcast. I told

Listening to the emperor's surrender broadcast, Yuasa Battery Company, Osaka, on August 15, 1945. Photo courtesy of the *Mainichi shinbun*.

myself that the war had ended but had no real sense of it. That day I went to a meeting. By the time I was on the way back to the temple, the sun had set, and I was ambling along the country road with a few other teachers, dragging my heavy legs. Suddenly a lamp was turned on in the second floor of a large house ahead of us.

"Hey, that's bright. I guess the war has really ended." The person lit by the light wasn't wearing the familiar work pants and was an older woman who wore a dress. There was no blackout covering on the lamp, and it shone brightly through the open window. We chorused as one, "The war has really ended. We can take a bath. Now we can go home."

My steps grew light. We sang our usual song of the mountain cedar at a faster tempo and with a lighter beat than usual.[15]

Kawamoto Michiji, the farmer from Osaka, described one person's response to the surrender announcement:

The August 15 newspaper. There is someone who took until ten o'clock in the evening to read it. He read it from the first page to the last. He is usually busy and hardly reads the newspaper at all. In many households, [though,] that day's newspaper was used, even in the toilet. This person who recognized that Japan's fate was his own let this sad fate seep in until ten in the evening. There probably has never been a newspaper that related such dramatic news.[16]

Tanaka Jingo wrote a long account of what happened after he and his family and friends heard the surrender broadcast:

Right at the stroke of twelve, there was a broadcast: "Imperial Headquarters Announcement. Today at noon we formally accepted the Potsdam Declaration."

Just when we were wondering "what sort of thing a formal acceptance of the Potsdam Declaration was," we were told that "right now there will be a broadcast of the jeweled sound of His Imperial Highness."

The high-pitched, unclear, and faltering words and the somber tone made it clear that he was informing us of the defeat. As we listened, our chests got warm, the women suppressed tears, and we could hear sobbing voices.

The jeweled sound broadcast ended. Although we did not hear the word "surrender," we realized that this was a rescript informing us of that.

Our lives have been difficult and tragic for nine [sic] years since the Sino-Japanese incident. We persevered until today in order to win the war, and now we hear the sad announcement of [our] defeat. The Great Feelings [the emperor] bore responsibility for this defeat and transmitted the sad announcement of it to the country. The emperor was pitiful.

Kayo's sad response was simply, "We've been defeated."

Even the usually cheerful Heitarō had a pained look on his face and muttered, "Jingo-san, Japan finally has been defeated," and Father, who looked stunned, chimed in, "Now that we have been defeated, what will happen?"

There was no change in the way we felt: we all felt the horror of being defeated and the inexpressible horror of being the citizens of a defeated country. What will happen now, I wondered. And as for the broadcast we came so eagerly to hear, we heard the sad announcement of the defeat. I thought now that Japan has surrendered, it will be tough going from now on. Everyone went home without saying a word.

I worried about how Masahito's unit was doing, and as far as Heitarō, Tokuo, and Kayo were concerned, the war had caused Inao's death in battle, and I sensed that today's announcement of the defeat made them feel more regret than sadness.

Sachiko asked, "How is older brother Masahito doing?" and worried the most about him.

"When a serviceman is victorious in war, he returns triumphantly, but when he loses and is in enemy territory, he becomes a prisoner. Masahito has probably become a prisoner."
"So when will he come home?"
"I don't know when he'll come home, but at least he won't die in the war."
"But I worry that he won't be coming home soon," added Sachiko.

In the village that afternoon, not a single person was out and about. The village was enveloped not by quiet but by fear, and a dark silence.

I went to check the water in the terraced and paddy fields. Sachio and the carpenter who had been working furiously before noon on the air-raid shelter were deflated by the surrender rescript and were depressed.

"Sachio-san, the air-raid shelter is history."
"Everything and all things are over."
When evening arrived, both Chio and Sachiko were still in a daze, and neither did anything in the kitchen. When dinner[time] came, [one of them asked], "Now that Japan's been defeated by America, what will happen?"

"This means that because Japan surrendered, America will decide on policies, and they probably will be pretty strict."
"Scary, ain't it?"

That evening Chio asked, "What will happen to our savings in the union and the bank?"
"That's what I'm thinking about too."[17]

Tanaka reported that he could not get to sleep that night.

Listening to the emperor's surrender broadcast, rural community. Photo courtesy of the *Mainichi shinbun*.

Sachimoto Kyōko, a sixteen-year-old who lived on one of the Amami Islands south of Kyushu, was bathing her younger sister when two soldiers came rushing by. "Where is the postmaster's house?" they asked. She described what happened next:

About to answer, "My uncle is the postmaster. We live in the same house," I held my tongue. Had my uncle done something wrong? My body shook.

Running up to my uncle, the soldiers claimed, "You're a traitor. You have spread an outrageous rumor. We can't let you live. Can't you tell that the radio broadcast was an enemy plot?"

Slap! Slap! They hit my uncle's face so hard he fell down. Clinging to one of the soldier's legs, I wailed, "I'm sorry. I'm sorry. Forgive my uncle, forgive him please."

Lying face down, my uncle didn't say a word. I pounded on his back with both fists and shouted, "Uncle, did you really hear that the war has ended on the radio? Aren't we supposed to fight until the day of victory? I hate you, Uncle, I hate you."

"We'll take you in tomorrow. Consider yourself dead." With that, the soldiers left. That night no one in the village talked about the war's end. My uncle kept his silence. He didn't answer no matter what he was asked. Pressing his hand against his swollen cheeks, he straightened out the post office documents and his own belongings. All night long, I prayed that my uncle wouldn't be taken away.[18]

Apparently the soldiers never came back.

The reactions of the two soldiers who beat up Sachimoto Kyōko's uncle were typical. Many servicemen took the surrender announcement hard.[19] Nakahara Seiichi was a science student at the Number Five High School in Kumamoto when he was drafted in the middle of July 1945. He was assigned to a unit defending Birō Island in Shibushi Bay, sixty miles southeast of Kagoshima, where he and his comrades practiced antitank tactics that involved "carrying mock explosives and lying down on the tiny beach to be overrun by the enemy tanks" that were expected to land there. Many years later, he remembered that the men in his unit had different reactions to the surrender broadcast:

There were three different reactions to the defeat in our unit. The first group was relieved that the war was over. I was one of them. The second group burned with desire for revenge—but not revenge against the enemy. Now that the war was over, the officers were just men like everyone else. The soldiers who had been bullied by their superior officers now started to bully them back. The third group wanted to return to the mainland as soon as possible and desert. As soon as we landed on the mainland, they deserted en masse.[20]

Shimura Yūsaku was drafted in July 1945 and sent to "work on defensive positions" on the Pacific Ocean side of the Bōsō Peninsula, southeast of Tokyo.

Our orders for 14 August were to go to the seacoast, which was overgrown with reeds and weeds, to dig foxholes from which rifles and machine guns could be fired. On the fifteenth, we soldiers heard about the emperor's broadcast when we returned to the houses where we were billeted.

On the nineteenth, our commander ordered all of us ranked above noncommissioned officer to gather at the primary school. He said, "Now, I will teach you how to commit *seppuku*. Is there anyone here that knows how to commit *seppuku*?"

For an instant we held our breaths, steeped in doom. A captain went to the teaching platform and, taking off his uniform and undershirt, grabbed his saber with both hands and pressed its tip against his belly.

"Wait!" the commander said, stopping him. The entire company took a breath and relaxed our tensed-up shoulders in relief. The next day we were ordered to transfer to a different location, which we reached by night train. I was the paymaster. Borrowing the bathhouse, I handed out the final pay by candlelight.[21]

At the end of the war, Nakagawa Yoshio was one of twenty boys stationed in the southern Ogasawara Islands, Japan's easternmost line of defense in the western Pacific, which was six hundred miles from Tokyo. They knew nothing about the emperor's broadcast.

Our languid vacation on this southern island was shattered on August 15 by a huge seaplane that looked like a motor-powered sailboat with wings. Circling over us at such a low altitude that we could see the ruddy faces of the crew, they told us in English through a powerful microphone, "Japanese boys, the war is over." Whether as a warning or a joke, they dropped a few bombs, causing all the frightened birds on the island to fly up like so many leaves blown off branches in the wind. Restraining my friend's rash attempt at countering with a small rifle, we rushed barefoot down to the beach of sharp coral fragments and hid in a natural cave. Our faces were darker than coconut leaves. After that we saw daily the silver wings of the bombers glittering against the pure white cumulonimbus clouds and deep blue sky as large formations of them headed for the mainland. Gazing up at them naked, I came to the realization that Japan had fallen.[22]

These servicemen were relatively lucky. Others, not aware that the war had ended, fought on. Imperial Japanese Army Private Nomura Seiki was one of those stragglers.[23] He had survived the Allied invasion of Okinawa and was hiding with many other stragglers in caves and bunkers south of Shuri, long after the fighting officially ended on June 27, 1945. On September 12, pacification teams made contact with his group, and then the next day they brought evidence that the war had ended: a copy of the emperor's surrender rescript and recent issues of the *Asahi*, *Mainichi*, and *Yomiuri* newspapers. Nomura described what happened next:

The seven of us stared silently at the evidence; its meaning was all too clear. I felt as though my whole body had suddenly collapsed and I was being attacked by a dark loneliness.

Then after recovering this feeling of loneliness, I was assailed by an inexpressible anger. Who or what in the world was the object of my anger? I couldn't say.

I stamped my feet on the floor like a child and screamed words of anger. I felt the urge to run like a cannonball right into the center of the American camp.

In the end, even as I was attacked by these violent feelings, I agreed with everyone else that we should surrender.[24]

He and eleven other stragglers surrendered the next day.

Many servicemen took to heart *The Field Service Code*'s command to "not give up under any circumstances" and committed suicide.[25] Some are reported to have killed Allied POWs to keep them from testifying about war crimes. Terada Miyoko recorded in her diary the speeches that officers made to the civilian workers at Imperial Headquarters two days earlier before the emperor's surrender announcement, speeches that give us insight into military men's reactions to the "jeweled sound." The first speech was by a Lieutenant Kamaga, who announced:

It has come to pass that the situation has changed radically. In view of this, our job has become even more important. To fulfill our responsibility, it has been decided that we will evacuate. But those who come with us must forget everything and must be individuals who have made the great decision that enables them together with us, to unite life and death. Think dispassionately about this and give us your answer before you return home today. This is definitely a difficult path. We probably will have to work for about a month without eating and will find ourselves in a situation where all must die. You must be the one to make this decision.[26]

The second speech was by a Lieutenant Itō Daisuke, who disagreed with the first speaker's call for the civilians to join the military men:

I would like all of you to remain behind. Dying is what we will do. In this war, the end has been announced by a military power. But if it is correctly tied to spirit, we will be able to create a truly new Japan. In the "thought war," women will fight, and the task of those who remain behind will be to construct a new, moral Japan and, in turn, the world. Soldiers will fight to the absolute end and commit *gyokusai* and display the spirit of Lord Kusunoki. Women have an obligation to survive, even if they are cruelly treated as slaves, and to pass on the Japanese spirit to the next generation. Dying is the easier thing to do. Consider living under the ugly enemy. It will be harrowing and painful. There is no question that you will be treated as slaves, but because our opponents are a civilized country, you probably will not be treated as slaves forever. Although Japan has prevailed by force since the Sino-Japanese War, it was defeated in the thought war. Even though we have been defeated by force, we must prevail in the thought war. It will not be easy to live though the dark ages and to transmit our culture to the next age. But if this is not done, there will not be an age when the Japanese people are truly awakened. It is the task assigned to women to see that all our citizens wake up spiritually and create a moral world.[27]

The third speech was by a Captain Machii, who came right to the point: "The male war has ended. From now on, it is a female war. In order for the Japanese people to endure in perpetuity, those who survive will have to bear all sorts of hardships to carry this out. We will commit *gyokusai*. We will die believing in a future Japan."[28]

At 1:00 P.M. on August 15, Terada and the other mobilized students working at Imperial Headquarters were released from service. That night she wrote in her diary, "Our efforts were not rewarded. We are full of the feeling that everything has been destroyed and of the pain [of realizing] that we have completely wasted our time."[29] What is important to note is that civilians like Terada were released from the interlocking wartime discourses that had been pointing to a "decisive battle" and the "death of the One Hundred Million."

The evacuated schoolchildren took the surrender hard. Nine-year-old Nakane Mihoko heard the news on August 16, and that night she wrote in her diary:

Today at breakfast we heard very sad news from Miyaji-sensei. At long last, Japan was forced to surrender unconditionally to the Soviet-American-British alliance. It was because of the atomic bomb. On August 15, His Majesty said, "We have endured hardships and sadness, but we have been defeated by that atomic bomb, and all Japanese could be injured or killed. It is too pitiful for even one of my dear subjects to be killed. I do not care what happens to me." We heard that he then took off the white gloves he was wearing and began to cry out loud. We cried out loud too. Watch out, you terrible Americans and British! I will be sure to seek revenge. I thought to myself, I must be more responsible than I have been.[30]

Satō Shizuko, who had been urging her parents back in Tokyo to endure "for the sake of the country," wrote in a postcard sent to them on August 17: "I read your letter and it's wonderful that you are fine. Mother, did you hear the important announcement at noon on the fifteenth? What do you think of it? I am truly grateful for the Great Heart [the emperor's compassion], and I also listened intently. It was horrible, horrible, and unbearable. But we will surely recover. And Naoyuki [her older brother] is probably raring to go."[31]

Two days later, she sent a birthday postcard to her grandmother on which she wrote, "Grandmother, congratulations! Today is your birthday, isn't it? Grandma, how old are you this year? I really want to see you, but it will be a little longer. You were probably really exhausted by the despicable enemy's air raids, weren't you? At long last Japan has surrendered. We will be sure to get revenge."[32]

Owada Kazuko's father wrote to his evacuated daughter four days after the surrender announcement: "The long, long war has ended. Japan was, in the end, defeated. This is really regrettable. Kazuko and your fellow little citizens, please become great individuals and make Japan the kind of great country that it once was."[33]

No one was more disappointed by the surrender, however, than the special attack pilots still alive at the time of the emperor's broadcast. Tsuchida Shōji, the young army pilot stationed at Tachiarai Airbase, had been waiting for nearly two weeks for the order to fly off on a special attack. At eleven o'clock on the morning of August 15, the Sixty-Sixth Combat Squadron's headquarters issued the order to attack:

Cape Sata, 280° 280 kilometers 400-ship enemy task force proceeding north.
  The order to attack is issued. Attack scheduled for 20:00 tonight, with bomb attached. After government-issued articles and personal belongings are returned, stand by.[34]

Tsuchida was waiting to leave when he got news of the surrender, which he called "the height of sadness."[35] The next day he wrote in his diary:

I feel the evanescence of the fate of defeat. The eyes of locals seem to be appealing to us for something, but the truth is that we have been stained with the stigma of defeat. Who is to blame? Not servicemen, and not our countrymen. All 100 million of us were at fault. We were not sufficiently self-aware. We lacked power. None should be blamed for the defeat.

The Great Lord's Sacred Decision was absolute. We had to swallow our tears and listen intently. For a whole day I had no hope. Not to mention the pain of simply passing the time idly. When I think about it, ours was a strange fate: a state that was an imperial country for 3,000 years is not a state today.[36]

Two days later, Tsuchida left Tachiarai on the 5:55 P.M. train:

The train was chock-full of returning servicemen and was unbearably hot. I changed trains at Kido Station, passed across the problematic Kanmon Strait without incident, and spent a whole night on the Osaka-bound train. I couldn't get to sleep, and the air was extremely foul.

In the train my thoughts raced back. . . . That day when I left my home village in such high spirits. The glorious Jinbu Special Attack Unit members whose bodies had carried the expectations of the nation were now hollow figures tainted with defeat and returning at the end of their journey.[37]

The next day, Tsuchida arrived at Osaka and boarded the train for Niigata. "The trains were as full as ever," he wrote, "and I was sleepy and famished. Fought off my hunger with salt and water." He also was struck by how pathetic those who wanted to board the train were. After changing trains at Naoetsu and Nagaoka, Tsuchida arrived at Niitsu Station in southeastern Niigata city. Once there, he looked up a friend of his squadron commander and had dinner and a bath. He left the house at 2:00 A.M. and started walking home. He reached home at 5:00 A.M. "My younger brothers and sisters got out of bed and were surprised," he wrote in his diary that night. "They immediately called my uncle and Sakai Kiyoko to announce my homecoming."[38]

As happy as Tsuchida was to be home, he quickly realized that returning servicemen "bearing the dishonor of defeat" were not warmly welcomed and that "feelings for him were not particularly cordial." Nonetheless, family friends and his buddies were happy to see him, and he thanked them for everything they had done for his family during his absence and explained his return. Acutely aware of how others saw him, Tsuchida vowed not to do anything that would "sully the purity" of his relationship with others and closed his diary with the words, "I must not rush things."[39]

The End of the War

The emperor's surrender announcement brought an end to the colossal destruction and death that the war had visited on Japan, its colonies, and occupied areas. Nearly two and a half million Japanese perished in the war, more than two million servicemen and three hundred thousand civilians. Most Japanese never imagined that the war would end in defeat. Many refused to believe what they had heard at noon on August 15, and some chose to take their own lives as a final act of loyalty to their ruler, their sacred cause, and their deceased comrades.

Nine high-ranking military men killed themselves in the weeks after the surrender. General Anami Korechika, the war minister, committed *seppuku* on the evening of August 15; Admiral Ōnishi Takijirō, creator of the first navy special attack units, did the same a day later, leaving a suicide note addressed to the men who gave their lives and their families. General Tanaka Seiichi had been asked by Anami to maintain order in the Tokyo area at the time of the surrender. Tanaka did this and then shot himself on August 24. General Sugiyama Hajime, war minister in the Koiso Cabinet (July 1944–April 1945) shot himself on September 12, and his wife, Keiko, committed *seppuku* the next day, dressed resplendently in white.[40] Others killed themselves rathern than face prosecution for war crimes.[41]

The responses of lower-ranking servicemen to the end of the war differed, depending on where they were on August 15, whether in the home islands or overseas. Their responses also reflected the values, sensibilities, and even personalities of their officers and their relationships with the enlisted men they commanded. Although the officers often had to persuade their men to stop fighting, sometimes the enlisted men defied their officers' orders to keep fighting. In addition, when hearing that the war was over, many enlisted men turned on their officers to vent their long-suppressed resentment and anger.

In contrast, most of the adults on the home front readily accepted the surrender. They had been driven to the edge of physical and mental collapse and were too hungry, tired, or weak to resist. Most of them also recognized that the defeat was inevitable, and accordingly, they began to talk about fighting the war in another form and about reconstruction. However, a few chose to commit suicide to demonstrate their loyalty to the emperor.[42] Perhaps the luckiest survivors of the war were the teenagers who were mobilized to work in the factories that were continually being bombed or who were sent to serve in the coastal units that would have been the first line of defense against the Allied invaders. Finally, the "jeweled sound" saved many thousands of evacuated children from themselves.

akebi	fruit (*Akebia quinata*) eaten in autumn
barnyard millet	*hie* (*Echinochloa utilis*)
banzai	celebratory cheer that means, literally, "ten thousand years"
bentō	portable meal consisting usually of cooked rice, entrées, and pickles
bog rhubarb	*fuki* (*Petasites japonicus*)
bracken fern	*warabi* (*Pteridium aquilinum* var. *latiusculum*)
brown rice	*genmai* (*Oryza sativa*)
Chinese cabbage	*hakusai* (*Brassica campestris* var. *amplexicaulis*)
chirashi sushi	type of sushi that mixes cooked or raw ingredients with vinegared rice
chub mackerel	*saba* (*Scomber japonicus*)
Classic of Changes	Chinese classic dating from the first millennium BCE and originally used for divination
cutlass fish	*tachiuo* (*Trichiurus lepturus*)
daizu-iri	dish made with soybeans
Date Masamune (1567–1636)	the lord of Sendai Domain in northern Japan
dropwort	*seri* (*Oenanthe javanica*)
fava bean	*soramame* (*Vicia faba*)
fiddlehead ferns	*kusa sotetsu* (*Matteuccia struthiopteris*)
flowering ferns	*zenmai* (*Osmunda japonica*)
freshwater eel	*unagi* (*Anguilla japonica*)
furikake	topping made of toasted *nori* and sesame seeds, dried fish, and salt
giant white radish	*daikon* (*Raphanus sativus*)
gizzard shad	*konoshiro* (*Clupanodon punctatus*); juveniles called *kohada* in Tokyo
Great Thanksgiving Festival	*daijōsai*; performed by new emperors on the occasion of the New Rice Ritual
gyokusai	literally, "shattering the jewel"; collective suicide
Hachiman	a god who is regarded as the protector of warriors, Japan, and the Japanese people
Hagakure	literally, "within hidden leaves"; a warrior classic compiled in 1716 by two warriors from Saga Domain in Kyushu: Yamamoto Tsunetomo (1659–1719) and Tashiro Tsuramoto (1678–1748)

hamachi	juvenile yellowtail
herring roe	*kazunoko*; roe of *nishin* (*Clupea pallasii*), typically salted or dried
horsetail	*tsukushi*; shoot of the *sugina* (*Equisetum arvense*)
iri-mame	fried and lightly salted peas or soybeans
kaidashi	to buy food directly from farmers
kama-age	one-pot dish
kami-shibai	a type of portable theater that used picture cutouts
kanme	unit of weight, approximately 8.3 pounds
kanten	confection made with jellied agar-agar (*Gelidium amansii*)
karasu mame	"crow's beans"
karintō	a confection dating from the Heian period
kasuzuke	pickled in saké lees
kelp	*konbu* (*Laminaria* spp.)
kinako	roasted soybean flour
kinton	sweet confection of chestnuts and sweet potato
kiriboshi daikon	dried, thinly cut strips of giant white radish
kokutai	national polity; a concept first articulated by scholars associated with the Mito Domain and used to define the modern Japanese state
konnyaku	tuber (*Amorphophallus rivieri*, var. *konjac*) made into a gelatinous substance added to simmered and one-pot dishes
kumi	an organization like the neighborhood association
Kusunoki Masashige (1294–1336)	a warrior whose loyalty to the reigning emperor is legendary
lotus root	*renkon* (*Nelumbo nucifera*)
mackerel	*aji* (*Trachurus japonicus*)
mame gohan	soybean rice
Matsuo Bashō (1644–1694)	a seventeenth-century poet famous for his haiku
matsutake	a prized mushroom (*Tricholoma matsutake*) picked in fall
miso	fermented paste made with soybeans and either barley or rice
mitsumame	popular dish made with sweet beans, fruit, and jellied agar-agar
mizuame	confection made from glucose syrup
mochi	steamed glutinous rice that has been pounded and shaped into small, round cakes

monpe	a type of cotton trousers traditionally worn by farm women that the wartime government encouraged women to wear
mugwort	*yomogi* (*Artemisia princeps*)
mushroom	*kinoko*
namasu	vinegared dish made with seafood or meat
natto	fermented soybeans
niboshi	dried fish, usually anchovies, used to make stock
nishime	simmered stew-like dish typically served at New Year's
nori	laver (*Porphyra* spp.)
ohagi	type of rice cake covered with paste made with sugar and *azuki* bean (*Vigna angularis*) or potato
okara	tofu lees
omiyage	gifts brought by travelers and visitors
onigiri	cooked rice formed into small balls or triangles
porridge	*kayu*; typically made with rice
pumpkin squash	*kabocha* (*Cucurbita moschata*)
red beans	*azuki* (*Vigna angularis*)
red-bean rice	*sekihan*; a celebratory dish made with cooked rice and red beans
rocamble	*asatsuki* (*Allium* ledebourianum); a kind of chive
sandfish	*hatahata* (*Arctoscopus japonicus*)
sansai	literally, "mountain vegetables"; wild herbs and plants gathered in spring
satori	Zen Buddhist enlightenment
Senjinkun	*Field Service Code*, issued to all servicemen beginning in 1941
seppuku	ritual suicide
shi	poem
shinigurui	frenzied death; described in *Hagakure*
short-necked clams	*asari* (*Tapes philippinarum*)
sōmen	thin wheat noodles
sōsu	shorted form of *usutā sōsu*; Japanese variety of Worcestershire sauce
stone parsley	*mitsuba* (*Cryptotaenia japonica*)
striped marlin	*nairage* (*Tetrapturus audax*)
suiton	wheat dumplings; served in soup
sweetfish	*ayu* (*Plecoglossus altivelis*); small freshwater fish caught in summer
sweet potato	*satsuma imo* (*Ipomoea batatas*); brought to Japan in 1597
tai-atari	literally, "body-crashing"; a tactic in traditional Japanese fencing that has the attacker moving directly against his opponent

tangerine	*mikan* (*Citrus unshiu*)
tanka	traditional thirty-one-syllable poem
taro	*satoimo* (*Colocasia esculenta*)
tatami	mats made of straw and rush and edged with a cloth border; used in traditional Japanese rooms
tatsukuri	dish made with sardines, fried in soy sauce with sesame seeds
tororo konbu	dish made with kelp; also natural variety of *konbu* (*Kjellmaniella aniella*)
tsubo	unit of measure (3.9 square yards)
tsukemono	vegetables pickled with salt, vinegar, saké lees, miso, or rice bran
tsukudani	salty-sweet preserve made by simmering fish, shellfish, or vegetables with soy sauce, sugar, and sweet saké
udo	Japanese asparagus (*Aralia cordata*)
udon	thick white noodle made with wheat
umeboshi	salt-pickled Japanese apricot (*Prunus mume* [*Armeniaca* mume])
unagi	freshwater eel (*Anguilla japonica*)
wrapping cloth	*furoshiki*
yamaudo	wild version of *udo*
yellowtail	*buri* (*Seriola quinqueradiata*)
zōni	traditional rice cake soup served at New Year's
zōsui	rice gruel

Introduction

1. Samuel Hideo Yamashita, *Leaves from an Autumn of Emergencies: Selections from the Wartime Diaries of Ordinary Japanese* (Honolulu: University of Hawai'i Press, 2005).

2. See Alf Lüdtke, ed., *The History of Everyday Life: Reconstructing Historical Experiences and Ways of Life*, trans. William Templer (Princeton, NJ: Princeton University Press, 1995), 3–4, 16, 18–19. Good examples of *Alltagsgeschichte* are Detlev Peukert, *Inside Nazi Germany: Conformity, Opposition, and Racism in Everyday Life*, trans. Richard Deveson (New Haven, CT: Yale University Press, 1987); and Christopher Browning, *Ordinary Men: Reserve Police Battalion 101 and the Final Solution in Poland* (New York: Harper Collins, 1992).

3. See Chino Toshiko, *Ashi orenu* (Tokyo: Ōtsuki shoten, 1947), 273–281.

4. Yoshizawa Hisako, *Shūsen made*, in *Shimin no nikki*, vol. 14 of *Shōwa sensō bungaku zenshū*, ed. Agawa Hiroyuki et al. (Tokyo: Shūeisha, 1965), 358–388. Note that Japanese names in this book follow the Japanese convention, with the surname preceding the given name. For example, Takahashi is the surname of a diarist and Aiko is her given name. The names of Japanese authors whose articles and books are written in a Western language are, however, listed in the Western order.

5. Midori Yamauchi and Joseph L. Quinn, *Listen to the Voices from the Sea* (Scranton, PA: University of Scranton Press, 2005).

6. John W. Dower, *War without Mercy: Race and Power in the Pacific War* (New York: Pantheon, 1986), 80–81, 84–85, 95, 124–131.

7. See Richard Tregaskis, *Guadalcanal Diary* (New York: Random House, 1943); John Hersey, *Hiroshima* (New York: Knopf, 1946); and Frank Gibney, *Five Gentlemen of Japan: The Portrait of a Nation's Character* (New York: Farrar, Straus & Young, 1953).

8. This passage appeared in the first postwar Japanese history textbook published by the Ministry of Education: Monbushō, *Kuni no ayumi* [The progress of the country] (Tokyo: Monbushō, 1946), 3:51.

9. Susan Sontag, *Regarding the Pain of Others* (New York: Farrar, Straus & Giroux, 2003), 94.

10. See Samuel Hideo Yamashita, "Pictures for 'Our Honorable American Friends,'" *Cross-Currents: East Asian History and Culture Review* 6 (Spring 2013): 175–185.

11. Lisa Yoneyama, *Hiroshima Traces: Time, Space, and the Dialectics of Memory* (Berkeley: University of California Press, 1999), 122.

12. Kinryō Sugihara, "Diary of First Lieutenant Sugihara Kinryō: Iwo Jima, January–February 1945," *Journal of Military History* 59, no. 1 (1995): 97–133.

13. Kiyoshi Kiyosawa, *A Diary of Darkness: The Wartime Diary of Kiyosawa Kiyoshi*, trans. Eugene Soviak and Kamiyama Tamie (Princeton, NJ: Princeton University Press, 1999).

14. Arthur C. Danto, *Narration and Knowledge* (New York: Columbia University Press, 1985).

15. Yoshizawa, *Shūsen made*, 359.

16. Frank Ankersmit, *Historical Representation* (Stanford, CA: Stanford University Press, 2001), 10.

17. Ibid.

18. Joan Scott, "The Evidence of Experience," *Critical Inquiry* 17, no. 4 (1991): 773–797.

19. Ibid.

20. Sontag, *Regarding the Pain of Others*, 52–55.

21. Ibid.

22. Eric Hammel, *Iwo Jima* (St. Paul, MN: Zenith Press, 2006), 148.

23. Sontag, *Regarding the Pain of Others*, 72.

Chapter 1: We Are All Home-Front Soldiers Now

1. Louise Young, *Japan's Total Empire: Manchuria and the Culture of Imperialism* (Berkeley: University of California Press, 1999), 58–68.

2. Radio ownership was still largely an urban phenomenon—40 percent of all urban homes had a radio, whereas only 10 percent of rural households had one. The government encouraged listening to the radio by distributing posters that urged people "to pull together for the defense of the nation; [listen] together on the radio." Simon Partner, *Toshié: A Story of Village Life in Twentieth-Century Japan* (Berkeley: University of California Press, 2004), 68.

3. Thomas R. H. Havens, *Valley of Darkness: The Japanese People and World War Two* (New York: Norton, 1978), 21–23; and Ben-Ami Shillony, *Politics and Culture in Wartime Japan* (New York: Oxford University Press, 1981), 94.

4. Rekishigaku kenkyūkai, comp., *Taiheiyō sensō, 1940–1942*, vol. 4 of *Taiheiyō sensōshi* (Tokyo: Aoki shoten, 1972), I, 248.

5. Havens, *Valley of Darkness*, 11–20.

6. Samuel Hideo Yamashita, "Confucianism and the Japanese State, 1904–1945," in *Confucian Traditions in East Asian Modernity: Moral Education and Economic Culture in Japan and the Four Mini-Dragons*, ed. Tu Wei-Ming (Cambridge, MA: Harvard University Press, 1996), 147–153.

7. Ibid., 151–152.

8. The numbers are 79,028 in the cities and 118,430 in the countryside. Havens, *Valley of Darkness*, 37–43.

9. In all, 1,323,473 neighborhood associations were created. Havens, *Valley of Darkness*, 77.

10. Havens, *Valley of Darkness*, 84.

11. Peter Duus, ed., *The Twentieth Century*, vol. 6 of *The Cambridge History of Japan* (Cambridge: Cambridge University Press, 1988), 485.

12. Higuchi Kiyoyuki, *Nihon shokubutsu shi: shoku seikatsu no rekishi* (Tokyo: Shikita shoten, 1989), 283; and Shimomura Michiko, "Senchū-sengo no shoku jittai," in *Hijō no shoku*, vol. 11 of *Nihon no shoku bunka*, ed. Noboru Haga et al. (Tokyo: Yusankaku, 1999), 170.

13. Rekishigaku kenkyūkai, comp., *Taiheiyō sensō, 1942–1945*, vol. 5 of *Taiheiyō sensōshi* (Tokyo: Aoki shoten, 1973), 103, 105–106.

14. Ibid., 100.

15. Ibid., 101.

16. Shillony, *Politics and Culture*, 92.

17. Shillony, *Politics and Culture*, 93–94; and Rekishigaku kenkyūkai, *Taiheiyō sensō, 1942–1945*, 135.

18. Later the government prohibited the use of American musical instruments such as steel guitars, banjos, ukuleles, and jazz percussion instruments. The government did permit music "that simply manifested the way of the gods, adorned the war gods, and elevated the Japanese war spirit." Rekishigaku kenkyūkai, *Taiheiyō sensō, 1942–1945*, 136.

19. Rekishigaku kenkyūkai, *Taiheiyō sensō, 1942–1945*, 105.

20. Inoue Mitsusada, *Kindai*, vol. 5 of *Nihon rekishi taikei* (Tokyo: Yamakawa shoten, 1984), 722. The Japanese government even taught its people how to hull rice using a beer bottle and a stick. See Takahashi Aiko, *Kaisen kara*, in *Shimin no nikki*, vol. 14 of *Shōwa sensō bungaku zenshū*, ed. Agawa Hiroyuki et al. (Tokyo: Shūeisha, 1972), 331.

21. Rekishigaku kenkyūkai, *Taiheiyō sensō, 1942–1945*, 120–121. For an account of a high school student mobilized to work at a balloon-making factory in Yamaguchi Prefecture, see Theodore F. Cook and Haruko Taya Cook, *Japan at War: An Oral History* (New York: New Press, 1992), 187–192.

22. Kodera Yukio, comp., *Senji no nichijō: aru saibankan fujin no nikki* (Tokyo: Hakubunkan, 2005), 117, 119.

23. Ibid., 118.

24. Ibid., 118, 119–120.

25. Ibid., 120. The Imperial Declaration of War was recited on the eighth of every month from January 8, 1942, through the end of the war.

26. Shima Rieko, *Senjika no haha: Ōshima Shizuko jūnen o yomu* (Tokyo: Tenbōsha, 2004), 40.

27. Kodera, *Senji no nichijō*, 122, 124, 125.

28. Shima, *Senjika no haha*, 40.

29. Ibid., 42.

30. Kodera, *Senji no nichijō*, 126, 138–139.

31. Manabe Ichirō, "Manabe Ichirō no nikki," in *Shiryō de kataru gakudō sokai*, vol. 5 of *Gakudō sokai no kiroku*, comp. Zenkoku sokai gakudō renraku kyōgikai (Tokyo: Ōzorasha, 1994), 282.

32. Peter Sano, *One Thousand Days in Siberia: The Odyssey of a Japanese-American POW* (Lincoln: University of Nebraska Press, 1997), 26–28.

33. Nakamura Shigetaka, *Sato ni utsurite: tegami to nikki ni nokosareta shūdan sokai no kiroku* (Kobe: Shinpōsha, 2006), 140. The Naval Preparatory Flight Training Pro-

gram (Yokaren) was created in 1930, and a large number of the navy men who died in special attacks in the last year of the war were graduates of this program.

34. Toshima ku-ritsu kyōdo shiryōkan, comp., *Toshima no shūdan gakudō sokai shiryōshū*, 10 vols. (Tokyo: Toshima-ku kyōiku iinkai, 1993), 5:67, hereafter cited as *TNSGSS*.

35. Kodera, *Senji no nichijō*, 127.

36. Shima, *Senjika no haha*, 47.

37. Kodera, *Senji no nichijō*, 130.

38. Ibid., 127, 138–139.

39. Ibid., 138–139.

40. Kodera, *Senji no nichijō*, 157; and Shima, *Senjika no haha*, 65.

41. Kodera, *Senji no nichijō*, 157–158; and Shima, *Senjika no haha*, 66.

42. Kodera, *Senji no nichijō*, 157–158. Gyokusai, "shattered jewel," is a word taken from a sixth-century Chinese classic that the wartime government used to describe the collective deaths of Japanese servicemen.

43. Shima, *Senjika no haha*, 66.

44. Kodera, *Senji no nichijō*, 166–167. The term "One Hundred Million" was used by the wartime government to refer to all Japanese citizens and subjects.

45. Takahashi, *Kaisen kara*, 334–335.

46. Lüdtke, introduction to *History of Everyday Life*, 5–6.

47. Kodera, *Senji no nichijō*, 163.

48. Minami-Tori Shima (Marcus Island) is a coral atoll located 1,148 miles southeast of Tokyo and 787 miles east of the Ogasawara Islands; a small Japanese force was stationed there during the war.

49. Kodera, *Senji no nichijō*, 164–171.

50. Shima, *Senjika no haha*, 79–82.

51. *TNSGSS*, 4:44, 48.

52. Takahashi, *Kaisen kara*, 332–334.

53. Ibid., 327–328, 329–330.

54. Tanaka Jingo, "Hyakushō nikki: Shōwa nijūnen ichi gatsu tsuitachi kara sono toshi no hachigatsu jūgonichi made," in "Sensōchō no kurashi no kiroku," special issue, *Kurashi no techō* 96 (August 1968): 220–221, 228, 230, 236, 238.

55. Yasumura Shizu, *Ippan sokai Yasumura Shizu nikki: aza Tengan kara Miyazaki e* (Gushikawa-shi: Gushikawa-shi kyōiku iinkai, kyōiku-bu shi-shi hensanshitsu, 1998), 3.

56. See Yasumura's entries from September 16, 18, 20, and 25, 1944; and October 6 and 8, 1944, in *Ippan sokai Yasumura Shizu nikki*, 16–17, 19, 22–23.

57. Takahashi, *Kaisen kara*, 327–328.

58. Tamura Tsunejirō, *Shinzan: Senchō sengo-kyō no ichishōmin no nikki* (Tokyo: Minerva shobō, 1980), 17.

59. Kodera, *Senji no nichijō*, 175.

60. Ibid., 175–176.

61. Ibid., 178.

62. Ibid., 146.

63. Ibid., 154.

64. Ibid.

65. Ibid., 165.

66. Ibid., 180. Also see her diary entries for August 10 and December 23, 1942; February 27, April 28, June 21, September 9, October 29, and December 19, 1943, in *Senji no nichijō*, 132, 146. 150, 154, 158–159, 166, 173, 177, 182.

67. Tamura, *Shinzan*, 55–56.

68. Rekishigaku kenkyūkai, *Taiheiyō sensō, 1942–1945*, 99.

69. Quoted in Akimoto Ritsuo, *Sensō to minshū: Taiheiyō sensōka to toshi seikatsu* (Tokyo: Gakuyō shobō, 1974), 111.

70. Kodera, *Senji no nichijō*, 121.

71. Ibid., 179.

Chapter 2: *"No Luxuries until the War Is Won"*

1. Dower, *War without Mercy*, 295–296.

2. Ibid., 297–298.

3. Katarzyna Cwiertka, *Modern Japanese Cuisine: Food, Power and National Identity* (London: Reaktion Books, 2006), 128–233; Owen Griffiths, "Need, Greed, and Protest in Japan's Black Market, 1938–1949," *Journal of Social History* 35, no. 4 (2002): 826–834; Havens, *Valley of Darkness*, 50–51, 115–117, 124–132; Saburō Ienaga, *The Pacific War: World War II and the Japanese*, trans. Frank Baldwin (New York: Pantheon Books, 1978), 193–194, 196; Bruce Johnston, *Japanese Food Management in World War II* (Stanford, CA: Stanford University Press, 1953), 151–164; Ian Nish, "Japan," in *The Civilian in War: The Home Front in Europe, Japan and the USA in World War II*, ed. Jeremy Noakes (Exeter, UK: University of Exeter Press, 1992), 93–103; Shunsuke Tsurumi, *An Intellectual History of Wartime Japan, 1931–1945* (London: KPI, 1986), 85–93.

4. Higuchi, *Nihon shokubutsu shi*, 283.

5. Shimomura, "Senchū-sengo no shoku jittai," 169–200.

6. Shimomura, "Senchū-sengo no shoku jittai," 170; Havens, *Valley of Darkness*, 50.

7. Rekishigaku kenkyūkai, *Taiheiyō sensō, 1942–1945*, 102.

8. Akimoto, *Sensō to minshū*, 103.

9. Rekishigaku kenkyūkai, *Taiheiyō sensō, 1942–1945*, 102.

10. Shima, *Senjika no haha*, 48; Sōmushō tōkei kyoku, *Shimpan Nihon chōki tōkei sōran* (Tokyo: Nihon tōkei kyōkai, 2006), 160.

11. Rekishigaku kenkyūkai, *Taiheiyō sensō, 1942–1945*, 110–111.

12. Ibid., 105.

13. Inoue, *Kindai*, 722.

14. Rekishigaku kenkyūkai, *Taiheiyō sensō, 1942–1945*, 105–106.

15. Ibid., 111.

16. Rekishigaku kenkyūkai, *Taiheiyō sensō, 1942–1945*, 111; and Inoue, *Kindai*, 723.

17. United States Strategic Bombing Survey, *Medical Division*, 50, 61–62; and Havens, *Valley of Darkness*, 131–132.

18. Takahashi, *Kaisen kara*, 324.

19. Inoue, *Kindai*, 723.

20. Shima, *Senjika no haha*, 61–62, 67–68.

21. Kiyosawa, *Diary of Darkness*, 168, 206; and Higuchi, *Nihon shokubutsu shi*, 283.
22. Kiyosawa, *Diary of Darkness*, 142, 156.
23. Watanabe Minoru, *Nihon shoku seikatsushi* (Tokyo: Kōbunkan, 1995), 310.
24. Tamura, *Shinzan*, 8, 79.
25. Kiyosawa, *Diary of Darkness*, 157, 174, 178, 207.
26. Sōmushō tōkei kyoku, *Shimpan Nihon chōki tōkei sōran*, 161, 172–173.
27. Inoue, *Kindai*, 722; and Yoshizawa, *Shūsen made*, 366.
28. Tamura, *Shinzan*, 4–5.
29. Rekishigaku kenkyūkai, *Taiheiyō sensō, 1942–1945*, 107–109.
30. Rekishigaku kenkyūkai, *Taiheiyō sensō, 1940–1942*, 109.
31. Shima, *Senjika no haha*, 53.
32. Tamura, *Shinzan*, 51.
33. Rekishigaku kenkyūkai, *Taiheiyō sensō, 1942–1945*, 109. Apparently many of those buying directly from farmers were black marketeers who sold what they procured at highly inflated prices. United States Strategic Bombing Survey, *Manpower, Food and Civilian Supplies Division*, 28.
34. Manabe, "Manabe Ichirō no nikki," 279–280, 282, 284.
35. Kiyosawa, *Diary of Darkness*, 145, 159, 206, 252.
36. Ibid., 192.
37. Hamada Akiko, *Sokai kyōshi 20-sai no nikki: Shōwa 19-nen 8-gatsu—20-nen 3-gatsu* (Tokyo: Ōmura shoten, 1994), 67, 86, 102.
38. Kamiyama Mitsuo, *Taiheiyō sensō senji nikki-shō—haisen no yoken* (Tokyo: Kindai bungeisha, 1995), 40.
39. Terada Miyoko, *Watakushi no gakutō dōin nikki* (Tokyo: Shūōsha, 1995), 73–74.
40. *TNSGSS*, vols. 5 and 6.
41. Kawamoto Michiji, *Sensō taiken nikki* (Takatsuki: Nishikasa insatsujo, 1984), 99.
42. Kodera, *Senji no nichijō*, 119–120.
43. Shima, *Senjika no haha*, 90–91.
44. Kiyosawa, *Diary of Darkness*, 207.
45. Ibid., 212.
46. Tamura, *Shinzan*, 19, 60–61.
47. Ibid., 6.
48. Frank Gibney, *Sensō: The Japanese Remember the Pacific War: Letters to the Editor of Asahi Shimbun*, trans. Beth Carey (Armonk, NY: Sharpe, 1995), 195.
49. Tanaka, "Hyakushō nikki," 243.
50. Gibney, *Sensō*, 187; and Yoshizawa, *Shūsen made*, 382.
51. Yoshizawa, *Shūsen made*, 352.
52. Gibney, *Sensō*, 205.
53. Ibid., 192.
54. Ibid., 256.
55. Kiyosawa, *Diary of Darkness*, 131, 142, 200–201.
56. E. Bartlett Kerr, *Flames over Tokyo: The U.S. Army Air Forces' Incendiary Campaign against Japan, 1944–1945* (New York: Donald I. Fine, 1991), 324–335, 337–338.
57. Kiyosawa, *Diary of Darkness*, 337.
58. Gibney, *Sensō*, 204.

59. Shima, *Senjika no haha*, 67–68, 82, 92, 61–62, 68.

60. United States Strategic Bombing Survey, *Manpower, Food and Civilian Supplies Division*, 29.

61. Shima, *Senjika no haha*, 49, 75, 81, 84, 90.

62. Ibid., 72, 78, 95, 102.

63. Ibid., 63, 95, 98.

64. Ibid., 72–73, 77, 81, 93, 95, 97, 99.

65. Ibid., 81, 95.

66. Ibid., 77, 80–81, 93.

67. Yasumura, *Ippan sokai Yasumura Shizu nikki*, 12, 14, 16–19, 22–23, 28–30, 35.

68. Hamada, *Sokai kyōshi 20-sai no nikki*, 112.

69. Hirakata-shi kikaku chōsashitsu, comp., *Gakudō shūdan sokai no seikatsu: insotsu kyōin no nikki* (Hirakata-shi: Hirakata-shi, 1993), 113.

70. Tanaka, "Hyakushō nikki," 220.

71. Ibid., 231.

72. Nakane Mihoko, *Sokai gakudō no nikki: kyōsai no shojo ga toraeta shōsen zengo* (Tokyo: Chō kōronsha, 1965), 26.

73. Tanaka, "Hyakushō nikki," 243.

74. Nakane, *Sokai gakudō no nikki*, 70.

75. Yasumura, *Ippan sokai Yasumura Shizu nikki*, 34.

76. Nakane, *Sokai gakudō no nikki*, 70.

77. Tanaka, "Hyakushō nikki," 221, 235, 274.

78. Partner, *Toshié*, 12, 14, 20; and Tanaka, "Hyakushō nikki," 226, 228, 230, 238.

79. Cwiertka, *Modern Japanese Cuisine*, 131; and Higuchi, *Nihon shokubutsu shi*, 283.

80. Tanaka, "Hyakushō nikki," 12–13, 20, 220–221, 228, 230, 236, 238.

81. Ibid., 247, 239, 244.

82. Ibid., 222–223, 239, 241, 242–243. For an account of a Korean mobilized for war work, see Cook and Cook, *Japan at War*, 192–199.

83. United States Strategic Bombing Survey, *Manpower, Food and Civilian Supplies Division*, 10–11.

84. Tanaka, "Hyakushō nikki," 228, 230–231, 234, 237, 241, 243, 245, 222.

Chapter 3: Making "Splendid Little Citizens"

1. The cities were Tokyo, Yokohama, Nagoya, Kyoto, Osaka, Kobe, and seven cities in northern Kyushu.

2. Gregory Johnson, "Mobilizing the 'Junior Nation': The Mass Evacuation of School Children in Wartime Japan" (PhD diss., Indiana University, 2009), 2–3, 169–207, 220, 243–247.

3. Ibid., 232.

4. In contrast, much has been written about the experiences of children in the European Theater of World War II, especially the Jewish children who were killed in German concentration camps, sheltered by sympathetic families, or safely evacuated to Britain. Important work is now being done on children in wartime China by Lily Li, who, under the direction of Rana Mitter at the University of Oxford, recently completed a doctoral dissertation on children in wartime Shanghai.

5. See Kaigo Tokiomi, "Shūshin kyōkasho sōkaisetsu," in *Nihon kyōkasho taikei: kindaihen*, ed. Kaigo Tokiomi (Tokyo: Kōdansha, 1965), 3:616–617; hereafter cited as *NKT*.

6. *NKT*, 3:618–619.

7. Ibid., 3:620.

8. Kaigo Tokiomi, "Shoshū kyōkasho kaidai," in *NKT*, 3:494–501.

9. *NKT*, 3:10–21, 31, 57–58, 63, 81, 88–89, 119, 128, 135, 152, 162, 175–176, 219, 229–230, 257–258, 276–277, 300–301, 366.

10. For entries on "diligence," see *NKT*, 3:18, 29, 69, 127, 145, 163–164, 179–180, 208–209, 250–251, 303–304; for those on "industriousness," see *NKT*, 3:39, 46, 86–87; and for "independence and initiative," see *NKT*, 3:18–19, 44–45, 115, 162, 199, 279–280, 335–336.

11. The entries on "enterprise" are found in *NKT*, 3:39, 101, 178–179, 198, 307–308; and for those on "starting industries," see *NKT*, 3:43, 58–59, 100, 117, 177, 306.

12. For entries on "honesty," see *NKT*, 3:13, 20, 40, 55, 65–66, 72, 77, 129–130, 137–138, 146, 221, 256–257; for those on "obeying rules and laws," see *NKT*, 3:78, 93, 115–116, 142, 148, 160–161, 168, 237, 260, 273–276; for those on "universal love," see *NKT*, 3:48, 92, 106–107, 166–167, 189, 286–287, 317–319; for those on "keeping promises," see *NKT*, 3:12, 73, 139, 243–244; for those on "not inconveniencing others," see *NKT*, 3:15, 67, 131, 222; and for those on "being orderly," see *NKT*, 3:11, 45, 64, 70, 134, 146, 221, 252, 365.

13. See *NKT*, 3:43, 99–100, 147, 176–177, 248–249, 304–306.

14. See *NKT*, 3:27–28, 97, 112–113, 171–172, 195–196, 330–333.

15. For entries on Katō Kiyomasa, see *NKT*, 3:97–98, 187–188; for those on Nakae Tōju, see *NKT*, 3:50, 104, 188–189, 324–326; for those on Kaibara Ekken, see *NKT*, 3:81, 152, 281–282; for those on Arai Hakuseki, see *NKT*, 3:103–104, 184–185, 313–315; for those on Ogyō Sorai, see *NKT*, 3:94, 169, 291–292; for those on Ninomiya Sontoku, see *NKT*, 3:68–69, 144–145, 250–252; and for those on Yoshida Shōin, see *NKT*, 3:21, 183–184, 320–321.

16. For entries on Florence Nightingale, see *NKT*, 3:47–48, 92, 166–167, 317–319; for those on Abraham Lincoln, see *NKT*, 3:54–55; for those on Benjamin Franklin, see *NKT*, 3:45–46, 116–117, 199–200, 336–340; for those on Christopher Columbus, see *NKT*, 3:46–47, 102, 182–183; for those on William Jenner, see *NKT*, 3:163, 274–275, 308–310; and for those on Socrates, see *NKT*, 3:30, 168, 277–278.

17. Carol Gluck, *Japan's Modern Myths: Ideology in the Late Meiji Period* (Princeton, NJ: Princeton University Press,1985), 102.

18. Ibid., 102.

19. See *NKT*, 3:39, 85–86, 111–112, 138, 144, 263.

20. Ibid., 3:14–15.

21. Ibid., 3:34.

22. For entries on Kusunoki Masashige, see *NKT*, 3:27–28, 97, 112–113, 171–172, 195–196, 320–321; and for those on other historical figures, see *NKT*, 3:17, 53, 85–86, 114–115, 144, 149, 348–350.

23. *NKT*, 3:19, 75.

24. Ibid., 3:15, 73, 112–113, 138, 242–243, 263.

25. Ibid., 3:35–36, 107–108, 120–121, 184, 207–208, 322–323.

26. Ibid., 3:18.

27. Ibid., 3:68.

28. Ibid., 3:133–134.

29. E. M. Forster, *Aspects of the Novel* (London: Harcourt, Brace & Company, 1927).

30. *NKT*, 3:75.

31. Ibid., 3:150.

32. Ibid., 3:131.

33. Ibid.

34. Michel Foucault, "The Subject and Power," *Critical Inquiry* 8, no. 4 (1982): 781–782. Foucault calls voluntary subjectification a process of "individualization."

35. *NKT*, 3:331.

36. Ibid., 3:248.

37. Maruyama Masao, *Thought and Behavior in Modern Japanese Politics* (Oxford: Oxford University Press, 1963), 2–19.

38. *NKT*, 3:227.

39. Ibid., 3:226–227.

40. Ibid., 3:640.

41. Ibid., 3:367, 370–371, 382, 385–386, 389–390, 399–401, 403–404, 409–416, 420.

42. For an entry on the rising sun see *NKT*, 3:382; for those on the flag see *NKT*, 3:367, 380, 403–404, 416, 446–447; for those on the imperial house see *NKT*, 3:363, 382, 386, 389–392, 407–410, 413–414, 419–423, 425, 429–432; for the one on the national anthem see *NKT*, 3:409–410; and for those on shrines see *NKT*, 3:396–397.

43. *NKT*, 3:413–414, 420.

44. Ibid., 3:386.

45. Ibid., 3:389–390.

46. Ibid., 3:374, 381–382, 402–403.

47. Ibid., 3:370–380, 398–400, 403–404, 407–410.

48. *NKT*, 3:370–380, 398–400, 403–404, 407–410. See Edward Said's discussion of Jane Austen's *Mansfield Park*, in his *Culture and Imperialism* (New York: Knopf, 1993), 80–97.

49. *NKT*, 367–368, 370–371, 374–375, 378–380.

50. Ibid., 3:371, 373–374, 379–382.

51. Ibid., 3:645.

52. Louis Althusser called this form of address "interpellation," and Edward Said identified it as a feature of nineteenth-century British fiction. See Louis Althusser, *Lenin and Philosophy, and Other Essays*, trans. Ben Brewster (New York: Monthly Review Press, 1972), 109; and Said, *Culture and Imperialism*, 61.

53. *NKT*, 3:373.

54. Ibid., 3:403–404.

55. Ibid., 3:387.

56. Johnson, "Mobilizing the 'Junior Nation,'" 136–144.

57. Hirakata-shi, *Gakudō shūdan sokai no seikatsu*, 48.

58. Ibid., 9, 12, 17.

59. Ibid., 16–19.

60. Ibid., 50.

61. Richard Wilhelm and Cary Baynes, trans., *The I Ching or Book of Changes* (Princeton, NJ: Princeton University Press, 1950), 6.

62. Hirakata-shi, *Gakudō shūdan sokai no seikatsu*, 69.

63. Ibid., 79.

64. Johnson, "Mobilizing the 'Junior Nation,'" 45.

65. Hirakata-shi, *Gakudō shūdan sokai no seikatsu*, 119.

66. Ibid., 96–98, 104, 107, 112, 117–118.

67. Ibid., 100–101. *Hyakunin isshu* is a collection of *waka* (short poems) compiled by the poet Fujiwara Teika (1162–1241).

68. Hirakata-shi, *Gakudō shūdan sokai no seikatsu*, 111.

69. Kiyosawa, *Diary of Darkness*, 323.

70. Nakane, *Sokai gakudō no nikki*, iv.

71. Ibid., 15.

72. Ibid., 15–16.

73. Ibid., 16.

74. Ibid., 25–26.

75. *NKT*, 3:403–404.

76. Nakane, *Sokai gakudō no nikki*, 30–31.

77. Ibid., 31, 46.

78. Ibid., 46, 65, 81. For more on the "reality effect," see Roland Barthes, *The Rustle of Language*, trans. Richard Howard (Berkeley: University of California Press, 1989), 141–148.

79. Nakane, *Sokai gakudō no nikki*, 17–18.

80. Ibid., 66–67.

81. Ibid., 69.

82. Ibid., 70. The italicized words were written by the teacher who checked her diary.

83. Ibid., 71–72.

84. Johnson, "Mobilizing the 'Junior Nation,'" 238.

85. Nakane, *Sokai gakudō no nikki*, 32, 64, 72.

86. Ibid., 22.

87. Ibid., 36, 72.

88. Ibid., 27.

89. Ibid., 31–32.

90. Ibid., 58–59.

91. Ibid., 73.

92. Ibid., 21.

93. Ibid., 30.

94. Ibid., 32.

95. Ibid., 38.

96. Ibid., 39.

97. Ibid., 42.

98. Ibid., 47.

99. Ibid., 50.

100. Ibid., 51–52.

101. Ibid., 53.

102. Ibid., 58.

103. Ibid., 30.

104. Ibid., 40–41.

105. Ibid., 44–45.

106. Ibid., 50–51.

107. Ibid., 75.

108. In 1945, Nakane's teachers practiced flying gliders on April 23, May 28, and June 10. See Nakane, *Sokai gakudō no nikki*, 22, 39, and 47–48.

Chapter 4: Monitoring the Evacuated Children

1. Nakane, *Sokai gakudō no nikki*, 27.

2. Ibid., 59.

3. Ibid., 60.

4. Ibid., 60.

5. Ibid., 74.

6. Ibid., 76.

7. Ibid., 77.

8. *TNSGSS*, 4:63.

9. Ibid., 4:43.

10. Ibid., 4:49.

11. Ibid., 4:53.

12. Ibid., 4:79.

13. Ibid., 4:78.

14. Ibid., 4:99.

15. Ibid., 4:100.

16. Ibid., 4:110. The sweets are called *karintō* and are a form of candy that dates from the Heian period (794–1185).

17. Ibid., 5:15.

18. Ibid., 5:39.

19. Ibid., 5:43.

20. Ibid., 5:46.

21. Ibid., 4:45.

22. Ibid., 4:55.

23. Ibid., 4:66.

24. Ibid., 5:28. She does this by writing "Shizuko" much smaller than everything else.

25. Nakamura, *Sato ni utsurite*, 63.

26. Ibid., 72.

27. Ibid., 185.

28. *TNSGSS*, 4:41–116 and 5:5–111.

29. For Satō Shizuko's entries on food, see *TNSGSS*, 4:45–47, 58–59, 63–64, 70–71, 74, 81, 89, 106–107, 109, and 5:7, 9, 15, 19, 33, 71, 84; for her entries on daily life, see 4:46–47, 53–54, 92; for her entries on hikes, see 4:47, 59, 69–70, 75, 77, and 5:87; for entries on foraging expeditions, see 4:63, 69–71, 76; for her entries on special events, see 4:45–47, 53–54, 58–60, 69, 74, 81, 85; for her entries on military drills, see 4:63–64, 100, and 5:15; for her entries on visitors, see 4:69–71, 74, 88; and for her account of how she and her classmates were faring, see 4:74, 109.

30. *TNSGSS*, 4:45, 81, 110, and 5:27, 46, 74, 83.

31. Nakamura, *Sato ni utsurite*, 45.

32. Ibid., 45–46.

33. Ibid., 51.

34. Ibid., 47–48.

35. Ibid., 83, 101.

36. Ibid., 61.

37. Ibid., 67, 117–118.

38. Ibid., 65.

39. Ibid., 144–145.

40. Ibid., 144.

41. Ibid., 88.

42. *TNSGSS*, 4:42.

43. Ibid., 4:42. "Fuku-chan" was a former teacher who became a special attack pilot and eventually died.

44. Ibid., 4:42–43.

45. Ibid., 4:43.

46. Ibid., 4:44, 48; 5:12, 73, 89.

47. Ibid., 4:48.

48. Ibid., 4:48, 69, 83, 87, 95; 5:21–22, 67, 75.

49. Ibid., 5:73.

50. Ibid., 4:75, 88–89.

51. Nakamura, *Sato ni utsurite*, 40, 76.

52. Ibid., 98, 129.

53. Ibid., 55–56, 71.

54. Ibid., 150.

55. Ibid., 187.

56. *TNSGSS*, 4:61.

57. Nakamura, *Sato ni utsurite*, 70–71. *Ano hata o ute* was directed by Abe Yutaka and released by Tōhō Studio in 1944. *Nikudan teishintai* was directed by Tanaka Shigeo and also released in 1944. The making of *Ano hata o ute* is discussed at length in Abé Mark Nornes and Fukushima Yukio, eds., *The Japan/America Film Wars: WWII Propaganda and Its Cultural Contexts* (Reading, UK: Harwood Academic Publishers, 1994), 235–241.

58. Ibid., 68.

59. Ibid., 97–98.

60. Ibid., 94.

61. Ibid., 100.

62. Ibid., 139.

63. Ibid., 130. The Boeing B-29 Superfortress was a large four-engine, propeller-driven bomber developed in the United States at great expense over the course of four years (1941–1945). Capable of flying at 350 mph and at an altitude of 31,850 feet, it was beyond the reach of most Japanese aircraft and antiaircraft weapons. B-29s were used almost exclusively in the Asia-Pacific Theater and with great effect, beginning in June 1944.

64. Ibid., 149.

65. Ibid., 180.

66. Ibid., 187.

67. *TNSGSS*, 4:84.

68. Ibid., 4:89–90.

69. Ibid., 4:97.

70. Ibid., 4:97.

71. Ibid., 5:32.

72. Ibid., 5:35.

73. Ibid.

74. Ibid., 5:44.

75. Ibid., 5:45.

76. Ibid., 5:46.

77. Ibid.

78. Ibid., 5:51. "Excerpts for Shizuko" was a collection of *shi* and *tanka* that Shizuko's teachers left for her when they were inducted. See *TNSGSS*, n166, 109.

79. Ibid., 5:52, 59.

80. Ibid., 5:61.

81. Ibid., 5:69.

82. Ibid., 5:79.

83. Ibid., 5:80.

84. Ibid., 5:83.

85. Ibid., 5:88.

86. Ibid., 4:49.

87. Ibid., 4:57.

88. Ibid., 4:73.

89. Ibid., 4:83.

90. Ibid., 4:85.

91. Ibid., 4:86.

92. Ibid., 4:93.

93. Ibid., 4:96.

94. Ibid., 4:97.

95. Ibid., 4:98.

96. Nakamura, *Sato ni utsurite*, 41.

97. Ibid., 55, 57.

98. Ibid., 58.

99. *TNSGSS*, 5:8.

100. Ibid., 5:13.

101. Ibid., 5:15.

102. Ibid., 5:18.

103. Nakamura, *Sato ni utsurite*, 168.

104. Ibid., 170.

105. Ibid., 179.

106. Ibid., 219, 224–225.

107. Ibid., 231.

108. *TNSGSS*, 5:30.

109. Ibid., 5:41.

110. Ibid., 5:46–47.

111. Ibid., 5:52.

112. Ibid., 5:53.

113. Ibid., 5:61.

114. Ibid., 5:63.

115. Ibid., 5:62.

116. Ibid., 5:77.

117. Ibid., 5:78.

118. Ibid., 5:88.

119. Nakamura, *Sato ni utsurite*, 102.

120. Ibid., 133.

121. Ibid., 151.

Chapter 5: The "Food Problem" of Evacuated Children in Wartime Japan

1. Johnson, "Mobilizing the 'Junior Nation,'" 2–3, 169–207, 220, 243–247.

2. Irisu no kai, ed., *Shimizu no sokai hōkoku: Kakuto sokai o shita nishi-ushioda kokumin gakkō* (Yokohama: Irisu no kai, 1986), 634.

3. Hamada, *Sokai kyōshi 20-sai no nikki*, 11; Kugahara shōgakkō-shōwa nijūnen sotsugyōsei dōkikai "Sensō taiken" bunshō henshō iinkai, comp., *Taiheiy sensō to Kugahara no kodomo-tachi* (Tokyo: Kugahara shōgakkō-shōwa nijūnen sotsugyōsei dōkikai "Sensō taiken" bunshō henshō iinkai, 1997), 187; Kyoto zeminaru hausu, ed., *Yamabōshi: Kita kuwata no gakudō sokai kiroku-shō* (Kyoto: Kita kuwata, 1996), 55, 59.

4. Hirakata-shi, *Gakudō shūdan sokai no seikatsu*, 18.

5. Johnson, "Mobilizing the 'Junior Nation,'" 276–279.

6. Kugahara, *Taiheiyō sensō to Kugahara no kodomo-tachi*, 182.

7. Aoki Kiminao, *Kōbe Saigō kokumin gakkō no baai*, vol. 1 of *Gakudō shūdan sokai no kiroku* (Kobe: Aoki Kiminao, 1991–1992), 110.

8. Ibid., 111.

9. Ōmura Izō, *Yamagata-ken Yonezawa Ringō gakudō sokai shashin-shō* (Kashiwa: Yonezawa gakudō omoidekai, 2009), 93.

10. Mizutani Hiroshi, *Gakudō sokai no kiroku: Nagoyashi kara* (Nagoya: Chūnichi shinbunsha, 1991), 314.

11. Aoki, *Kōbe Saigō kokumin gakkō no baai*, 2:111; Mizutani, *Gakudō sokai no kiroku*, 314.

12. Kugahara, *Taiheiyō sensō to Kugahara no kodomo-tachi*, 182; Kyoto zeminaru hausu, ed., *Yamabōshi*, 55.

13. Shioniri Mansaku, *Gakudō sokai no kiroku: Shioniri Mansaku* (Tokyo: Aoi torisha, 2006), 171–172.

14. Aoki, *Kōbe Saigō kokumin gakkō no baai*, 2:124; Kyoto zeminaru hausu, *Yamabōshi*, 55.

15. Ōmura, *Yamagata-ken*, 92; Yamada Seiji, *Sannensei no gakudō sokai senki* (Tokyo: Kindai bungeisha, 1994), 75; Kyoto zeminaru hausu, *Yamabōshi*, 60.

16. Aoki, *Kōbe Saigō kokumin gakkō no baai*, 2:142–143.

17. Gibney, *Sensō*, 191.

18. Nakagawa Suzushi, *Tōkyō-to Itabashi dai-go kokumin gakkō gakudō sokai "kaizō-ryō" no kiroku* (Urawa: Kaizōji-kai, 1995), 12. Johnson explains that these older students were put in charge of groups of younger students and abused their power ("Mobilizing the 'Junior Nation,'" 296–297).

19. Aoki, *Kōbe Saigō kokumin gakkō no baai*, 2:137.

20. Nakagawa, *Tōkyō-to*, 10.

21. Yamada, *Sannensei no gakudō sokai senki*, 76.

22. Mizutani, *Gakudō sokai no kiroku*, 320.

23. Aoki, *Kōbe Saigō kokumin gakkō no baai*, 2:149.

24. Ōmura, *Yamagata-ken*, 86.

25. Hirakata-shi, *Gakudō shūdan sokai no seikatsu*, 48–49.

26. Ibid., 55.

27. Ibid., 81.

28. Mizutani, *Gakudō sokai no kiroku*, 177–179, 189, 316–317.

29. Ibid., 178.

30. Ibid.

31. Hamada, *Sokai kyōshi 20-sai no nikki*, 9.

32. Ibid., 87, 93.

33. Yamada, *Sannensei no gakudō sokai senki*, 75.

34. Hamada, *Sokai kyōshi 20-sai no nikki*, 37, 45, 54, 57, 58, 71, 107, 150.

35. Mizutani, *Gakudō sokai no kiroku*, 189.

36. Ōmura, *Yamagata-ken*, 87.

37. Mizutani, *Gakudō sokai no kiroku*, 189.

38. Aoki, *Kōbe Saigō kokumin gakkō no baai*, 2:136, 145; Ōmura, *Yamagata-ken*, 87, 93; Yamada, *Sannensei no gakudō sokai senki*, 75–76.

39. Ōmura, *Yamagata-ken*, 69.

40. Irisu no kai, *Shimizu no sokai hōkoku*, 27.

41. Mizutani, *Gakudō sokai no kiroku*, 174.

42. Ibid., 320.

43. Shioniri, *Gakudō sokai no kiroku*, 172.

44. Mizutani, *Gakudō sokai no kiroku*, 179–180.

45. Ibid., 182.

46. Aoki, *Kōbe Saigō kokumin gakkō no baai*, 2:125.

47. Mizutani, *Gakudō sokai no kiroku*, 187.

48. Kugahara, *Taiheiyō sensō to Kugahara no kodomo-tachi*, 124.

49. Mizutani, *Gakudō sokai no kiroku*, 187.

50. Aoki, *Kōbe Saigō kokumin gakkō no baai*, 2:125; Hidaka Katsuyuki, *Ōkusunoki: kokoro atatamaru gakudō sokai* (Tokyo: Bungeisha, 1999), 39; Kugahara, *Taiheiyō sensō to Kugahara no kodomo-tachi*, 124–125, 189; Nakagawa, *Tōkyō-to*, 10, 12; Yorozu Haruo, *Bokutachi no gakudō sokai* (Tokyo: Nansōsha, 1991), 64.

51. Mizutani, *Gakudō sokai no kiroku*, 182.

52. Nakagawa, *Tōkyō-to*, 12.

53. Kugahara, *Taiheiyō sensō to Kugahara no kodomo-tachi*, 183.

54. Ōmura, *Yamagata-ken*, 69.

55. Mizutani, *Gakudō sokai no kiroku*, 180.

56. Yorozu, *Bokutachi no gakudō sokai*, 45.

57. Kugahara, *Taiheiyō sensō to Kugahara no kodomo-tachi*, 182; Kyoto zeminaru hausu, ed., *Yamabōshi*, 57; Yorozu, *Bokutachi no gakudō sokai*, 47.

58. Aoki, *Kōbe Saigō kokumin gakkō no baai*, 2:125; Nakagawa, *Tōkyō-to*, 10–11; Kyoto zeminaru hausu, ed., *Yamabōshi*, 57; Yorozu, *Bokutachi no gakudō sokai*, 45.

59. Nakagawa, *Tōkyō-to*, 11.

60. Mizutani, *Gakudō sokai no kiroku*, 185.

61. Yorozu, *Bokutachi no gakudō sokai*, 45.

62. Aoki, *Kōbe Saigō kokumin gakkō no baai*, 2:125.

63. Nakagawa, *Tōkyō-to*, 10.

64. Aoki, *Kōbe Saigō kokumin gakkō no baai*, 2:139; Kugahara, *Taiheiyō sensō to Kugahara no kodomo-tachi*, 189.

65. Aoki, *Kōbe Saigō kokumin gakkō no baai*, 2:144; Mizutani, *Gakudō sokai no kiroku*, 44, 183.

66. Mizutani, *Gakudō sokai no kiroku*, 320.

67. Ibid., 183.

68. Nakagawa, *Tōkyō-to*, 11; Kyoto zeminaru hausu, ed., *Yamabōshi*, 55.

69. Kugahara, *Taiheiyō sensō to Kugahara no kodomo-tachi*, 189.

70. Ibid., 182.

71. Mizutani, *Gakudō sokai no kiroku*, 95.

72. Nakagawa, *Tōkyō-to*, 12.

73. Aoki, *Kōbe Saigō kokumin gakkō no baai*, 2:140, 143; Kugahara, *Taiheiyō sensō to Kugahara no kodomo-tachi*, 95; Nakagawa, *Tōkyō-to*, 10–11.

74. Yorozu, *Bokutachi no gakudō sokai*, 46.

75. Aoki, *Kōbe Saigō kokumin gakkō no baai*, 2:143.

76. Ibid., 142–143.

77. Johnson, "Mobilizing the 'Junior Nation,'" 287.

78. Ikeda Kiyoko, *Higashiyama sokai gakudō no nikki* (Tokyo: Tōkyō-to taitō-kuritsu yanaka shōgakkō, 1995), 13.

79. Nakagawa, *Tōkyō-to*, 11.

80. Kyoto zeminaru hausu, *Yamabōshi*, 56.

81. Ibid., 55.

82. Nakagawa, *Tōkyō-to*, 11; Aoki, *Kōbe Saigō kokumin gakkō no baai*, 2:148.

83. Momosan sokai no kai, ed., *Ina-rō: nijōisseiki ni kataru: Nakano-ku ritsu mo-mozono dai-san gakkō kaikō hachijō shōnen kinen gakudō sokai kiroku* (Tokyo: Momo-san sokai no kai, 2000), 50. The sinking of the *Tsushima Maru*, which was carrying school administrators, teachers, and children from Okinawa to the home islands resulted in the death of 767 children. I would like to thank Professor Ebara Ayako, who brought the sinking of the *Tsushima Maru* to my attention and supplied copies of the documents that record the numbers of *sokaiji* deaths and their causes.

Chapter 6: Learning How to Die

1. *Tokkō*, "special attack," is the abbreviated form of *tokubetsu kōgekitai*, "special attack units," the official designation for these units.

2. See navy special attack pilot Itabashi Yasuo's diary: *Kaigun tokubetsu kōgekitaiin no nikki*, in *Ware tokkō ni shisu: yokaren no isho*, ed. Orihara Noboru (Tokyo: Keizai Ōraisha, 1973), 358–399. My translation can be found in Yamashita, *Leaves from an Autumn of Emergencies*, 51–80.

3. "Ōnishi kaigun chūshō jijin," *Asahi shimbun* (Tokyo), August 18, 1945; "Ōnishi gunreibu shichō jijin su," *Mainichi shimbun*, August 18, 1945; "Ōnishi gunreibu shichō jijin," *Yomiuri shimbun*, August 18, 1945.

4. Rikihei Inoguchi and Tadashi Nakajima, with Roger Pineau, *The Divine Wind: Japan's Kamikaze Force in World War II* (New York: Bantam Books, 1960).

5. See Emiko Ohnuki-Tierney, *Kamikaze, Cherry Blossoms and Nationalisms: The Militarization of Aesthetics in Japanese History* (Chicago: University of Chicago Press, 2002), and *Kamikaze Diaries: Reflections of Japanese Student Soldiers* (Chicago: University of Chicago Press, 2007).

6. Yuki Tanaka, "Japan's Kamikaze Pilots and Contemporary Suicide Bombers: War and Terror," *Asia-Pacific Journal: Japan Focus* (2005), available at http://www.japanfocus.org/-yuki-tanaka/1606.zzlzz.

7. Historian Aaron Moore was given access to the wartime diaries of Imperial Japanese Navy special attack pilots housed at the Kanoya Self-Defense Forces Museum in Kanoya, Kyushu. See Aaron W. Moore, *Writing War: Soldiers Record the Japanese Empire* (Cambridge, MA: Harvard University Press, 2013).

8. Inoguchi and Nakajima, *Divine Wind*, 23, 25–26.

9. Bōeichō kenshōjo senshishitsu, comp., *Kaigun shōgo sakusen (2) filipin oki-nawasen* (Tokyo: Asagumo shimbunsha, 1972), 107.

10. Inoguchi and Nakajima, *Divine Wind*, 22–23; and Ikuta Makoto, *Rikugun kōkū tokubetsu kōgekitai* (Tokyo: Bizunesha, 1977), 28–29.

11. The word *tai-atari* was borrowed from kendo, a Japanese martial art that uses bamboo or wooden swords, and is a tactic that has the attacker moving his or her body directly into an opponent.

12. Inoguchi and Nakajima, *Divine Wind*, 26–27; and Ikuta, *Rikugun kōkū tokubetsu kōgekitai*, 70.

13. Ikuta, *Rikugun kōkū tokubetsu kōgekitai*, 35–37. In July 1944, the Inspector General of Army Air Forces was instructed to develop attack forces with special duties

(*tokubetsu ninmu kōgekitai*). Bōeichō kenshūjo senshishitsu, comp., *Rikugun kōkū sakusen—Okinawa, Taiwan, Iwojima hōmen* (Tokyo: Asagumo shimbunsha, 1970), 249–251.

14. Ikuta, *Rikugun kōkū tokubetsu kōgekitai*, 25, 18–19, 68, 70; and Bōeichō kenshūjo senshishitsu, *Kaigun shōgo sakusen (2) filipin okinawasen*, 106–107.

15. Mark Peattie, *Sunburst: The Rise of Japanese Naval Air Power, 1909–1941* (Annapolis, MD: Naval Institute Press, 2007), 189–205.

16. Ikuta, *Rikugun kōkū tokubetsu kōgekitai*, 43; and Inoguchi and Nakajima, *Divine Wind*, 3–9.

17. Inoguchi and Nakajima, *Divine Wind*, 10.

18. Ikuta, *Rikugun kōkū tokubetsu kōgekitai*, 80, 85–95. Army pilot Tsuchida Shōji recorded that the army headquarters in Tokyo issued a report that army special attackers had been successful and that the army units were formed just over ten days after the navy units had been formed; see Tsuchida Shōji, *Tokkō nisshi* (Ōsaka: Tōhō shuppan, 2003), x.

19. Tanaka, "Japan's Kamikaze Pilots," 1; Ikuta's appendices report that 1,404 army pilots perished in special attacks. Ikuta, *Rikugun kōkū tokubetsu kōgekitai*, 277, 291, 296, 298, 300.

20. Gerald Astor, *Wings of Gold: The U.S. Naval Air Campaign in World War II* (San Francisco: Presidio Press, 2005), 16–17.

21. Heinz Knoke, *I Flew for the Führer: The Story of a German Fighter Pilot* (New York: Henry Holt, 1954), 14, 22–29.

22. Ikuta, *Rikugun kōkū tokubetsu kōgekitai*, 19; and Yasuo Kawahara, *Kamikaze: A Japanese Pilot's Own Spectacular Story of the Infamous Suicide Squadrons* (Clearfield, UT: American Legacy Media, 2007), 20–26, 38, 53, 65, 69–72, 76.

23. Saburō Sakai, *Samurai!* (New York: Dutton, 1957), 18–19.

24. Ibid., 27.

25. Ikuta, *Rikugun kōkū tokubetsu kōgekitai*, 18.

26. Kazuko Tsurumi offers a psychological analysis of training in the Imperial Japanese Army in her *Social Change and the Individual: Japan Before and After Defeat in World War II* (Princeton, NJ: Princeton University Press, 1970), 114–126. Edward Drea offers a detailed account of the training of Imperial Japanese Army recruits in his *In the Service of the Emperor: Essays on the Imperial Japanese Army* (Lincoln: University of Nebraska Press, 1998), 75–90.

27. "Wakao Tatsuo nikki," in *Bansei tokkōtaiin no isho*, comp. Naemura Shichirō (Tokyo: Gendai hyōronsha, 1976), 202–206. Hereafter cited as *BTNI*.

28. Historian Alvin Coox points out that the Japanese army had long believed in the power of the "Japanese spirit." "Army leaders always argued that Japan's inferiority in raw materials, finances, and demographic base was counterbalanced by its moral and psychological superiority." See Coox, "The Pacific War," in Duus, *The Twentieth Century*, 322. Akira Iriye argued as well that this belief in the spiritual superiority of the Japanese was implicit in much of the prewar writing that predicted a decisive war with the United States. See Akira Iriye, *Across the Pacific: An Inner History of American-East Asian Relations* (New York: Harcourt, Brace & World, 1967), 230–231.

29. Tsuchida, *Tokkō nisshi*, 5.

30. This brings to mind Alf Lüdtke's observation about the purposefulness of everyday activities in which an element of "repetitiveness" predominates in such a way as to eliminate "constant uncertainty or doubts" (Lüdtke, *History of Everyday Life*, 5–6).

31. Tsuchida, *Tokkō nisshi*, 17.

32. See ibid., 44, 59, 71, 90, 91–92, 93, 114, 120, 122, 127, 130–131, 132, 135, 137, 142, 148, 150, 153, 161.

33. Tsuchida, *Tokkō nisshi*, 86, 161.

34. Ibid., 74, 88, 92, 94, 157.

35. Ibid., 54, 94, 135.

36. Ibid., 96, 102.

37. Ibid., 72, 78, 84, 98, 104, 132, 133, 160, 162.

38. Ibid., 25, 124.

39. Ibid., 23, 68, 262.

40. Ibid., 150, 153.

41. Ibid., 37–39, 122, 159.

42. Ibid., 123.

43. Ibid., 142.

44. Ibid., 198, 201.

45. Ibid., 122, 125, 133, 156.

46. Tsuchida, *Tokkō nisshi*, 161. The command "find a good place to die" alludes to Yamamoto Tsunetomo's *Hagakure* (In the shade of leaves) and the Imperial Japanese Army's *Senjinkun* (*Field Service Code*).

47. Tsuchida, *Tokkō nisshi*, 186, 189, 196, 234, 249, 252, 263, 280–281, 286, 296.

48. Ibid., 182, 206, 208, 223, 235, 244, 246, 254, 256, 260, 266, 269, 271, 300, 304, 305.

49. Ibid., 258, 282.

50. Ibid., 185, 206, 215.

51. Rikugunshō, *Senjinkun* (Tokyo: Tokyo Gazette, 1941), 9.

52. Tsuchida, *Tokkō nisshi*, 17.

53. Ibid., 34 (italics added).

54. Ibid., 51.

55. Tsuchida, *Tokkō nisshi*, 121. See Yamamoto, *Hagakure*, 42–43.

56. Tsuchida, *Tokkō nisshi* , 161.

57. Ibid., 204.

58. Ibid., 218–219.

59. Ibid., 181.

60. Ibid., 185, 188, 190, 199.

61. Ibid., 204, 221.

62. Ibid., 181.

63. Ibid., 182.

64. Ibid., 186.

65. Ibid., 188.

66. Ibid., 190.

67. Ibid., 193.

68. Naemura, *BTNI*, 497–499. For a discussion of the strategy behind the movement of Imperial Japanese Army units from Manchuria to the Japanese home islands, see Drea, *In the Service of the Emperor*, 40–41.

69. Tsuchida Shōji's diary confirms this (see 337–338, 340–341, 348, 350).

70. Tsuchida, *Tokkō nisshi*, 331–332, 334, 335, 340–341, 348, 350–352.

71. Naemura, *BTNI*, 508–519.

72. Ibid., 170, 174, 181.

73. For a discussion of the modern readings of this poem offered by Nishi Amane, Nitobe Inazō, and Tsubuouchi Shōyō, see Ohnuki-Tierney, *Kamikaze, Cherry Blossoms and Nationalisms*, 106–107, 115–120.

74. Naemura, *BTNI*, 200–201.

75. Ibid., 240.

76. Ibid., 222.

77. Ibid., 167, 174, 175, 178, 184.

78. Ibid., 229–230, 231, 168.

79. Ibid., 244.

80. Ibid., 177, 179, 180.

81. Tsuchida, *Tokkō nisshi*, 51.

82. Ibid., 34, 51, 228.

83. Naemura, *BTNI*, 198.

84. Ibid., 171.

85. William Theodore de Bary, *Sources of East Asian Tradition* (New York: Columbia University Press, 2008), 1:67–68.

86. Naemura, *BTNI*, 171, 229.

87. Ibid., 167.

88. For more on "death in life," see Zenkei Shibayama, *A Flower Does Not Talk: Zen Essays*, trans. Sumiko Kudo (Rutland, VT: Tuttle, 1970), 46–47.

89. Naemura, *BTNI*, 175–176.

90. Ibid., 200.

91. Ibid., 213.

92. Ibid., 172.

93. Ibid.

94. Ibid., 224, 268.

95. Ibid., 179, 183–184.

96. Ibid., 184.

97. Ibid., 185, 189.

98. Ibid., 166, 489, 515; and Ikuta, *Rikugun kōkū tokubetsu kōgekitai*, 288.

99. Tsuchida, *Tokkō nisshi*, 324.

100. Ibid.

101. Ibid., 326.

102. Ibid., 329.

103. Ibid.

104. Ibid., 333.

105. Ibid., 339.

106. Ibid., 340.

107. Ibid., 345.

108. Ibid.

109. Because military units were regionally based and composed mostly of men from a specific locale, there was considerable pressure on the conscripts to do well and to not bring shame to their families. Drea, *In the Service of the Emperor*, 80.

110. Tsuchida, *Tokkō nisshi*, 345–346.

111. Ibid., 346.

112. Ibid., 345, 348, 350–352.

113. Ibid., 352.

114. Naemura, *Rikugun saigo no tokkō kichi*, 513, 515.

115. Ibid.

116. Tsuchida, *Tokkō nisshi*, 352.

117. Ibid., 353.

118. Ibid.

119. Ibid.

120. Ibid., 353–354.

121. Ibid., 354.

122. See Itabashi, *Kaigun tokubetsu kōgekitaiin no nikki*, 358–399.

123. Gerald F. Linderman, *The World within War: America's Combat Experience in World War II* (New York: Free Press, 2003), 263–299.

124. Kiyosawa, *Diary of Darkness*, 301, 304. Lieutenant General Nakai Ryōtarō had been the commander of the 106th Division at the battle of Changsha (August–October 1939). See Richard Fuller, *Shōkan: Hirohito's Samurai: Leaders of the Japanese Armed Forces, 1926–1945* (London: Arms and Armour, 1992), 165, 323.

Chapter 7: Popular Resistance to the Wartime Government and Its Policies

1. Gibney, *Sensō*, 176–177.

2. Monbushō, *Kuni no ayumi*, 3:51.

3. Carol Gluck, "The Idea of Showa," *Daedalus* 119, no. 3 (1990): 13.

4. Ben-Ami Shillony, "Wartime Japan: A Military Dictatorship?" in *Shōwa Japan: Political, Economic and Social History, 1926–1989*, ed. Stephen Large, Routledge Library of Modern Japan (New York: Routledge, 1998), 16–17.

5. Ienaga, *Pacific War*, 222.

6. Shillony, *Politics and Culture*, 9–10, 56–57, 63–64.

7. Incidents involving workers, though not as violent as the right-wing plots, also expressed opposition to the wartime government and its policies.

8. Rekishigaku kenkyūkai, *Taiheiyō sensō, 1940–1942*, 299; and Ienaga, *Pacific War*, 209.

9. Bunsō Hashikawa, "The 'Civil Society' Ideal and Wartime Resistance," in *Authority and the Individual in Japan*, ed. J. Victor Koschmann (Tokyo: University of Tokyo Press, 1978), 131–142; Ienaga, *Pacific War*, 203–228; and Shillony, *Politics and Culture*, 120–133. John Dower catalogs the groups that opposed wartime policies, in his *Japan in War and Peace: Selected Essays* (New York: New Press, 1993), 103–124.

10. Ienaga, *Pacific War*, 213–214. I. C. B. Dear, general editor, *The Oxford Companion to World War II* (New York: Oxford University Press, 1995), 297.

11. Foucault, "Subject and Power," 780; and Lüdtke, *History of Everyday Life*, 3–25.

12. Shima, *Senjika no haha*, 89, 98.

13. Inoue, *Kindai*, 109.

14. Inoue, *Kindai*, 72; and Shima, *Senjika no haha*, 45.

15. Tamura, *Shinzan*, 51.

16. Tanaka, "Hyakushō nikki," 228.

17. Ienaga, *Pacific War*, 215–216.

18. Tanaka, "Hyakushō nikki," 222–223, 228–229, 230–231, 235, 310.

19. Shima, *Senjika no haha*, 90, note.

20. Nakamura, *Sato ni utsurite*, 106–107.

21. Gibney, *Sensō*, 41.

22. Kiyosawa, *Diary of Darkness*, 61, 87, 100.

23. Ibid., 87, 124.

24. Ibid., 100.

25. Ibid., 145, 168, 180, 196, 307.

26. Ibid., 189–190.

27. Nakamura, *Sato ni utsurite*, 55–56.

28. Imperial Japanese Army recruits were paid $0.65 a month, which meant they could not buy food or meals off-base. See Drea, *In the Service of the Emperor*, 86.

29. Kiyosawa, *Diary of Darkness*, 194–195.

30. Ibid., 355.

31. Kiyosawa Kiyoshi, *Ankoku nikki* (Tokyo: Chikuma shobō, 2002), 2:165.

32. Yoshizawa, *Shūsen made*, 381.

33. Kiyosawa, *Diary of Darkness*, 310.

34. Kawamoto, *Sensō taiken nikki*, 159–160.

35. "No-arashi no moto kyōjū ni gonen," *Asahi Shimbun* (Osaka), August 4, 1945.

36. Gibney, *Sensō*, 188.

37. Aoki Kiminao, *Kōbe Saigo Kokumin gakkō no baai*, vol. 2 of *Gakudō shūdan sokai no kiroku* (Kobe: Aoki Kiminao, 1992), 143.

38. Ochanomizu gakudō sokai no kai, comp., *Tōkyō joshikōtō shihan gakkō fuzoku kokumin gakkō*, vols. 7 and 8 of *Dai niji sekai taisen gakudō sokai kiroku-shū* (Tokyo: Ochanomizu gakudō sokai no kai, 1989), 17.

39. Tamura, *Shinzan*, 17.

40. Absenteeism was a serious problem in Japanese industry in the closing months of the war. See Dower, *Japan in War and Peace*, 114.

41. Satō Kazumasa, *Numazu kaigun kōshō tsūnen dōin nikki*, in *Numazu-shiritsu suruga toshokan* (Numazu: Numazu shiritsu suruga toshokan, 1976), 88–90.

42. Terada, *Watakushi no gakutō dōin nikki*, 55–56, 83, 88, 95, 104–105, 107.

43. Satō, *Numazu kaigun kōshō tsūnen dōin nikki*, 54–55, 59.

44. Tamura, *Shinzan*, 18–19, 29–30.

45. Takahashi, *Kaisen kara*, 335.

46. Tamura, *Shinzan*, 55–56.

47. Takahashi, *Kaisen kara*, 329.

48. Akimoto, *Sensō to minshū*, 80–81.

49. Hamada, *Sokai kyōshi 20-sai no nikki*, 186.

50. Takahashi, *Kaisen kara*, 331–332.

51. Isoko Hatano, comp., *Mother and Son: The Wartime Correspondence of Isoko and Ichiro Hatano* (Boston: Houghton Mifflin, 1962), 12.

52. Kiyosawa, *Diary of Darkness*, 102.

53. Ibid., 231.

54. Takahashi, *Kaisen kara*, 334–335, 337–338.

55. Ibid., 339.

56. Yoshizawa, *Shūsen made*, 361, 367, 370–371, 378–380. The American authorities believed that by November 1944, one-tenth of the Japanese population "believed that defeat was inevitable," "one-half by June 1945," and "two-thirds by the time of surrender." See Dower, *Japan in War and Peace*, 130.

57. *Tokkō geppō* (Monthly gazette of the Special Higher Police), the semimonthly report issued by the Special Higher Police, records an impressively large number of antigovernment rumors. For example, the wartime authorities investigated 1,603 rumors suspected of violating the Military Code between August 1937 and April 1943, prosecuting 646 individuals. See Dower, *Japan in War and Peace*, 124–140.

58. Kiyosawa, *Diary of Darkness*, 199.

59. Gibney, *Sensō*, 178.

60. Yoshimi Yoshiaki, *Kusa no ne no fashizumu: Nihon minshū no sensō taiken* (Tokyo: Tōkyō daigaku shuppankai, 1987), 10.

61. Tanaka, "Hyakushō nikki," 220, 222, 228.

62. Tanaka, "Hyakushō nikki," 231. Koiso Kuniaki (1880–1950) succeeded Tōjō Hideki as prime minister in July 22, 1944, and served until April 5, 1944.

63. Kiyosawa, *Diary of Darkness*, 295.

64. Ienaga, *Pacific War*, 221–222.

Chapter 8: The "Jeweled Sound"

1. Action reports confirm that 118 aircraft from six aircraft carriers attacked designated targets in eastern Japan on the morning of August 15. United States Strategic Bombing Survey, *The Records of the Carrier-Based Navy and Marine Corps Aircraft Action Reports, 1944–1945*, Entry 55. USB-06.

2. Yoshizawa, *Shūsen made*, 384–385.

3. Ibid.

4. Takahashi, *Kaisen kara*, 356–357.

5. Yoshizawa, *Shūsen made*, 385.

6. Gibney, *Sensō*, 258.

7. Kawamoto, *Sensō taiken nikki*, 164–165.

8. Ibid.

9. Tanaka, "Hyakushō nikki," 248.

10. Takahashi, *Kaisen kara*, 385.

11. Yoshizawa, *Shūsen made*, 385.

12. Terada, *Watakushi no gakutō dōin nikki*, 144.

13. Inoue Tarō, *Kyūsei kōkosei no Tokyo haisen nikki* (Tokyo: Heibonsha, 2000), 186.

14. Kamiyama, *Taiheiyō sensō senji nikki-shō*, 56.

15. Gibney, *Sensō*, 254.

16. Kawamoto, *Sensō taiken nikki*, 166.

17. Tanaka, "Hyakushō nikki," 249.

18. Gibney, *Sensō*, 256–257.

19. Japanese POWs also took the news of the surrender hard. See Ulrich Straus, *The Anguish of Surrender: Japanese POWs of World War II* (Seattle: University of Washington Press, 2003), 222–225.

20. Gibney, *Sensō*, 260–262.

21. Ibid., 259.

22. Ibid., 260.

23. For the account of another straggler on Okinawa, see Cook and Cook, *Japan at War*, 367–372.

24. Nomura Seiki, *Okinawa haisenhei nikki* (Tokyo: Taihei shuppansha, 1974), 221–222.

25. *The Field Service Code (Senzinkun)* (Tokyo: Tokyo Gazette Publishing House, 1941), 9.

26. Terada, *Watakushi no gakutō dōin nikki*, 139.

27. Ibid., 140.

28. Ibid., 141.

29. Ibid., 145.

30. Nakane, *Sokai gakudō no nikki*, 85–86.

31. *TNSGSS*, 5:90.

32. Ibid.

33. Owada Kazuko and Shinohara Eita, *Kazuko-chan no tegami: gakudō sokaiji no kiroku* (Tokyo: Hikari shobō, 1979), 174.

34. Tsuchida, *Tokkō nisshi*, 355.

35. Ibid., 356.

36. Ibid.

37. Ibid., 355, 356.

38. Ibid., 357.

39. Ibid.

40. "Anami rikusō jijin," *Asahi shimbun* (Tokyo), August 16, 1945; "Ōnishi kaigun chūshō jijin," *Asahi shimbun* (Tokyo), August 18, 1945; "Tanaka Seiichi taishō, jiketsu," *Asahi shimbun* (Osaka), September 21, 1945; "Sugiyama gensui kyojū de jiketsu," *Asahi shimbun* (Osaka), September 13, 1945; "Shira shōzoku kite jijin," *Asahi shimbun* (Osaka), September 14, 1945.

41. "Shirokura chūshō jiketsu," *Asahi shimbun* (Osaka), September 16, 1945; and "Hamada chūshō banya de jiketsu," *Asahi shimbun* (Osaka), September 20, 1945.

42. See "Josei mo jijin," *Asahi shimbun* (Tokyo), August 29, 1945; "Isshi, kōkoku o mamoru," *Mainichi shimbun* (Tokyo), August 29, 1945; and "Isshi, kōkoku ni junzu," *Yomiuri shimbun* (Tokyo), August 29, 1945.

BIBLIOGRAPHY

Newspapers

Asahi shimbun

"Anami rikusō jijin." *Asahi shimbun* (Tokyo), August 16, 1945.

"Hamada chūshō banya de jiketsu." *Asahi shimbun* (Osaka), September 20, 1945.

"No-arashi no moto kyōjū ni gonen." *Asahi shimbun* (Osaka), August 4, 1945.

"Ōnishi kaigun chūshō jijin." *Asahi shimbun* (Tokyo), August 18, 1945.

"Shira shōzoku kite jijin." *Asahi shimbun* (Osaka), September 14, 1945.

"Shirokura chūshō jiketsu." *Asahi shimbun* (Osaka), September 16, 1945.

"Sugiyama gensui kyojū de jiketsu." *Asahi shimbun* (Osaka), September 13, 1945.

"Tanaka Seiichi taishō, jiketsu." *Asahi shimbun* (Osaka), September 21, 1945.

Mainichi shimbun

"Ōnishi gunreibu shichō jijin su." *Mainichi shimbun*, August 18, 1945.

Yomiuri shimbun

"Ōnishi gunreibu shichō jijin." *Yomiuri shimbun*, August 18, 1945.

Primary Sources

Agawa Hiroyuki et al., eds. *Shōwa sensō bungaku zenshū*. Tokyo: Shūeisha, 1972.

Aoki Kiminao. *Kōbeshi Saigō kokumin gakkō no baai*. Vols. 1 and 2 of *Gakudō shūdan sokai no kiroku*. Kobe: Aoki Kiminao, 1991–1992.

Arai Kazuo. "Arai Kazuo nisshi." In *Bansei tokkōtaiin no isho*, compiled by Naemura Shichirō. Tokyo: Gendai hyōronsha, 1976.

Chino Toshiko. *Ashi orenu*. Tokyo: Ōtsuki shoten, 1947.

The Field Service Code [*Senzinkun*]. Tokyo: Tokyo Gazette Publishing House, 1941.

Gibney, Frank. *Sensō: The Japanese Remember the Pacific War: Letters to the Editor of Asahi Shimbun*. Translated by Beth Carey. Armonk, NY: Sharpe, 1995.

Hamada Akiko. *Sokai kyōshi hatachi no nikki: Shōwa 19-nen 8-gatsu—20-nen 3-gatsu*. Tokyo: Ōmura shoten, 1994.

Hatano, Isoko, comp. *Mother and Son: The Wartime Correspondence of Isoko and Ichiro Hatano*. Boston: Houghton Mifflin, 1962.

Hidaka Katsuyuki. *Ōkusu no ki: kokoro atatamaru gakudō sokai*. Tokyo: Bungeisha, 1999.

Hirakata-shi kikaku chōsashitsu, comp. *Gakudō shūdan sokai no seikatsu: insotsu kyōin no nikki*. Hirakata-shi: Hirakata-shi, 1993.

Ikeda Kiyoko. *Higashiyama sokai gakudō no nikki*. Tokyo: Tōkyō-to taitō-kuritsu yanaka shōgakkō, 1995.

Inoue Tarō. *Kyūsei kōkōsei no Tokyo haisen nikki*. Tokyo: Heibonsha, 2000.

Irisu no kai, ed. *Shimizu no sokai hōkoku: Kakuto sokai o shita nishi-ushioda kokumin gakkō*. Yokohama: Irisu no kai, 1986.

Itabashi Yasuo. *Kaigun tokubetsu kōgekitaiin no nikki.* In *Ware tokkō ni shisu: yokaren no ikō.* Edited by Orihara Noboru. Tokyo: Keizai Ōraisha, 1973.

Kaigo Tokiomi, ed. *Nihon kyōkasho taikei: kindaihen.* 27 vols. Tokyo: Kōdansha, 1965.

Kamiyama Mitsuo. *Taiheiyō sensō senji nikki-shō—haisen no yoken.* Tokyo: Kindai bungeisha, 1995.

Kawahara, Yasuo. *Kamikaze: A Japanese Pilot's Own Spectacular Story of the Infamous Suicide Squadrons.* Clearfield, UT: American Legacy Media, 2007.

Kawamoto Michiji. *Sensō taiken nikki.* Takatsuki: Kawamoto Michiji, 1983.

Kiyosawa, Kiyoshi. *A Diary of Darkness: The Wartime Diary of Kiyosawa Kiyoshi.* Translated by Eugene Soviak and Tamie Kamiyama. Princeton, NJ: Princeton University Press, 1999.

Kiyosawa Kiyoshi. *Ankoku nikki.* 3 vols. Tokyo: Chikuma shobō, 2002.

Kodera Yukio, comp. *Senji no nichijō: aru saibankan fujin no nikki.* Tokyo: Hakubunkan, 2005.

Kugahara shōgakkō-shōwa nijūnen sotsugyōsei dōkikai "Sensō taiken" bunshū henshū iinkai, comp. *Taiheiyō sensō to Kugahara no kodomo-tachi.* Tokyo: Kugahara shōgakkō-shōwa nijūnen sotsugyōsei dōkikai "Sensō taiken" bunshū henshū iinkai, 1997.

Kuguricha Takashi. "Kuguri Takashi nisshi." In *Rikugun saigo no tokkō kichi: bansei tokkōtaiin no isho-iei,* compiled by Naemura Shichirō. Osaka: Tōhō shuppan, 1979.

Kurosawa Yoshiko. *Watakushi-tachi no gojūnen: yanaka shōgakkō de mananda (Shōwa nijūnen-sotsu) shōjotachi no kiroku-shū-Higashiyama sokai gakudō no nikki.* Tokyo: Tōkyō-to Taitō-kuritsu Yanaka chū-shōgakkō "Yanaka-shō de manada (Shōwa nijūichi-nen sotsu) shōjotachi no kirokushū" henshū iinkai, 1995.

Kyoto zeminaru hausu, ed. *Yamabōshi: Kita kuwada no gakudō sokai kiroku-shū.* Keihoku: Kyoto zeminaru hausu, 1996.

Manabe Ichirō. "Manabe Ichirō no nikki." In *Shiryō de kataru gakudō sokai.* Vol. 5 of *Gakudō sokai no kiroku.* Compiled by Zenkoku sokai gakudō renraku kyōgikai. Tokyo: Ōzorasha, 1994.

Mizutani Hiroshi. *Gakudō sokai no kiroku: Nagoyashi kara Yokkaichi e.* Nagoya: Chūnichi shinbunsha, 1998.

Momozono sokai no kai, ed. *Imaji: nijūisseiki ni kataru: Nakano-ku ritsu momozono dai-san shōgakkō kaikō hachijū shūnen kinen gakudō sokai kiroku.* Tokyo: Momozono sokai no kai, 2000.

Monbushō. *Kuni no ayumi.* Vol. 3. Tokyo: Monbushō, 1946.

Munemiya Akihira. "Munemiya Akihira nisshi." In *Bansei tokkōtaiin no isho,* compiled by Naemura Shichirō. Tokyo: Gendai hyōronsha, 1976.

Naemura Shichirō, comp. *Bansei tokkōtaiin no isho.* Tokyo: Gendai hyōronsha, 1976.

———, comp. *Rikugun saigo no tokkō kichi: Bansei tokkōtaiin no isho-iei.* Osaka: Tōhō shuppan, 1993.

Nakagawa Suzushi. *Tōkyō-to Itabashi dai-go kokumin gakkō gakudō sokai "kaizōji-ryō" no kiroku.* Urawa: Kaizōji-kai, 1995.

Nakamura Shigetaka. *Sato ni utsurite: tegami to nikki ni nokosareta shūdan sokai no kiroku.* Kobe: Shinpūsha, 2006.

Nakane Mihoko. *Sokai gakudō no nikki: kyūsai no shōjo ga toraeta shūsen zengo.* Tokyo: Chūō kōronsha, 1965.

Nomura Masaki. *Okinawa senpaihei nikki.* Tokyo: Taihei shuppansha, 1974.

Ochanomizu gakudō sokai no kai, comp. *Tōkyo joshikōtō shihan gakkō fuzoku kokumin gakkō.* Vols. 7 and 8 of *Dai niji sekai taisen gakudō sokai kiroku-shū.* Tokyo: Ochanomizu gakudō sokai no kai, 1989.

Ōmura Keizō. *Yamagata-ken Yonezawa Ringō gakudō sokai shashin-shū.* Kashiwa: Yonezawa gakudō omoidekai, 2009.

Orihara Noboru, ed. *Ware tokkō ni shisu: yokaren no ikō.* Tokyo: Keizai Ōraisha, 1973.

Ōtsuka Kaname. "Otsuka Kaname nisshi." In *Bansei tokkōtaiin no isho,* compiled by Naemura Shichirō. Tokyo: Gendai hyōronsha, 1976.

Ōwada Kazuko and Shinohara Eita. *Kazuko-chan no tegami: gakudō sokaiji no kiroku.* Tokyo: Hikari shobō, 1979.

Rikugunshō. *Senjinkun.* Tokyo: Tokyo Gazette, 1941.

Sakai, Saburō. *Samurai!* New York: Dutton, 1957.

Sano, Peter. *One Thousand Days in Siberia: The Odyssey of a Japanese-American POW.* Lincoln: University of Nebraska Press, 1997.

Satō Kazumasa. *Numazu kaigun kōshō tsūnen dōin nikki.* In *Numazu-shiritsu suruga toshokan.* Numazu: Numazu shiritsu suruga toshokan, 1976.

Shibayama, Zenkei. *A Flower Does Not Talk: Zen Essays.* Translated by Sumiko Kudo. Rutland, VT: Tuttle, 1970.

Shima Rieko. *Senjika no haha: Ōshima Shizuko jūnen o yomu.* Tokyo: Tenbōsha, 2004.

Shimura Hatsuo. "Shimura Hatsuo nisshi." In *Bansei tokkōtaiin no isho.* Compiled by Naemura Shichirō. Tokyo: Gendai hyōronsha, 1976.

Shinoiri Mansaku. *Gakudō sokai no kiroku: Tokiwamatsu shōgakkō.* Tokyo: Aoi torisha, 2006.

Sugihara, Kinryū. "Diary of First Lieutenant Sugihara Kinryū: Iwo Jima, January–February 1945." *Journal of Military History* 59, no. 1 (1995): 97–133.

Takahashi Aiko. *Kaisen kara.* In *Shimin no nikki.* Vol. 14 of *Shōwa sensō bungaku zenshū.* Edited by Agawa Hiroyuki et al. Tokyo: Shūeisha, 1965.

Tamura Tsunejirō. *Shinsan: Senchū sengo-kyō no ichishomin no isho.* Tokyo: Minerva shobō, 1980.

Tanaka Jingo. "Hyakushō nikki: Shōwa nijūnen ichi gatsu tsuitachi kara sono toshi no hachigatsu jūgonichi made." In "Sensōchū no kurashi no kiroku," special issue, *Kurashi no techō* 96 (August 1968).

Terada Miyoko. *Watakushi no gakuto dōin nikki.* Tokyo: Shūosha, 1995.

Toshima ku-ritsu kyōdo shiryōkan, comp. *Toshima no shūdan gakudō sokai shiryōshū.* 10 vols. Tokyo: Toshima ku kyōiku iinkai, 1993–2000.

Tsuchida Shōji. *Tokkō nisshi.* Osaka: Tōhō shuppan, 2003.

United States Strategic Bombing Survey. *Civilian Defense Division* (1). Vol. 2 of *Taiheiyō sensō hakusho.* Tokyo: Nihon tosho senta, 1992.

———. *Manpower, Food and Civilian Supplies Division.* Vol. 16 of *Taiheiyō sensō hakusho.* Tokyo: Nihon tosho senta, 1992.

———. *Medical Division.* Vol. 6 of *Taiheiyō sensō hakusho.* Tokyo: Nihon tosho senta, 1992.

———. *The Records of the Carrier-Based Navy and Marine Corps Aircraft Action Reports,* Entry 55. USB-06.

Wakao Tatsuo. "Wakao Tatsuo nikki." In *Bansei tokkōtaiin no isho,* compiled by Naemura Shichirō. Tokyo: Gendai hyōronsha, 1976.

Wilhelm, Richard, and Cary Baynes, trans. *The I Ching or Book of Changes.* Princeton, NJ: Princeton University Press, 1950.

Yamada Seiji. *Sannensei no gakudō sokai senki.* Tokyo: Kindai bungeisha, 1994.

Yamamoto, Tsunetomo. *Hagakure: The Secret Wisdom of the Samurai.* Translated by Alex Bennett. Rutland, VT: Tuttle, 2014.

Yasumura Shizu. *Ippan sokai Yasumura Shizu nikki: aza Tengan kara Miyazaki e.* Gushikawa-shi: Gushikawa-shi kyōiku iinkai, kyōiku-bu shi-shi hensanshitsu, 1998.

Yorozu Haruo. *Bokutachi no gakudō sokai.* Tokyo: Nansōsha, 1991.

Yoshizawa Hisako. *Shūsen made.* In *Shimin no nikki,* vol. 14 of *Shōwa sensō bungaku zenshū,* edited by Agawa Hiroyuki et al. Tokyo: Shūeisha, 1965.

Zenkoku sokai gakudō renraku kyōgikai, comp. *Gakudō sokai no kiroku.* 6 vols. Tokyo: Ōzorasha, 1994.

Secondary Sources

Akimoto Ritsuo. *Sensō to minshū: Taiheiyō sensōka to toshi seikatsu.* Tokyo: Gakuyō shobō, 1974.

Althusser, Louis. *Lenin and Philosophy, and Other Essays.* Translated by Ben Brewster. New York: Monthly Review Press, 1972.

Ankersmit, Frank. *Historical Representation.* Stanford, CA: Stanford University Press, 2002.

Astor, Gerald. *Wings of Gold: The U.S. Naval Air Campaign in World War II.* New York: Presidio Press, 2005.

Barthes, Roland. *The Rustle of Language.* Translated by Richard Howard. Berkeley: University of California Press, 1989.

Bōeichō kenshūjo senshishitsu, comp. *Rikugun kōkū sakusen—Okinawa, Taiwan, Iwojima hōmen.* Tokyo: Asagumo shimbunsha, 1970.

Browning, Christopher. *Ordinary Men: Reserve Police Battalion 101 and the Final Solution in Poland.* New York: HarperCollins, 1992.

Cook, Theodore F., and Haruko Taya Cook. *Japan at War: An Oral History.* New York: New Press, 1992.

Coox, Alvin. "The Pacific War." In *The Twentieth Century.* Vol. 6 of *The Cambridge History of Japan.* Edited by Peter Duus. Cambridge: Cambridge University Press, 1988.

Cwiertka, Katarzyna. *Modern Japanese Cuisine: Food, Power and National Identity.* London: Reaktion, 2006.

Danto, Arthur C. *Narration and Knowledge: Including the Integral Text of* Analytical Philosophy of History. New York: Columbia University Press, 1985.

Dear, I. C. B., general editor, *The Oxford Companion to World War II* (New York: Oxford University Press, 1995).

De Bary, William Theodore. *Sources of East Asian Tradition.* Vol. 1. New York: Columbia University Press, 2008.

Dower, John W. *Japan in War and Peace: Selected Essays.* New York: New Press, 1993.

———. *War without Mercy: Race and Power in the Pacific War.* New York: Pantheon, 1986.

Drea, Edward J. *In the Service of the Emperor: Essays on the Imperial Japanese Army.* Lincoln: University of Nebraska Press, 1998.

Duus, Peter, ed. *The Twentieth Century.* Vol. 6 of *The Cambridge History of Japan.* Cambridge: Cambridge University Press, 1988.

Forster, E. M. *Aspects of the Novel.* London: Harcourt, Brace & Company, 1927.

Foucault, Michel. "The Subject and Power." *Critical Inquiry* 8, no. 4 (1982): 777–795.

Fuller, Richard. *Shōkan: Hirohito's Samurai: Leaders of the Japanese Armed Forces, 1926–1945.* London: Arms and Armour, 1992.

Gibney, Frank. *Five Gentlemen of Japan: The Portrait of a Nation's Character.* New York: Farrar, Straus & Young, 1953.

Gluck, Carol. "The Idea of Showa." *Daedalus* 119, no. 3 (1990): 1–26.

———. *Japan's Modern Myths: Ideology in the Late Meiji Period.* Princeton, NJ: Princeton University Press, 1985.

Griffiths, Owen. "Need, Greed, and Protest in Japan's Black Market, 1938–1949." *Journal of Social History* 35, no. 4 (2002): 825–858.

Hammel, Eric. *Iwo Jima.* St. Paul, MN: Zenith Press, 2006.

Hashikawa, Bunsō. "The 'Civil Society' Ideal and Wartime Resistance." In *Authority and the Individual in Japan: Citizen Protest in Historical Perspective,* edited by J. Victor Koschmann. Tokyo: University of Tokyo Press, 1978.

Havens, Thomas R. H. *Valley of Darkness: The Japanese People and World War Two.* New York: Norton, 1978.

Hersey, John. *Hiroshima.* New York: Knopf, 1946.

Higuchi Kiyoyuki. *Nihon shokubutsu shi: shoku seikatsu no rekishi.* Tokyo: Shikita shoten, 1987.

Hosking, Richard. *A Dictionary of Japanese Food: Ingredients and Culture.* Rutland, VT: Tuttle, 1996.

Ienaga, Saburō. *The Pacific War: World War II and the Japanese, 1931–1945.* Translated by Frank Baldwin. New York: Pantheon, 1978.

Ikuta Makoto. *Rikugun kōkū tokubetsu kōgekitaishi.* Tokyo: Bijinesusha, 1977.

Inoguchi, Rikihei, and Tadashi Nakajima, with Roger Pineau. *The Divine Wind: Japan's Kamikaze Force in World War II.* New York: Bantam, 1958.

Inoue Mitsusada. *Kindai.* Vol. 5 of *Nihon rekishi taikei.* Tokyo: Yamakawa shoten, 1984.

Iriye, Akira. *Across the Pacific: An Inner History of American–East Asian Relations.* New York: Harcourt, Brace & World, 1967.

————. *Power and Culture: The Japanese-American War, 1941–1945.* Cambridge, MA: Harvard University Press, 1981.

Johnson, Gregory. "Mobilizing the 'Junior Nation': The Mass Evacuation of School Children in Wartime Japan." PhD diss., Indiana University, 2009.

Johnston, Bruce. *Japanese Food Management in World War II.* Stanford, CA: Stanford University Press, 1953.

Kaigo Tokiomi. "Shūshin kyōkasho sōkaisetsu." In *Nihon kyōkasho taikei: kindaihen.* Edited by Kaigo Tokiomi. Tokyo: Kōdansha, 1962.

Kasza, Gregory J. *The State and the Mass Media in Japan: 1918–1945.* Berkeley: University of California Press, 1988.

Kerr, E. Bartlett. *Flames over Tokyo: The U.S. Army Air Forces' Incendiary Campaign against Japan, 1944–1945.* New York: Donald I. Fine, 1991.

Knoke, Heinz. *I Flew for the Führer: The Story of a German Fighter Pilot.* New York: Henry Holt, 1954.

Linderman, Gerald F. *The World within War: America's Combat Experience in World War II.* New York: Free Press, 1997.

Lüdtke, Alf, ed. *The History of Everyday Life: Reconstructing Historical Experiences and Ways of Life.* Translated by William Templer. Princeton, NJ: Princeton University Press, 1995.

Masao, Maruyama. *Thought and Behavior in Modern Japanese Politics.* Translated by Ivan Morris et al. Oxford: Oxford University Press, 1963.

Moore, Aaron William. *Writing War: Soldiers Record the Japanese Empire.* Cambridge, MA: Harvard University Press, 2013.

Nish, Ian. "Japan." In *The Civilian in War: The Home Front in Europe, Japan and the USA in World War II,* edited by Jeremy Noakes. Exeter, UK: University of Exeter Press, 1992.

Nornes, Abé Mark, and Fukushima Yukio, eds., *The Japan/America Film Wars: World War II Propaganda and Its Cultural Contexts* (Reading, UK: Harwood Academic Publishers, 1994).

Ohnuki-Tierney, Emiko. *Kamikaze, Cherry Blossoms and Nationalisms: The Militarization of Aesthetics in Japanese History.* Chicago: University of Chicago Press, 2002.

————. *Kamikaze Diaries: Reflections of Japanese Student Soldiers.* Chicago: University of Chicago Press, 2007.

Partner, Simon. *Toshié: A Story of Village Life in Twentieth-Century Japan.* Berkeley: University of California Press, 2004.

Peattie, Mark. *Sunburst: The Rise of Japanese Naval Air Power, 1909–1941.* Annapolis, MD: Naval Institute Press, 2007.

Peukert, Detlev. *Inside Nazi Germany: Conformity, Opposition, and Racism in Everyday Life.* Translated by Richard Deveson. New Haven, CT: Yale University Press, 1987.

Rekishigaku kenkyūkai, comp. *Taiheiyō sensō, 1940–1942.* Vol. 4 of *Taiheiyō sensōshi.* Tokyo: Aoki shoten, 1972.

————, comp. *Taiheiyō sensō, 1942–1945.* Vol. 5 of *Taiheiyō sensōshi.* Tokyo: Aoki shoten, 1973.

Said, Edward. *Culture and Imperialism*. New York: Knopf, 1993.

Scott, Joan. "The Evidence of Experience." *Critical Inquiry* 17, no. 4 (1991): 773–797.

Shillony, Ben-Ami. *Politics and Culture in Wartime Japan*. New York: Oxford University Press, 1981.

———. "Wartime Japan: A Military Dictatorship?" In *Shōwa Japan: Political, Economic and Social History, 1926–1989*, edited by Stephen Large. Routledge Library of Modern Japan. New York: Routledge, 1998.

Shimomura Michiko. "Senchū-sengo no shoku jittai." In *Hijō no shoku*. Vol. 11 of *Nihon no shoku bunka*. Edited by Noboru Haga et al. Tokyo: Yusankaku, 1999.

Sōmushō tōkei kyoku, ed. *Shimpan Nihon chōki tōkei sōran*. Tokyo: Nihon tōkei kyōkai, 2006.

Sontag, Susan. *Regarding the Pain of Others*. New York: Farrar, Straus & Giroux, 2003.

Straus, Ulrich. *The Anguish of Surrender: Japanese POWs of World War II*. Seattle: University of Washington Press, 2003.

Tanaka, Yuki. "Japan's Kamikaze Pilots and Contemporary Suicide Bombers: War and Terror." *Asia-Pacific Journal: Japan Focus* (2005). http://www.japanfocus .org/-yuki-tanaka/1606.zzlzz.

Tregaskis, Richard. *Guadalcanal Diary*. New York: Random House, 1943.

Tsuji, Shizuo. *Japanese Cooking: A Simple Art*. Tokyo: Kodansha International, 1980.

Tsurumi, Kazuko. *Social Change and the Individual: Japan Before and After Defeat in World War II*. Princeton, NJ: Princeton University Press, 1970.

Tsurumi, Shunsuke. *An Intellectual History of Wartime Japan, 1931–1945*. London: KPI, 1986.

Watanabe Minoru. *Nihon shoku seikatsushi*. Tokyo: Kōbunkan, 1995.

Yamashita, Samuel Hideo. "Confucianism and the Japanese State, 1904–1945." In *Confucian Traditions in East Asian Modernity: Moral Education and Economic Culture in Japan and the Four Mini-Dragons*, edited by Tu Wei-Ming. Cambridge, MA: Harvard University Press, 1996.

———. *Leaves from an Autumn of Emergencies: Selections from the Wartime Diaries of Ordinary Japanese*. Honolulu: University of Hawai'i Press, 2005.

———. "Pictures for 'Our Honorable American Friends.'" *Cross-Currents: East Asian History and Culture Review* 6 (Spring 2013): 175–185.

Yamauchi, Midori, and Joseph L. Quinn, eds. *Listen to the Voices from the Sea: Writings of the Fallen Japanese Students*. Scranton, PA: University of Scranton Press, 2000.

Yoneyama, Lisa. *Hiroshima Traces: Time, Space, and the Dialectics of Memory*. Berkeley: University of California Press, 1999.

Yoshimatsu Masahire, comp. *Kaigun shōgo sakusen (2) filipin okinawasen*. Tokyo: Asagumo shimbunsha, 1970–1972.

Yoshimi Yoshiaki. *Kusa no ne no fashizumu*. Tokyo: Tōkyō daigaku shuppankai, 1987.

Young, Louise. *Japan's Total Empire: Manchuria and the Culture of Imperialism*. Berkeley: University of California Press, 1998.

food, grains and grain products,
continued
"perseverance flour," 52
rice, 14, 37, 39–40, 44–55, 113,
115–116, 118–119, 121, 123–124,
160–161
wheat, 39, 54–55, 119, 121
meat and poultry, 14, 38, 48, 51, 55, 117
beef, 17, 55, 113
chicken, 42, 54, 98, 119, 160
ham, 49–50
pigeons, 120
pork, 17
sparrows, 117
noodles
dried noodles, 16, 37, 40
sōmen, 47, 49–50, 113
udon, 45, 52, 54, 116–117
nuts, 120
chestnuts, 51, 95, 114, 117, 119–120
dried chestnuts, 119
hedama, 120
walnuts, 120
other
crackers, 47, 49–50
eggs, 54, 98
grasshoppers, 55, 116, 120–121
ground beetles, 120
quail eggs, 52
prepared dishes
chirashi sushi, 48–49, 51
daizu-iri, 117
fish cake, 47–48, 50
ground sardine dumplings, 48–49,
51
iri-mame, 121
kelp rolls, 42
kiriboshi daikon, 41
konnyaku, 41
mame-iri, 25
miso soup, 77, 85, 87, 113–114, 123
namasu, 42
nishime, 42, 52, 54
onigiri, 47, 85, 119, 124
red-bean porridge, 52

red-bean rice, 25, 52, 54, 111
rice cakes, 42–44, 51–52, 54, 82, 87,
117–119
rice crackers, 51
roasted barley flour, 50
roasted soybeans, 52
sashimi, 42
Scotch egg, 116
soup, 114
soybean rice, 113
Spanish omelet, 116
suiton, 116
sukiyaki (one-pot dish), 42
sushi, 25, 44, 54
sweet potato rice, 54
tatsukuri, 42
tempura, 39
tsukudani, 39, 47–51
zōni, 17–18, 42
zōsui, 40, 52, 117, 119
reptiles
frog, 55, 120–121
snake, 120
seaweed
kelp, 25, 47–48, 50–51, 123
nori, 25, 52, 124
tororo konbu, 85
wakame (seaweed), 123
shellfish
dried clams, 52
freshwater shrimp, 120
oysters, 48, 50
shrimp, 17, 42, 120
snails, 120
soybeans and soybean products
miso, 16, 38, 45–46, 54, 113, 118
natto, 54
soybean, 25, 39–40, 47, 49–50, 52,
54, 115, 117, 119, 121, 123
soybean bran, 40
soybean flour, 25, 48, 52
soybean meal, 122–123
soy sauce, 16, 38, 48–50, 54, 118
tofu, 25, 47, 49–50, 53–54, 119
tofu lees, 26, 47, 49, 51, 114